Shattered Voices

Pennsylvania Studies in Human Rights

Bert B. Lockwood, Jr., Series Editor

A complete list of books in the series is available from the publisher.

Shattered Voices

Language, Violence, and the Work of
Truth Commissions

Teresa Godwin Phelps

To Stephen and Barbara,
With affection and
admiration.
Do good work —
Pray for peace.

Terry

PENN

University of Pennsylvania Press

Philadelphia

10 9 8 7 6 5 4 3 2 1

Published by
University of Pennsylvania Press
Philadelphia, Pennsylvania 19104–4011

Library of Congress Cataloging-in-Publication Data

Phelps, Teresa Godwin.
   Shattered voices : language, violence, and the work of truth
commissions / Teresa Godwin Phelps.
      p.   cm.—(Pennsylvania studies in human rights)
   ISBN 0-8122-3797-8 (alk. paper)
   Includes bibliographical references and index.
      1. Truth commissions.   2. Human rights.   3. Reconciliation.
   4. Governmental investigations.   I. Title.   II. Series
JC580 .P48   2004
323.4′9—dc22   2004041498

For Bill

Contents

Prologue for Paulina

In the winter of 1992 in London, I attended one of the first performances in English of *Death and the Maiden*, a play by Chilean writer Ariel
Dorfman. Juliet Stevenson's brilliant depiction of Paulina Salas presented a transfixed audience with a compelling question: what happens
when a new and tenuous democracy, because of political necessity, turns
its back on some of the victims of the regime it has replaced? Paulina is
just such a victim, and the play provides a troubling answer.

The play opens when Gerardo, Paulina's husband, returns very late to
the isolated house he shares with Paulina. He is late because he had a
flat tire and was rescued and driven home by a considerate stranger, Dr.
Roberto Miranda. Paulina hears only voices outside as she waits inside
the darkened house, clutching a gun and "rolled into a foetus-like position."[1] Gerardo, a lawyer, is returning from a meeting with the country's
president, the most "important meeting of my whole life,"[2] in which he
has been named head of a commission that will investigate some crimes
committed by the recently displaced military dictatorship. The initial
dialogue between Paulina and Gerardo reveals that Paulina's response
to the voices outside was typical: she has frequent breakdowns resulting
from her treatment when she, as an activist student fifteen years in the
past, was kidnapped and tortured. Rather than pleasing her, however,
Gerardo's appointment to head the commission further disturbs her:

Paulina: This Commission you're named to. Doesn't it only investi-
gate cases that ended in death?
Gerardo: It's appointed to investigate human rights' violations that
ended in death or the presumption of death, yes.
Paulina: Only the most serious cases?
Gerardo: The idea is that if we can cast light on the worst crimes, other
abuses will come to light.
Paulina: Only the most serious?

Gerardo:	Those beyond redemption.
Paulina:	Only those beyond redemption, huh?
Gerardo:	I don't like to talk about this, Paulina.
Paulina:	I don't like to talk about it either.[3]

Paulina's fragile emotional state is thrown into turmoil by this official pronouncement in which her husband is complicitous: her kidnapping and torture will not be investigated because they are not considered to be among the "most serious" crimes committed during the dictatorship. For all official purposes, her pain and humiliation did not happen and she is forced back into her ongoing silence—"I don't like to talk about this, Paulina." The "this" is ambiguous: does Gerardo not like to talk about the Commission's limited mandate or, more tellingly, does he not like to talk about what happened to Paulina? Paulina, in fact, has told Gerardo very little about her imprisonment and the treatment she received; she has not even told him that her torture included rape.[4] The political process, she now discovers, promises only that her silence must continue. The new government, the government in whose cause she refused to give over names, including Gerardo's, will not take retribution for her.

An hour later, after Gerardo and Paulina have gone to bed, Roberto Miranda, the stranger who assisted Gerardo with his flat tire, reappears to return Gerardo's patched tire, which was inadvertently left in his trunk *and* because he heard on his car radio that Gerardo Escobar, the very man he aided, has been named to head the president's Investigating Commission. Gerardo and Miranda discuss the Commission's charge and the fact that the army will resist the Commission's work, its officers having warned the president that the Commission will open old wounds. Miranda compares the army to the Mafia: "yes, a secret brotherhood, nobody gives out names and they cover each others' backs. The Armed Forces aren't going to allow their men to give testimony to your Commission and if you people call them in they'll just ignore the summons. Whatever they please . . . they've got the guns. . . ."[5] This late night exchange between the two men discloses the tenuous nature of the new government, the uneasy alliance that exists between the duly elected democratic leaders of a transitional democracy and the former regime that still has "the guns." It captures the difficult and dangerous process by which such a government attempts to provide redress to the victims of abuses committed on a massive scale, a process complicated by a military establishment that is in retreat but far from powerless.

Because of the late hour, Gerardo invites Dr. Miranda to spend the night. Paulina, who has been huddling in the hallway in a kind of post-traumatic stress reaction to any late night knock on the door, recognizes

Miranda's voice (she was blindfolded during her imprisonment) as that of the doctor who tortured and raped her fifteen years earlier, crimes that will be ignored by the president's Commission because she did not die. Confronting the failure of legal state retribution, she decides to take personal revenge. After the men have gone to sleep, she finds Gerardo's gun, ties up the doctor, and gags him. She then hides his car; in it she discovers a cassette recording of Schubert's string quartet "Death and the Maiden," the very music her torturer played repeatedly as he raped her.

The audience is left to wonder whether Miranda is actually Paulina's torturer or whether she has fallen past sanity into delusions. Small clues are dropped—like the cassette tape of "Death and the Maiden" and Paulina's memory of characteristic phrases the torturer used that Miranda also uses ("teensy-weensy bit")—but we can never be certain that Paulina is right. It may be that her damaged psyche and her new knowledge that she will have no chance for retribution combine to find someone—anyone—to blame.

When Gerardo awakens, he is, naturally, shocked at what Paulina has done to their guest, and he accuses her of being ill. Paulina responds: "All right then, I am. But I can be ill and recognize a voice. . . . It's his voice. . . . The way he laughed. Certain phrases he used. . . . It may be a teensy-weensy thing, but it's enough for me. During all these years not an hour has passed that I haven't heard it, that same voice, next to me, next to my ear, that voice mixed with saliva, you think I'd forget a voice like his?"[6] That Paulina identifies her torturer by his voice reflects the polarization of language that occurs in torture in which "the prisoner become[s] a colossal body with no voice and the torturer a colossal voice . . . with no body."[7] For fifteen years, Miranda has remained a "colossal voice," all language, to the silenced, purely sentient Paulina, who has been unable to tell even her husband the details of her torture. Language itself has become part of the disbalance that occurs with such a harm.

Gerardo asks Paulina what she intends to do with the bound and gagged Miranda, and she explains: "We're going to put him on trial, Gerardo, this doctor. Right here. Today. Or is your famous Investigating Commission going to do it?"[8] The curtain drops to end Act One.

In Act Two, the "trial" commences. Gerardo protests that Paulina is merely mirroring the tactics of her own kidnappers: "If something revolted me about them it was that they accused so many men and women, that they forged evidence and ignored evidence and did not give the accused any chance of defending themselves, so even if this man committed genocide on a daily basis, he has the right to defend himself."[9] In response, Paulina assigns Gerardo as Dr. Miranda's "defense counsel." Gerardo insists that Paulina's actions will destroy him, that he will have to resign his new government post on principle, even if no one finds out about Paulina's actions. Paulina replies: "Because of your mad wife, who was mad because she stayed silent and is now mad because she suddenly began to speak?"[10]

The lawyer Gerardo represents the prudent voice of the new democracy that must compromise to appease the army and must make practical decisions about the country's future. Its decisions mean that people like Paulina will never have a chance to speak out officially against their torturers, will never have an opportunity to tell their stories and have them officially acknowledged. The state has forgone retribution for them. Gerardo tries to explain the practicalities: "If he's guilty, more reason to let him go. Don't look at me like that. You want to scare these people and provoke them, Paulina, till they come back . . . ? Because that is what you're going to get. Imagine what would happen if everyone acted like you did. You satisfy your personal passion, you punish on your own, while the other people in this country with scores of other problems who finally have a chance to solve some of them, those people can go screw themselves—the whole transition to democracy can go screw itself—. . . . Let him go, Paulina. For the good of the country. . . ."[11] Miranda, in his own self-interest, also presents a compelling argument against any action: "So we go on and on with violence, always more violence. Yesterday they did terrible things to you and now you do terrible things to me and tomorrow the same cycle will begin all over again. Isn't it time we stopped?"[12]

Paulina is unconvinced and unwilling: "What about my good? . . . You're asking me to forget."[13] She lays out for Gerardo her emotional response when she first heard Miranda's voice that night. At first she wanted an eye for an eye; she wanted someone to rape him: "But I began to realize that wasn't what I really wanted. And you know what conclusion I came to, the only thing I really want? I want him to confess. I want him to sit in front of that cassette-recorder and tell me what he did—not just to me, everything, to everybody—and then have him write it out in his own handwriting and sign it and I would keep a copy forever—with all the information, the names and data, all the details. That's what I want."[14]

Gerardo later concedes that he understands Paulina's need: "It coincides with the need of the whole country. The need to put into words what happened to us."[15] And this, he realizes, should be the task of his Commission. As the scene ends, Paulina, with a gun aimed at the head of a kneeling Miranda, poses the question at the heart of the play: "Why is it always people like me who have to sacrifice, who have to concede when concessions are needed, biting my tongue, why?"[16] A giant mirror descends to the stage and the audience members are forced to look at themselves.[17]

Gerardo and Dr. Miranda are right, of course. Paulina's possible violence toward Miranda both mirrors and perpetuates the horrors committed against her. She remains enmeshed in a cycle of violence that may have no end. All the arguments are there: why dredge up the past and dwell on past wrongs? Why risk a backlash? Let bygones be bygones and move forward in a spirit of reconciliation.[18] But Paulina's needs are personal, not political. She seeks, as do most victims, a rebalancing. Her torture took something from her that she wants to take back. The Latin root of "retribution" is "retribuere" meaning "to pay back" (re + tribuere). Adequate retribution for Paulina will pay back to her something that she lost as a result of the crimes against her. The play symbolizes this loss by Schubert's string quartet, "Death and the Maiden," her favorite piece of music to which she cannot listen since her torture. In the play's final scene, Paulina is shown at a concert at which the musicians are tuning up for "Death and the Maiden." A surreally lighted Dr. Miranda is also present at the concert, and the audience is left to decide whether he exists only in Paulina's imagination or is real: whether she fired the gun or let him go after his confession. In either case, she has her Schubert back, but was the balancing gained through violence or language?

This book will argue that it was language, that Paulina lost language as well as Schubert.[19] Her ability to articulate her pain was taken away by her torture, and any adequate balancing she would achieve requires a restoration of that language. Pain and oppression destroy a person's ability to use language, and the rebalancing that is at the heart of revenge and retribution requires the recovery of that destroyed language. Paulina was surprised to discover that words were what she needed; she wanted Miranda's confession. She wanted the story of what happened to her to be heard and acknowledged.

So, what happens when a new and fragile democracy turns its back on some (or even all) of the victims of the regime it has replaced? The troubling and provocative answer that the play provides is this: if what happened to Paulina is ignored, if the state fails in its responsibility to enact retribution for her, she will take revenge into her own hands. If a new government turns its back on the victims, the victims will, in time, get their own back, becoming the perpetrators in the next stage of the cycle, the cycle of revenge that has no appropriate stopping place. If a state expects the Paulinas of the world to be the ones who make the concessions, it ignores critical truths about human history and psychology.

History shows us that revenge cycles end when the victims cede the right to take revenge to the state and the state properly fulfills this duty.

That is, the victims are somehow satisfied that they have retrieved something that they have lost. What they get back, of course, can in no way be commensurable with what was lost by the harm. Nonetheless, it must be in some measure satisfying. The first process is the subject of Chapter 1, a look backward at the evolution of private revenge into state retribution. It demonstrates that revenge was once at the heart of the idea of justice and that the taking of revenge was considered a noble duty. As nation-states emerged, that duty was given over to (or taken over by) central authorities and became state-sponsored judgment and punishment, but the human need for revenge remained acknowledged and served as the basis for state punishment. Revenge and justice continued to be aligned. Moreover, the giving over was tentative and reluctant and was frequently taken back by the individual or family, especially in those instances in which the state failed to take retribution.

Eventually, however, in order to insure its own security against the disorder and destructiveness of private revenge, it was in a state's best interest to go further and attempt to convince people that private revenge was not only imprudent but also evil. Thus, as part of the cultural *Zeitgeist*, a duality was created that put revenge and justice into a false opposition—not just the act of revenge but also even the feeling of wanting revenge. A state would benefit by making people ashamed of the human need for revenge and by characterizing it as immoral and excessive. It needed to buttress the transfer to the state with moral and religious arguments. Yet the passion for revenge remained powerful, albeit underground, and much of what was written about revenge was layered and ambiguous. Chapter 2 examines the attempted demonizing of revenge and the gradual removal of emotion from state responses to harms against people. It also discusses the undercurrent of opinions that acknowledge the potential problems if a state fails to take into account a desire for retribution and ignores the necessity of allowing personal passions into systems of justice. The chapter concludes by suggesting that discussions about revenge and retribution generally presume a state willing and capable of taking action (in the form of state-sponsored violence) on a victim's behalf. Few commentators take up the critical contemporary problem of a state incapable or unwilling to so act. Are there possibilities for adequate and satisfying balancing beyond violence for violence?

These background chapters ultimately show that the need to take revenge is a deeply rooted human need that cannot be moralized away; it is an inevitable and indestructible part of the human psyche. At the same time, it is a powerful emotion that can be contained in the appropriate forms. These chapters, meant to be allusive and suggestive rather than definitive historical analyses, lay the groundwork for the argument that a state must do something in response to wrongs against its people. Ignoring the needs of victims insures that the revenge cycle will continue. These chapters also lay bare the void that exists when a state will not or cannot act in its citizens' behalf. For all we know or think we know about revenge and retribution, we have not developed a way of thinking about alternatives to traditional violence for violence—whether personal or public. Our vision is limited by our history, but Paulina shows us another possibility.

The process described in Chapters 1 and 2 is revealed in Paulina's situation in *Death and the Maiden*. She turned her personal need for revenge over to the state and the state failed her. She thus takes back her "right" to revenge, seeking at first *lex talionis*, comparable violence, an eye for an eye, rape for rape. But then she discovers that she does not want violence, what she wants are words. In the middle of the night, when a bound and gagged former oppressor is at her mercy, Paulina discerns that more violence is *not* what she wants. Instead she requires an acknowledgment that something evil happened to her. She wants Miranda to say the words and she wants Gerardo to hear them. She wants them written down and she wants to keep the words forever.

The center of the book's theoretical project, in Chapters 3 and 4, is to answer the question as to whether there is any reason to think that stories can work in this way in actual transitional democracies—countries that have few choices as to the action they take as they make the transition from a violent past. Chapter 3 analyzes the relationship between language and the violence that accompanies oppression, arguing that the appropriation and manipulation of language are central to the technology of oppression. Chapter 4 asks whether stories can do anything of value in the wake of such oppression. Is there any reason to think that the solution that Paulina discovers she wants—her story told and acknowledged—can work over the long term? What are the relationships between language and power, language and pain, language and violence? Is language an appropriate balance for violence and pain? Can having a story told and acknowledged possibly satisfy the emotional needs of victims? And if so, what forms should this language take?

The question whether storytelling can work over the long term is not a theoretical one and the stakes are high. Transitional democracies are faced with a concrete and pressing problem, an "enormous, miserable task,"[20] of how to deal with the past without destroying the future. History, recent and long past, has shown that cycles of revenge are indeed unending if dealt with in primitive and unthought out ways. From southern Europe to Latin America, eastern Europe to South Africa, Rwanda and Bosnia, the solutions are varied and controversial. Should (and can) a country fully investigate, bring to trial, and punish former leaders and their lackeys? Are amnesties or pardons a better solution? An international tribunal? Truth commissions? Is it wise to impose on states an affirmative duty to investigate and prosecute?[21] Or does the best solution lie in turning the other cheek, putting the past behind and moving forward with the new government? Do states even have the right to forgive or is that "right" vested only in victims? Do amnesties and pardons perpetuate a culture of impunity? What is the appropriate way to move from lawlessness to the rule of law? Are any generalizations possible at all or does every case have a unique context?[22] A fledgling democracy is in the process of building a new moral community. What ways of dealing with the past can best achieve this goal? A spectrum of solutions has been tried: trials, both national and international; exclusion from government posts; the opening of secret files; commemorations in art and ceremony; forgiveness and reconciliation; confrontations; and storytelling contained in truth commission reports.[23]

Chapter 4 lays out seven potential benefits of storytelling in the context of transitional democracies: (1) translating chaotic events into a story not only provides therapy for victims (a claim that is well-documented), but the creation of story from experience also is an essentially human activity that enables all of us to make sense of our lives; (2) the restoration of the ability to use language for oneself in one's own way balances the loss of language effected by oppression and violence, and thus is a form of retribution in a basic semantic sense (a sense of the word that was lost as the philosophy of punishment shifted the focus from the victim to the perpetrator) of *giving back* that which was taken away; (3) the free and open telling of stories can reveal more truth than other responses, including trials; (4) stories can bring about communication between people who normally cannot understand each other; (5) the storytelling setting in some circumstances provides healing ritual, akin to *carnival*, in which the hierarchy is inverted and the people are empowered; (6) the stories are a visible manifestation of the invisible in a sacramental sense; and (7) the truth commission reports give the stories a plot (in the technical sense used in narrative theory) and result in the creation of a constitutive history for the emerging state. Chapter 4 discusses the first six of these potential benefits and argues that they offer an expanded vision of the worth of stories for a transitional democracy and that they provide new and hopeful ways of thinking about and using such stories.

In Chapters 5 and 6, I first relate the ubiquity of truth commissions to the turn to narrative in diverse disciplines and demonstrate that truth commission reports can be a promising kind of constitutive history for a transitional democracy. The book then revisits my initial question:

whether language can in any way adequately balance the harms of pain and oppression—can stories do any good?—in specific contexts. I analyze situations in which just such an attempt is being made: truth commissions and their reports. Looking in detail at commissions and reports from four countries—Argentina, Chile, El Salvador, and South Africa—I discuss the various layers of "stories" that are told by the commission reports, and, using narrative theory, I evaluate their relationship to justice. I ask, using a question generated in the work of James Boyd White: what kind of community does the report imagine and create?

Truth commission reports have come into existence in the final decades of the twentieth century, and they are seen as filling a gap when countries do not have the will or the resources to pursue more traditional forms of justice: investigations, trials, and punishment. As time passes though, truth commissions are being criticized as doing as much harm as good by some observers who assert that truth commissions are a poor substitute for traditional justice. These critics maintain that truth commissions offer an inadequate second-best and that truth commissions and their reports encourage premature closure. The first of these common criticisms I refute and instead argue that truth commission reports may constitute a radically new kind of justice, and that they are, in any event, a necessary component of any adequate understanding of justice. This book will argue that justice is not a single event that occurs for once and for all—"we were harmed and now we have 'justice' "—but is instead an ongoing, dynamic process, of which storytelling is a vital part. The second criticism—that the reports are a rush to closure—I engage in the final chapter and offer a cautionary word about narratives in general and the reports in particular: they can tempt us to a comfortable sense of closure more appropriate to fictions than actual political and human situations. I also engage two other potential problems: hearing or reading too many stories of violence may result in "psychic numbing," in which we shut off our empathetic response rather than feeling anything; and the appropriation of people's stories of pain, for whatever well-intentioned reasons, is a morally and ethically problematic act. As Hayden White and other narrative theorists warn, stories can be used to put across a moral vison of the world in the interests of power and manipulation. Is it possible to fashion truth commission reports in such ways to minimize their misuse in the interests of the new power structure? If the strengths of stories that I discuss in Chapter 4 are to be realized, we must be wary of the dark potentiality of storytelling as well.

Lingering doubts persist about the efficacy or propriety of language when confronting mass atrocity, that "radical evil seems to surpass the boundaries of moral discourse."[24] When I set out to look at truth commission reports through the lens of narrative theory (in a broad sense),[25]

I expected that such a view would provide a richer vision of the potentialities of the reports, and indeed this has proven the case. Truth commission reports are capturing the imagination because stories can achieve powerful ends, many of which have not been articulated or even brought into consciousness. This book begins the process of uncovering what stories can achieve in the context of transitional democracy, whether they represent the "simple drama of storytelling"[26] or something far more profound and significant.

There is certainly no dearth of published opinion about the various responses that countries have undertaken to reckon with the past.[27] The reports themselves, including the four on which I focus, continue to be discussed and evaluated.[28] One of the widely recognized problems in truth reports is the political agenda of their writers; one of the less-recognized problems in the critiques of truth reports is the political agenda of the critics. Looking at the reports through narrative theory allows us to see their strengths and weaknesses in an apolitical way—as, after all, *stories*. This book draws from but does not retrace the steps taken in previous works; instead it focuses on a particular somewhat neglected issue: What constitutes revenge and retribution and what role, if any, does language play in those processes? It seeks to develop a theory about the role of language in revenge and retribution and in so doing makes several claims. First, given the historical and psychological evidence about revenge, putting the past behind by attempting to draw a bright line between the past crimes and the new government, in other words, "getting on with it" with no action, is unworkable and unwise. The metaphor of balancing is at the heart of discussions about revenge and retribution, a metaphor that we should consider and take seriously. When grievous harms occur, a rebalancing will occur whether it is orderly and lawful or disorderly and unlawful. Second, adequate government action need not be state-sponsored violence in the form of prosecutions; as Paulina discovered, *lex talionis* may not be the rule. At the same time, a state should provide or assist victims in finding "*effective* alternative means of psychic support that provide the benefits sought in revenge: preserving self-esteem and honor, providing physical security, and satisfying the desire for justice" (italics original).[29] Third, in any case, state-enacted redress must not be decided upon from the top down; the desires and emotions of the victims must be taken into account and outlets provided for them. Fourth, language, if not necessarily the end-all of the retribution process, is requisite to any adequate balancing. This fourth claim has several implications that have to do with the work of truth commissions, and indeed all other responses to an oppressive past including trials. A solution is viable only if it provides an atmosphere in which storytelling and subsequent dialogue can flourish.

The book's final claim, and perhaps its most critical contribution, is that in the developing culture of ubiquitous truth reports, we need to become attentive to the form that these reports take. The form of the report and its use of victims' stories necessarily convey a political message to the citizens of the emerging democracy. The book's theoretical framework and its analysis of prominent truth reports reveals that some reports are better than others. Why? To what forms should the writers of truth reports aspire?

Gerardo's question—What would happen if everyone acted as you did?—is a compelling one to which we know the answer if we are attentive to history. Miranda's question—Isn't it time we stopped?—is the contemporary humanitarian response. But Paulina's question—What about my good?—is too often put aside. What is Paulina's "good" and can it be achieved without bringing down the country? That's what this book attempts to answer.

Chapter One
The Demise of Paulina's Good: From Personal Revenge to State Punishment

Blood cries for blood; and murder murder craves.
—John Marston, *Antonio's Revenge* (1599)

"What about *my* good?" Paulina's question embarrasses Gerardo, and it embarrasses most of us. If we or our loved ones are harmed, we call the police and thereafter depend upon the state to investigate, judge, and punish for us. As good citizens and emotionally stable individuals, we are taught to become procedurally and emotionally distanced from both the harm and its perpetrator. Victims who make a fuss about their own needs are treated as emotionally suspect.[1] Feeling and acting have collapsed into one impulse so that even when the state acts in our behalf, we are expected to relinquish an emotional response as well, to give up or repress any feelings about revenge, despite the fact that the impulse to get back for injuries is probably universal and often culturally sanctioned.[2] Feeling any desire for personal revenge is regarded as a character flaw. We say "we don't want revenge; we want justice," indicating by this duality our conviction that a desire for revenge is shameful. When we use "justice" to deny any desire for revenge, we demonstrate our belief that justice is completely distinct from revenge, unrelated in any way.

But it was not always so. In early societies, the taking of revenge was a sacred duty, a right, and a responsibility that was both individual and familial, depending on the structure of the society. If a person was harmed, he would have a natural right to return the harm. If a family or clan member was killed or harmed, it was not only a right but, in many societies,[3] the duty of a clan to avenge the wrong, to enter into a blood feud with the offender's clan.[4] The responsibility to avenge as well as the punishment was often personal but also collective, clan versus clan. Thus the actions of every person involved the clan: in killing someone, the offender brought the enmity of the victim's clan not only upon himself but also upon his entire familial group.[5]

This chapter tells the story of the shift away from private dutiful and honorable revenge to dispassionate state punishment, what we have come to call retribution. Although the focus is on trying to understand the human need for revenge, with all its nuances, I do not, of course, advocate the taking of violent revenge. Instead, I am interested in what it means to *want* revenge: to *feel* something, not necessarily to *do* something. Does the feeling necessarily mean desiring an act of violence? Or can wanting revenge mean—as I think it can—wanting something back that was lost as a result of the initial harm? What has happened to this impulse as the personal has given way to the public? Do state systems of punishment include or acknowledge any desire for revenge on the part of the victim or the victim's family? What becomes of Paulina's "good"? Within the larger argument I am making in this book about the role that stories can play in revenge and retribution, I am concerned with a reappraisal of the desire for revenge, in particular in the context of transitional democracies, in which there is a justifiable temptation to put the past behind. What are the consequences and possibilities of reintegrating the need (the *need*, not the *act*) for revenge into emerging and changing justice systems of new and fragile countries? What are the consequences of any state's efforts to repress a desire for redress as a legitimate, even necessary, part of the human psyche?

To answer these questions, we require a picture of what the desire for revenge looked like and how it was acted out before such a desire came to be considered reprehensible, before a harm against a person was the state's business at all. The progression (real and constructed) has three steps:[6] first, revenge as an honorable, measured act of balancing that focused on a victim's need; second, the state's appropriation of revenge in the form of state punishment and, along with that shift, personal revenge being characterized as always excessive and destructive; third, the change in focus from the victim's need to the perpetrator's desert—the contemporary understanding of *retributivism*[7]—and, concomitantly, the attaching of shame to a victim's desires. Some understanding of this progression and its hold on us will help us to appreciate why hearing Paulina ask about her "good" makes us feel puzzled and uncomfortable.

The evolution within cultures from private revenge to state punishment was anything but regular and linear, and any attempt to tell the story of this shift in the form of a chronological history is filled with problems.[8] The evolution occurred variously in different societies, depending upon such factors as geography, culture, and time. A pattern does emerge, nonetheless, in that societies develop laws concerning revenge at particular points in their evolution, regardless of when those points occur on some master calendar. Essentially (in an oversimplified way), the pattern develops along these lines: first, homicide and other crimes against people are personal matters appropriately settled by the family or clan, usually by the death of the killer or his relatives; next, the necessity of the death of the wrongdoer gives way to the willingness to accept other forms of restitution, usually, but not exclusively, money or property; then, crimes come to be seen not as personal matters but as wrongs against the community at large (an idea sometimes referred to as the "pollution doctrine"); and finally, as central authority strengthens, personal crimes become matters of concern to the state, the state assumes the duty to punish the wrongdoer, and personal revenge is outlawed.

The ancient Babylonian laws (the Code of Hammurabi), for example, demonstrate that blood feuds became more and more limited as the central government grew stronger. "The State by degrees forced composition [payment of a fine] and restricted gratification of vengeance. . . . This process of limitation by the State was slowly extended, and the injured party was only allowed to carry out the execution himself under the supervision of some central authority and sometimes merely to be present at it."[9] We see in these codes, perhaps for the first time, the notion of the state punishing a wrong against another person entering the civic imagination.

As states developed and legal codes were written, the right to private revenge was gradually ceded to official authorities, who assumed not merely the right but also the obligation to enact revenge for the victim and the victim's family. The gradual rise of central authority in kings moved the avenging of wrongs from the private and familial to the public, a difficult yet critical transference in that warring clans had the potentiality to undermine and even destroy a king's authority over the people. The advent of Christianity with its message of turning the other cheek in forgiveness may have played a small part,[10] but the major reason for the change was utilitarian rather than Christian. The destructive potentiality of blood feuds in addition to the emergence of nation-states made private vengeance an impracticable and unwise practice and, perhaps most critically, a threat to the centralized state. In time it became a ruler's right to seek revenge, by punishment, fine, or both, and crimes were seen not as private matters but as offenses against the king's peace.[11]

Yet the surrender of blood feud to state-controlled punishment was uneven and gradual, occurring at vastly different times in different cultures,[12] always revealing a struggle to balance revenge and restraint. The giving over was also reluctant and tentative because taking revenge was regarded as a sign of character. In heroic societies, for example, it was a right, an obligation, and a mark of character, particularly if a blood relative had been murdered, to enact revenge upon not only the murderer but also his relatives and even his descendants: "If someone kills you, my friend or brother, I owe you their death and when I have paid my debt to you their friend or brother owes them my death."[13] This loyalty and fidelity to duty was not condemned as emotional wrongheadedness but honored as virtue. Nor was seeking revenge evidence of lawlessness for it operated firmly within the established boundaries of customary law. In a kinship or friendship relationship, the virtues of courage and fidelity were paramount: courage assuring that a friend or kinsman had the power to respond and fidelity assuring the will to do so. These virtues held the social structure in place and thus blood vengeance was a duty and an honorable act.[14]

The tension between the customary power of revenge and the gradual ceding of the right to the state can be seen in numerous societies. For example, although England in the tenth and eleventh centuries saw a rapid growth in the power of kings and in the development and centralization of law, surrendering the right to revenge was still greatly resisted. Up until the Norman conquest, kinship was the strongest of bonds and that bond was never more palpable than in the blood feud. The blood feud was the visual equivalent of the strength of the familial bond. "A man's kindred are his avengers; and, it is their right and honour to avenge him. . . . Step-by-step, as the power of the State waxes, the self-centered and self-helping of the kindred wanes. Private feud is controlled, regulated, put . . . into legal harness."[15] Slowly, and only by degrees, did the principles of state retribution prevail, and only gradually did the members of a community or family become, at least overtly, content with the remedies afforded by law.

This transition from a culture's practice of personal revenge to a growing dependence on the state for retribution can be usefully illustrated through a look at the values reflected in the literature and history of pre-Christian Greek culture. The Greek word for avenging the dead is etymologically related to the word for honor, signifying that revenge is more than satisfaction for the revenger, but also a requisite restoration of honor.[16] This double meaning is reflected throughout both the *Iliad* and the *Odyssey*: "the objective of the Homeric heroes was always to ensure that they recovered from an aggressor the loss they had suffered."[17] Blood vengeance reestablished the balance lost as a result of the initiating harm; the revenge balanced the natural order and put the world back on the right track: "the balance of restorative transactions

. . . explains[s] the rhythmical exchanges of natural events."[18] This balancing should not be seen as actual, of course; even the life of another, taken in precisely the same way, in no way equals the life of a loved one. Nonetheless, the metaphor of balancing to restore a kind of natural order informs most of the discourse concerning revenge. Many Greek myths and legends express the idea that order rested on vengeance, and the Homeric poems of the heroic age for the most part reveal an undisputed approval of the right to revenge.

In the *Odyssey* (ca. 700 B.C.), for example, Odysseus' revenge on the suitors of his wife Penelope, which comprises the last eleven books, possesses no ambivalence. Odysseus does not suffer the tribulations of later revengers: he does not hesitate or fear for his life or his soul. He does not die or go mad or even require any sort of purification. He even seems to have heavenly approval as the goddess Athena serves as his ally while he wreaks his bloody revenge. And after the suitors are killed, Athena steps in to prevent their relatives from continuing the revenge cycle, which would be unending without divine intervention.

The *Iliad*, as well, is filled with stories of blood-for blood retaliation that are generally dealt with approvingly.[19] In some ways, the *Iliad* is all about revenge in its broad sense, that is, anger and resentment for even minor wrongs, slights, and insults. The great hero Achilles pouts in his tent, refusing to fight, because his slave girl was taken from him. Beyond relating these smaller acts of getting even, the *Iliad* explicitly celebrates blood revenge; in a gruesome scene, Patroclus makes the Trojans "pay in blood."[20] After Patroclus himself is killed, Achilles, his friend, takes specific payment for the slaying: "When Achilles' hands were sore from killing, / He culled twelve boys live from the river / To pay for the blood of dead Patroclus."[21] We are meant to recognize Achilles' great love for Patroclus in his act of revenge for Patroclus' death; we are also meant to admire Achilles' virtue in his willingness to so act.

Interwoven with these scenes, however, are intimations of the ultimate incommensurability of great loss and the necessity of accepting less than adequate recompense (because "adequate" is impossible). Ajax, in an attempt to convince Achilles to return to fight the Trojans, portrays a model of human behavior that involves self-restraint and acceptance of loss:

> A man accepts compensation
> For a murdered brother, a dead son.
> The killer goes on living in the same town
> After paying blood money, and the bereaved
> Restrains his proud spirit and broken heart
> Because he has received payment.[22]

This reference to "blood money," although arguably atypical for the Achaean society of both Ajax and Achilles,[23] foretells the gradual giving way of the custom of blood revenge that prevailed at the time. This very giving way occurs in the character of Achilles, who, initially unmoved by Ajax's story, apparently learns about restraint and forgiveness when he later bows to Priam's entreaties to return Hector's body for burial. Earlier, when Hector has suggested that the winner of their combat shall return the slain to his family, Achilles refuses the bargain, comparing himself to lions and wolves, wild creatures that would not observe such niceties. By the end of the *Iliad*, we see a slightly more compliant Achilles. When Priam comes as a suppliant to Achilles to get Hector's body, saying, "I have borne what no man / Who has walked this earth has ever yet borne. / I have kissed the hand of the man who killed my son,"[24] Achilles surrenders his overwhelming need further to avenge the death of his friend, Patroclus, even upon Hector's corpse. Instead, he opens himself to share with Priam the human experience of shared grief. In one of the final scenes of the *Iliad*, archenemies Priam and Achilles weep together, and the warrior Achilles promises Priam a temporary truce to give him time to bury his son properly.[25]

As the *Iliad* so movingly depicts in this surprising scene, although revenge was acknowledged as the hero's right, a true hero recognized limits. The unabashed acceptance of unlimited bloody revenge had dire consequences. Even small disputes could require families and clans to enter into blood feuds that continued indefinitely in a state of vendetta, thereby weakening the clan by the loss of most men of fighting age. Blood revenge was among the most common causes of war among primitive people, with "mutual extinction" a likely outcome.[26]

The utter destructiveness of unrestrained blood feuding gave rise to certain variations to bring about closure. By the time of the great Attic tragedies in the fourth century B.C., the natural right to revenge was clearly ambiguous[27] and the moral status of an act of revenge depended upon the individual context.[28] This ambiguity and contextuality become apparent through the contrast between the *Odyssey*'s version of the story of Orestes, who kills his mother and her lover in revenge for his father's murder, and the versions presented by Aeschylus and Euripedes some three centuries later. In the *Odyssey*, Zeus relates the tale of Orestes' revenge on Aegisthus with approval: Zeus told Aegisthus "not to kill the man [Agamemnon] and not to woo his wife, / Or payment would come through Orestes."[29] Orestes is described as "godly,"[30] and his act of revenge is viewed as expected, fully justified, and unambiguous. Orestes' revenge strictly accords with the operative Achaean system of vendetta: "Blood has been shed; blood is avenged by blood."[31]

Euripides, depicting the same story centuries later, makes Orestes an entirely different character—a revenge-seeking thug dispossessed of any nobility, let alone any godliness. In so doing, Euripides transforms vengeance into an evil impulse. What the *Odyssey* described as Orestes' duty to take revenge becomes in Euripides' drama a character flaw, a selfish emotional need. But in order to characterize Orestes' act of revenge as a failure of character, Euripides must offer an alternative to personal revenge and thereby indulge in an anachronism. He creates in his play a system of state punishment that did not actually exist when Orestes, according to legend, killed his mother. Of course, the system of state judgment and punishment did exist for Euripides' audience, so they would have fully comprehended the consequences of Orestes' repudiation of state retribution in favor of taking personal revenge.[32] Equally understood would have been Euripides' argument against Orestes' act of revenge as he presents it through the judgment passed by Tyndareus, Orestes' grandfather and Clytemnestra's father. Tyndareus claims that Orestes acted "stupidly" and outside the boundaries of the law or accepted custom:

What should he have done? When his father died—killed, I admit, by my own daughter's hand, an atrocious crime which I do not condone and never shall—he should have haled his mother into court, charged her formally with murder, and made her pay the penalty prescribed, expulsion from his house. Legal action not murder. That was the course to take. Under the circumstances, a hard choice, true, but the course of self-control and due respect for law, the better choice of two evils.[33]

Orestes, in Euripides' version, has demonstrated a lamentable lack of self-control and respect for law, traits that the audience would quickly condemn. His passion for revenge is given no place; it is unequivocally the foolhardy alternative to a court of law.

Aeschylus' more nuanced treatment of the Orestes story is situated, on the other hand, between the outright praise from Zeus found in the *Odyssey* and the condemnation found in Euripides. Aeschylus and Euripides differ critically in the role they accord to vengeance in relation to any system of state punishment. For Aeschylus the desire for revenge is an understandable, although problematic emotion. Instead of condemning it, he creates a complex compromise that includes a system of state punishment within the polis of Athens, but this system incorporates a responsibility to the human desire for revenge.

Aeschylus presents Orestes as trapped between Apollo's mandate that he avenge his father's murder and the inevitability that the Furies will relentlessly pursue him if he does kill; Orestes cannot do the right thing. In the second part of Aeschylus' trilogy, *The Libation Bearers*, Orestes is pressured by his sister, Electra, and by society (represented by the

Chorus), to kill his mother, Clytemnestra, and her lover, Aegisthus, because they have killed his father, Agamemnon. Electra and the Chorus both represent the values of heroic societies. Electra sees the problem as a simple one: a death for a death. As she prays at her father's tomb, the Chorus approaches her and instructs: "Say simply: 'one to kill them for the life they took.' May you not hurt your enemy when he struck first?"[34] Electra prays that Agamemnon's "avenger come, that they / who killed you shall be killed in turn, as they deserve."[35] When Orestes appears, she and the Chorus argue powerfully in an attempt to convince him to be that avenger, aligning revenge with justice and insisting that vengeance, in the form of a murder for a murder, is necessary to heal the "Swarming infection that boils within"[36] the land. For the gods, too, the situation is clear. Apollo's oracle orders Orestes to take revenge or he will experience "winters of disaster";[37] if Orestes fails to avenge his father he will "pay penalty / with [his] own life, and suffer much sad punishment."[38]

Once Orestes has killed his mother and her lover Aegisthus, however, he discovers that he has enmeshed himself in a cycle of revenge that is unending: one murder begets another. Unlike the unscathed Odysseus at the end of the *Odyssey* whose serial revenge has enabled him to regain his wife and his throne, Orestes suffers mightily for what appeared to be a god-sanctioned act of murder. The Furies (or Erinyes)[39] haunt him: "Women who serve this house, they come like gorgons, they / wear robes of black, and they are wreathed in a tangle / of snakes. I can no longer stay."[40] He becomes an outcast, and the Furies, "utterly repulsive,"[41] stalk him, demanding their own retribution.[42] Orestes cannot rule in his rightful place, and he flees his land unable to rest anywhere without the omnipresent Furies. The Furies are a unique composite image created by Aeschylus, who drew them partly from the Keres, the ghosts of those murdered who cry out for vengeance, and partly from an image depicting a source of physical infection capable of poisoning the land (in keeping with the pollution doctrine). The revenge sought by the Furies, then, is both individual representing a vengeful spirit of the slain Clytemenestra, and more widespread, in that Orestes' murders pollute the very land.

In the final play of the *Oresteia*, *The Eumenides*, Aeschylus depicts the difficulties and intricacies of a transition from private revenge to state judgment. Orestes, still fleeing the Furies, becomes a suppliant to Athena, the goddess of wisdom, a very different Athena than the vengeful goddess present in the final books of the *Odyssey*. Athena asks to hear both sides. The Furies' indictment is brief, to the point, and reflects the basic principle of blood feuds that the intent of the wrongdoer is irrelevant:[43] "He murdered his mother by deliberate choice."[44] Orestes then makes his argument:

> He [Agamemnon] died without honor when he came home. It was my mother of the dark heart, who entangled him in subtle gyves and cut him down, the bath is witness to his death. I was an exile in the time before this. I came back and killed the woman who gave me birth. I plead guilty. My father was dear, and this was vengeance for his blood. Apollo shares responsibility for this. He counter-spurred my heart and told me of pains to come if I should fail to act against the guilty ones. This is my case.[45]

Athena, in a dramatic shift away from earlier practices that left decisions about vengeance to individuals and families, characterizes the "matter as too big for any mortal man"[46] and that even she, a goddess, does not have the right "to analyze cases of murder where wrath's edge is sharp."[47] At the same time, Aeschylus presents her as wise enough to see the consequences of ignoring the Furies: "yet these, too, have their work. We cannot brush them aside, / and if this action so runs that they fail to win, / the venom of their resolution will return / to infect the soil, and sicken all my land to death."[48] Orestes' dilemma becomes Athena's dilemma when the Furies agree to turn their authority to avenge murder over to Athena. She, the goddess of wisdom, recognizes her problem and sets up a court: "Here is dilemma. / Whether I let them stay or drive / them off, it is a hard course and will hurt. Then, since / the burden to the case is here, and rests on me, / I shall select judges of manslaughter, and swear / them in, establish a court into all time to come."[49] Athena refers to the conception of the pollution doctrine that held that the harm would spread from the individual to the culture at large—"infect the soil." Yet she takes the expiation of the pollution away from the individuals seeking vengeance, the Furies, and places it in the hands of a jury of strangers to the matter.

The *Oresteia* provides insights into the problems that accompanied the transfer of the right to revenge to a central authority, even to the goddess of wisdom herself. The outcome may not deal well with the emotional needs of those seeking revenge.[50] The ballots of the jury that Athena has selected result in a tie, and Athena casts the deciding ballot for Orestes.[51] The Furies, having lost, threaten: "I, disinherited, suffering, heavy with anger / shall let loose upon the land / vindictive poison / dripping deadly out of my heart upon the ground."[52] Athena has foreseen their disappointed and angry reaction, and she placates them by offering "a place of [their] own, deep hidden under ground that is yours by right / where you shall sit on shining chairs beside the hearth / to accept devotions offered by your citizens."[53] Unconvinced at first, the Furies repeat their lament, claiming to be disinherited, mocked, dishonored. Athena pleads with them: "No, not dishonored. You are goddesses. Do not / in too much anger make this place of mortal men / uninhabitable."[54] Athena is patient with the Furies, promising that no household will prosper without their will, that she will let them have much influence and be honored. (It takes over 150 lines of dialogue between Athena and the Furies before they are convinced.) The Furies finally concede to Athena and utter these crucial lines: "I accept this home at Athena's side," thereby creating a complex image of vengeance at wisdom's side, of raw unrestrained emotion incorporated into justice.[55] In so doing, the Furies became transformed into the Eumenides, the "kindly ones," a critical aspect of institutionalized law.[56] They cease to be the Furies and become instead the local goddesses, contained by but also part of the legal system of Athens. As such, they are no longer frightful Gorgons but, as they came to be portrayed in artifacts, "gentle, staid, matronly figures."[57] Acknowledged and incorporated, they participate in justice but are not irrationally destructive.

But Aeschylus' vision was overly optimistic. As various cultures worked through the shift from private revenge to state punishment, the Furies were not always accorded a "home at Athena's side." Instead, revenge and justice became treated as polar opposites, and the urge toward revenge was deemed reprehensible and always excessive. But the change within any culture from Aeschylus' optimistic positioning of the Furies to their complete dismissal could not be accomplished in a single step. A culture steeped in a tradition of blood feud revenge needed transitional steps.

One of these transitional steps took on some form of the *lex talionis* argument, the eye-for-an-eye principle that requires that the punishment exacted equal in both form and harshness the harm received. While often interpreted as a permissive doctrine, *lex talionis* sanctioned equal punishment, thereby imposing a limit upon the revenge that could be taken:[58] a life for a life, an injury for an injury, property for property.[59] Such limitations in theory provided end points for blood feuds; once the original harm was balanced, the feud ended. In practice, of course, the parties often disagreed as to what was a fair and adequate balancing, and the feud continued indefinitely. Another means of balancing the harm was a payment of money to the victim's relative. As early as the eighteenth century B.C., for example, the Code of Hammurabi, while adhering generally to the principle of *lex talionis*, attempted to limit private revenge and blood feuds.[60] Many wrongs could be compensated by payment (composition) to the victim's family or clan, the amount varying with the offense and with the status of the victim.[61] Among the Assyrians and the Hittites, a rich killer could have himself replaced by another or could buy his way out of blood revenge.[62] The

Pelagasians of ancient Greece practiced a "tribal wergeld."[63] In Anglo-Saxon societies, the *wergeld*, the worth of a man, could "buy off the spear"[64] and was commonly used to avenge a death.[65] The consolidated laws of the Germanic tribes describe sums of money as compensations for homicides.[66]

In all these practices, the state acknowledged the desire for revenge, keeping the Furies by Athena's side, while it simultaneously worked to regulate and limit its fulfillment in action. The private settlements may be seen as an advancement over violence for violence yet these practices also met with disapproval and condemnation.[67] Although the state vied to interfere and to regulate, at this time it still remained unthinkable for any authority outside the kinship group to act; the state had neither the power nor the approval of the people to take action[68]—until the emergence of the "pollution doctrine."

The pollution doctrine was perhaps the most effective argument the state could make in its effort to regulate vengeance.[69] In effect, the pollution doctrine began the process of state retribution in that it depersonalized harm and spread the revenge requirement from the individual or the clan to the entire community. In this doctrine, a crime became an insult to and a stain against the community at large. "Much as the religions of the Athenians and Hebrews differed, their doctrine . . . was . . . that the land is polluted by the shedding of innocent blood and no expiation can be made for the land but by the death of the offender. It is the duty of the nearest kin to obtain revenge for the slain and the presence of the slayer in the land destroys its fertility."[70] The pollution doctrine may be seen as a bridge between private blood feud revenge and state retribution in that it expresses a compromise between tribal traditions and the slowly evolving power of the state.[71] Because the pollution doctrine saw the wrong as committed against the community, private settlement of any sort—violent revenge, compensation, or even pardon—was not exclusively a personal matter. Although the actual taking of revenge might still be enacted by a family member, this action would occur under state aegis.[72]

The conception of pollution was very Semitic and is essentially the biblical approach to revenge: a wrong is a stain against the community and no payment may be taken to balance the transgression.[73] God instructs Moses as the Israelites approach Canaan as to the appropriate sanctions for homicide: "Blood defiles the land, and expiation cannot be made on behalf of the land for blood shed on it except by the blood of the man that shed it."[74] Not the individual or the clan but God, as the ruler of the tribal Israelites, alone is entitled to take vengeance.[75] In this respect, revenge and justice are not contraries, but are related. While the God of the Old Testament is sometimes described as "compassionate [and] long-suffering,"[76] God is also depicted as having a "sword steeped in blood" awaiting a "day of vengeance"[77] and as showing "unfailing love" by causing enemies' "life-blood [to] spurt[ed] over [his] garments."[78] In the world revealed in the Old Testament, revenge seems requisite to reestablishing the natural order: "And the sun stood still and the moon halted until a nation had taken vengeance on its enemies."[79] Revered Old Testament figures such as Samson[80] and Deborah[81] are renowned for their acts of heroic revenge. The New Testament likewise ratifies God's right to avenge; Paul writes that God will "pay every man for what he has done. . . . [T]here will be the fury of retribution. . . . trouble and distress for every human being who is an evil-doer."[82] The principle of God's justice is inextricably aligned with willingness to take revenge.

Although virtues such as courage and fidelity remained important in early societies, with the emergence of the pollution doctrine, blood vengeance and the duty to one's clan was reluctantly ceded to the polis, or city-state. As the state managed to characterize itself as the victim, it could argue more effectively that the needs of the individual victim and family were less significant than a balancing within the state itself. If the state claims that *it* must reestablish the natural order that has been disrupted by the crime, then the importance of the victim's need for some personal balancing becomes virtually insignificant. Like Euripides' Orestes or Dorfman's Paulina, the victim must be willing to forgo any personal desire for vengeance so that the state can function in an orderly fashion for some larger good. State punishment, then, carried an important message related to the pollution doctrine: a wrong was committed not just against the individual but also against the social unit itself—in many cases the state embodied in the person of the king.[83]

Gradually, the complete suppression of private revenge came to be presented as being essential to the advancement of civilization, as requisite to an ordered society. When the state takes revenge in the form of retribution, however, the passion leaches out of it; revenge is passionate, retribution is dispassionate.[84] Over time, revenge, once an important component of justice systems, became justice's polar opposite. Thus the powerful image in Aeschylus' *Oresteia*, the emotional drive for revenge taking its rightful place at wisdom's side, is unrealized.

This ragged history reveals that revenge did not always have a bad reputation. Humankind was not always embarrassed by a desire to balance a harm with a comparable harm in an act of revenge. What, then, occurred that created the polarization? And why was it seen as necessary?

Chapter Two
The Demonizing of Revenge

If thou didst ever thy dear father love—
. . . .
Revenge his foul and most unnatural murder.
—William Shakespeare, *Hamlet, Prince of Denmark*

In the present age . . . we are inclined to think that civilized people are not given to hatred and to an anger so intense that it generates the desire for revenge.
—Jeffrie Murphy, *Forgiveness and Mercy*

The first quotation, spoken by the ghost of Hamlet's father at the initial meeting between the prince and the ghost, was written around 1600, the second in 1988. In less than 400 years, the beliefs, in Western culture at least, that surround the taking of revenge have metamorphosed from viewing revenge as a natural and necessary component of love and the requisite mark of kinship to an all-out condemnation of revenge as unfit for "civilized people." What happened in the interim? Revenge had a nearly sacrosanct place in early conceptions of justice. What changed the popular opinion concerning revenge from recognizing it as a mark of honor to judging it a desperate and illegal act?

The willingness of people to abdicate the right to take personal revenge was contingent upon the strength of the central authority. The people's obedience also depended on the sovereign's willingness and ability to take on revenge as a state responsibility. By the twelfth century, in most places in the Western world, the state had grown strong enough to fully usurp the right to take vengeance. Private revenge became extra-legal as the state claimed a monopoly on legal violence. Homicide ceased to be a private wrong calling for familial response in the form of a death or compensation, but rather became a capital offense, a crime against the state as well as the individual or family. Centralized in this way, revenge became what is commonly called retribution, that is, revenge enacted by the state.[1] Additionally, the state acting in a person's behalf—taking on one's violent act, so to speak—became synonymous with *justice.* To get justice meant getting the state to punish the wrong-doer.

The degree of private restraint, nonetheless, was always proportional to the strength of the sovereign. The strong arm of the law alone, however, could not convince people to give up what they had regarded as a sacred privilege and duty. The story of the state's usurpation includes great resistance from people accustomed to righting their own private wrongs. Because revenge was deeply connected to a sense of kinship, family loyalty, and courage, other more subtle maneuvers were necessary to complete the transfer.

While the pollution doctrine might provide the state with a rationale to justify its participation in punishment, that rationale alone cannot eliminate the desire for private revenge that has been so deeply part of human culture. Paulina does not argue against the state's *right* to prosecute, but she does insist that her own needs be taken into account. When she asks Gerardo (standing in for the official state as head of the government commission), "What about *my* good?" Gerardo has no reply except to ask for her sacrifice. How else can he respond? In the legal system he serves, Paulina's "good" has no standing. Paulina issues another unanswerable challenge: "Why is it always people like me who always have to sacrifice, who have to concede when concessions are needed, biting my tongue, why?" Clearly, it would be more convenient for the state if Paulina and others like her remained silent, bit their tongues and held their peace. Paulina's cooperative silence would be guaranteed if her desire for revenge were somehow eliminated. She is expected to suppress her own emotional requirements, her desire and need for some revenge. From the perspective of a less-than-stable state, Paulina should not only allow the government to determine crimes and punishments, she should also be willing to "put the past behind" if that is what the state requires of her.

As emerging states began to centralize their power and monopolize revenge, another development became necessary so that people would not readily reclaim their ancient right. This development was the removal of emotion from state punishment and the purgation of the victim's desire for punishment. States needed to insure that even the desire for revenge would be unacceptable. One of the most effective devices for this suppression and silencing was shame, the instructing of each citizen to be ashamed of any citizen, including himself or herself, who might give importance to a desire for revenge. Citizens were taught to believe that they could seek justice (dispassionate state punishment) but not revenge, severing any original nexus that the two might have shared. The situation in Western Europe, particularly in England from the sixteenth to the eighteenth centuries, provides an example of the cultural strategies employed to change the perception of revenge. Religion, philosophy, and literature were enlisted to convince people to keep the urge for personal revenge restrained. Wherever people gathered—in churches, theaters, and educational institutions—they encountered some sort of argument, subtle or otherwise, against personal revenge.

In their sermons and religious writings, ministers and theologians reinterpreted the biblical practice and approval of revenge depicted in both the New and Old Testaments. No longer was the emphasis on God's wrathful vengeance, on his "sword steeped in blood." Instead theologians roundly denounced revengers and predicted damnation for anyone who took revenge into his or her own hands; the revenger "strips himselfe of Gods protection."[2] Elizabethan England was described as a New Jerusalem, in which "there is now no thirsting for reuenge. The law of Retribution is disanuld amongst them. . . . An eie no longer for an eie; a tooth no longer for a tooth."[3] Influential theologian Joseph Butler (in an interesting foreshadowing of Nietzsche) preached that revenge, which stems from resentment, is contrary to religion and that while "every man naturally feels an indignation upon seeing instances of villainy and baseness,"[4] at the same time "indulgence of revenge"[5] has the tendency to propagate itself and thus must not be engaged in "by any one who considers mankind as a community or family, and himself a member of it."[6]

Much of the popular drama of the sixteenth and seventeenth centuries set up a similar stark contrast between revenge and justice, often with bloody depictions of revenge and equally bloody portrayals of its consequences. A culture bent on suppressing destructive revenge impulses had to encourage the emergence of stories that contrasted revenge with justice, stories that created the cautionary cultural narrative arguing that revenge and justice are mutually exclusive and, thus excluded, the desire for revenge is shameful and requires suppression. In seeking an extinction of the passion for revenge, the extremes of vengeful behavior were presented, with revenge often portrayed as being sought for trivial wrongs and in excess. Popular dramas portrayed revenge as an agonizing burden that invariably pushed even good people into madness with cataclysmic results. If the notion of revenge entered a hero's life, it would inevitably "warp his character [and] drive him to insanity."[7]

Thomas Kyd's *The Spanish Tragedy* (1589) was the "most prodigious success of any drama produced and printed between 1580 and 1642."[8] In *The Spanish Tragedy*, Kyd portrays a variety of revengers: the noble but paralyzed Hieronimo who must avenge his murdered son, as well as the malicious Balthazar and Lorenzo, who kill for selfish reasons and trivial wrongs. The actions of all the revengers, good and evil, bring down the state and result in multiple deaths. At the close of the play, the Ghost of Don Andrea, a slain warrior, speaks to a character called Revenge and delineates, with gruesome pleasure, the multiple revenge murders that have occurred:

I, now my hopes have end in their effects,
When blood and sorrow finnish my desires:
Horatio murdered in his Fathers bower,
Vilde *Serberine* by *Pedringano* slaine,
False *Pedringano* hangd by quaint device,
Faire *Isabella* by her selfe misdone,
Prince *Balthazar* by *Bel-imperia* stabd,
The Duke of Castile and his wicked Sonne,
Both done to death by olde *Hieronimo*.
My *Bel-imperia* falne as *Dido* fell,
And good *Hieronimo* slaine by himselfe:
I these were spectacles to please my soule.[9]

Nine deaths and the end of the possibility of peace between Spain and Portugal are the fruits of the drive for revenge. In *The Spanish Tragedy* and in many of the plays that the English audiences attended for several generations, "The act of revenge does not correct an imbalance and restore order . . . with the even exchange of an eye for an eye, tooth for tooth. Revenge is itself an act of excess."[10] In *The Spanish Tragedy*, revenge does not restore a balance; it destroys the possibility of one.

The perverse nature of revenge appears in another popular drama of the time, John Marston's *Antonio's Revenge* (ca. 1601). The evil Piero opens the play covered in blood having just murdered Andrugio because many years earlier Andrugio was his rival for the hand of Maria, who had chosen Andrugio. Piero brags, "I am great in blood, / Unequal'd in revenge"[11] and plots even more bloody acts. Andrugio's son, Antonio, bid by the ghost of his father to avenge his murder, acts, it would seem, out of an ancient sense of duty, honor, and justice. But those values become perverted as Antonio, as part of the revenge, murders Piero's completely innocent son Julio as Julio begs for his life— "Pray you do not hurt me."[12] The motive for revenge begins in duty and transforms into excess and cruelty.

A study of over twenty revenge plays produced in England between 1562 and 1607 concludes that in most of them revenge is "unmistakably condemned,"[13] and the plays constitute an intense propaganda campaign against revenge because of the establishment's fear of the civil disorder that could result from private revenge.[14] By the mid-seventeenth century, revenge had few advocates, and bloody acts of revenge in dramas were put into the hands of villains, buttressing a general and unceasing propaganda against revenge.[15]

By the eighteenth century, the original connection between personal revenge and state punishment had become obscured to the extent that the focus of any rationale for the state's right to punish bypassed the victim and focused on the duty of the sovereign and the moral status of the perpetrator. The philosophical stances of Kant and Hegel toward punishment capture the prevalent mood of the late eighteenth and early nineteenth centuries. In Kant's work, for example, punishment by the state is deontological, the absolute right and duty of the state. The law concerning punishment is one of Kant's categorical imperatives. The state has a duty to punish and for a sovereign to fail to punish, to grant clemency, is itself an act of injustice: "woe to him who rummages around in the winding path of a theory of happiness looking for advantage to be gained by releasing the criminal from punishment or by reducing the amount of it."[16] A victim's personal emotions, regarded as "brute forces" by Kant, have no place in punishment, either for severity or mercy. Human beings may be forgiving (*placabilitas*), but being forgiving should not be confused with tolerating wrongs, "for then a human being would be throwing away his rights and letting others trample on them, and so would violate his duty to himself."[17]

Hegel developed Kant's advocacy of the deontological nature of punishment by refining the idea of balancing that was originally found in feelings about revenge: "crime . . . contains within itself its own nullification, and this appears in the form of punishment."[18] Rather than the "absurdity" of "specific equality" required by *lex talionis* ("so that one can even imagine the miscreant as one-eyed or toothless"), Hegel argued that punishment should result in an "inner equality"—the negating of the original negative (crime): "punishment is merely a manifestation of the crime, i.e. it is one half which is naturally presupposed by the other."[19] Hegel shifted the focus to the wrongdoer by arguing that offenders had the *right* to be punished, that punishing those who do wrong treats them as responsible moral agents making free choices: "In so far as the punishment . . . is seen as embodying *the criminal's own right*, the criminal is *honoured* as a rational being" (original italics).[20] In addition, punishment should be derived from the criminal's own act, so that he is not "regarded simply as a harmful animal which must be rendered harmless," but as a rational being.[21] Hegel emphasized the personal/impersonal distinction between revenge and retribution and also distinguished the two as immoral and moral respectively: "What is at first sight objectionable about retribution is that it looks like something immoral, like revenge, and may thus be interpreted as a personal matter."[22] For Hegel, state punishment was justified not because it satisfied the victim but because it treated the criminal with dignity.

While Kant's and Hegel's theories remain the bedrock for contemporary retributive theories of punishment that argue for treating criminals as responsible moral agents,[23] it was Nietzsche's introduction of the notion of *ressentiment* that thoroughly condemned the kinds of emotions that would desire revenge. *Ressentiment* is not merely the anger and resentment that would result from a personal injury. It includes a litany of negative emotions: hate, envy, ill will, suspicion, rancor, revenge, hostility, prejudice, and greed. Saying we want revenge, then, categorizes us as the kind of people who surrender to these primitive urges, and the "emotions that give rise to retributive judgments are always pathological."[24] Wanting revenge, even in the form of state retribution, dooms us, in Nietzsche's judgment, to be creatures of *ressentiment*. A good justice system for him does not incorporate such emotions in an Aeschylean vision but shuts them down and stops the "senseless raging of *ressentiment*."[25] This shutting down is accomplished by disallowing a role for the victim, by providing other compensations for victims, and by using the law to define and restrict what penalties might be exacted. Above all, such a justice system "trains" the minds and perceptions of victims away from any personal feeling about an injury:

> But the most decisive thing the higher power does and forces through against the predominance of counter- and after-feelings . . . is the establishment of the *law*, the imperative declaration of what in general is to count in its eyes as permitted, as just, what as forbidden, as unjust: after it has established the law, it treats infringements and arbitrary actions of individuals or entire groups as wanton acts against the law, as rebellion against the highest power itself, thereby diverting the feeling of its subjects away from the most immediate injury caused by such wanton acts and thus achieving in the long run the opposite of what all revenge wants, which sees only the viewpoint of the injured one, allows only it to count—from now on the eye is trained for an ever *more impersonal* appraisal of deeds, even the eye of the injured one himself. (original italics)[26]

Nietzsche disparages any tendency "to hallow *revenge* under the name of *justice*" (original italics).[27] Distinctions, nuances, or subtleties between the just anger felt by an Aeschylean Orestes against a real wrong committed against oneself or one's kin and the crazed anger and other negative emotions that lead to excessive, illegal acts of revenge have fallen under the weight of Enlightenment philosophy. In a series of maneuvers, the original relationship between revenge and justice and the victim's emotional response to a harm have disappeared and been replaced by *ressen-*

timent. In the law of punishment, "reasonable emotion" and "just anger" are oxymorons.

By the time the nineteenth century closed, in some of the most widely read literature of the age, Dickens portrayed the "corrosive powers"[28] of revenge and retribution, mirroring the trend in jurisprudence that had begun to abandon retribution as a justification for punishment. This trend gave retributivist theories of punishment the same moral taint that attached to revenge in Elizabethan times. While it is difficult, if not impossible, to generalize about the various theories of punishment that were vigorously debated, the debate was largely between deontology and consequentialism. Many strong retributivists gave in to Darwinian ideas that in some ways echoed the pollution doctrine and maintained that "the good of the social organism" was the morally superior justification for punishment rather than a personal, vindictive need for revenge.[29] Any state "responsibility" to victims had entirely disappeared and was, in fact, a disreputable notion.

The twentieth century ushered in a reluctance to acknowledge revenge as a human need, and even the reformed Kantian-Hegelian retributivist position became suspect in intellectual circles.[30] The desire for revenge and for using the state as a mechanism for retribution met with increasing disapproval, being seen as a "wilful substitution of passion for reason as a guide of conduct, and a kind of passion which, in the form of private revenge, civilised society has agreed to condemn."[31] Retribution became a "polite name for revenge . . . vindictive, inhumane, barbarous, and immoral."[32] Backward-looking retributive theories of punishment were displaced by forward-looking utilitarian and consequentialist rationales that justified punishment largely as deterrence and rehabilitation, and perhaps to deter those who, in the absence of state retribution, would enact private revenge.[33] Those opposed to retributivism argued also that the incommensurability of harms made it impossible to inflict an appropriate punishment in the name of retribution, adhering, it seems, to the ancient *lex talionis* as an impossible necessity.[34] For a variety of reasons, retributivism was "destroyed by criticism,"[35] was "no longer the dominant objective of the criminal law,"[36] and, in the words of a leading hornbook, was "the least accepted [justification for punishment] today by theorists."[37] The sacred personal right that was reluctantly transferred to the state has become the natural right of the state; the victim has disappeared. Jeffrie Murphy sums up the contemporary attitude toward retributive theories of punishment: "In the present age, most of us do not feel comfortable talking about the criminal law in such terms, for we are inclined to think that civilized people are not given to hatred and to an anger so intense that it generates the desire for revenge. . . . We prefer to talk highmindedly of our reluctantly advocating punishment of criminals perhaps because social utility or justice demands it and tend to think that it is only primitives who would actually *hate* criminals and want them to suffer to appease an anger or outrage that is felt toward them" (original italics).[38]

What the Athena of Aeschylus' *Oresteia* recognizes and honors in the Furies is lost, and we see this plainly in the character of the lawyer Gerardo in *Death and the Maiden*. Fury and passion have no appropriate place in a legal system. Gerardo's position is the rational voice of civilization that has held, at least since Elizabethan times, that vengeance is personally fruitless, socially destructive, and aligned with madness, if not symptomatic of it. To Gerardo, Paulina's emotional need for something from the state is at best selfish and misguided, at worst deranged. "Imagine what would happen if everyone acted like you did. You satisfy your personal passion . . . the whole transition to democracy can go screw itself." Miranda buttresses Gerardo's rationality with "Isn't it time we stopped?" Paulina's newly recovered voice is that of passion, reason's alleged opposite, that requires, indeed demands, some sort of balancing to recover the natural order destroyed by her torture. "What about my good?" The two "goods," societal order and personal emotional need for redress, are deemed antithetical, with our contemporary notion "justice" squarely on the side of societal order and the repression of the emotions of resentment and hatred that lead to revenge. Additionally, any original sense of the meaning of retribution as giving something back to the victim has disappeared; retribution has come to mean punishment directed at the perpetrator. The state punishes because the perpetrator *deserves* it.[39]

This transfer to the state advocated by theologians, philosophers, and dramatists assumes a strong central state capable and willing to act on a victim's behalf. Yet interwoven with these staunch positions against revenge, we find more layered and ambiguous positions about revenge. For some, the presence and possibility of private revenge remained an imminent possibility, especially if the state failed in its duty to enact an appropriate rebalancing. Machiavelli wrote that while the power to avenge ought properly to be vested in those with the requisite authority, that authority must lead to action: "if an individual is grievously offended either by the public or by a private person, and does not receive due satisfaction, he will, if he lives in a republic, seek to avenge himself, even if it lead to the ruin of that republic."[40] While Francis Bacon deplored revenge, writing in a much-quoted line "Revenge is a kind of wild justice, which the more man's nature was to it, the more ought law weed it out,"[41] he also tempered his harsh judgment of revenge by adding in a less quoted line "The most tolerable sort of revenge is for those wrongs which there is no law to remedy."[42] An influential Elizabethan writer maintained that private revenge was appropriate "when violence is offered, and the Magistrate is absent. . . . In this case, God puts the sword into the priuate mans hands."[43] These writers supported the view that the state was the appropriate enactor of punishment for a wrong, but if the state failed to act, an individual was justified in taking revenge. Despite the predominant cultural voice that condemned revenge, there existed another countervoice that insisted that the desire for revenge was not per se evil and even tolerated revenge under some circumstances. Such writers arguably attempted to restore the collapsed distinction between just feelings of resentment and barbarous emotions run amok.

Some, in fact, saw the desire for revenge as a noble and worthwhile emotion. Adam Smith, who, unlike Kant and Hegel, promoted the guidance of the emotions as being critical to good judgment,[44] found resentment and hatred against someone who has wronged us to be a necessary part of human nature. He, nonetheless, qualified those instances in which the urge for revenge is appropriate: "if we yield to the dictates of revenge, it is with reluctance, from necessity, and in consequence of great and repeated provocations. When resentment is guarded and qualified in this manner, it may be admitted to be even generous and noble."[45] Smith sees anger and resentment, as long as they are legitimately provoked, as part of the underpinnings of a moral community, as safeguards against wrongdoing "to protect the weak, to curb the violent, and to chastise the guilty."[46] Smith's position on revenge draws its imagery from Senecan revenge tragedies:

His blood [one slain], we think, calls aloud for vengeance. The very ashes of the dead seem to be disturbed at the thought that his injuries are to pass unrevenged. The horrors which are supposed to haunt the bed of the murderer, the ghosts which, superstition imagines, rise from their graves to demand vengeance on those who brought them to an untimely end, all take their origin from this natural sympathy with the imaginary resentment of the slain. . . . Nature . . . has in this manner stamped upon the human heart . . . an immediate and instinctive approbation of the sacred and necessary law of retaliation.[47]

For Smith, there is something natural in humankind that needs some kind of revenge, something "stamped upon the human heart" that requires a state with laws and procedures that can fulfill the "sacred and necessary law of retaliation."[48]

Carlyle, who deplored reformers arguing for humane prisons, declined euphemistic language and openly defended the urge for revenge: "'Revenge,' my friends! revenge, and the natural hatred of scoundrels, and the ineradicable tendency to *revancher* oneself upon them and pay them what they have merited: this is forevermore intrinsically a correct, and even a divine feeling in the mind of every man. Only the excess of it is diabolical; the essence I say is manlike, and even god-like."[49] Similarly, the Victorian jurist James Fitzjames Stephen resisted the move into viewing punishment as for deterrence alone and insisted that the desire for revenge was natural to "healthily constituted minds."[50] A good criminal justice system recognizes this need and should be "an emphatic assertion of the principle that the feeling of hatred and the desire for vengeance   are important elements of human nature which ought . . . to be satisfied in a regular and legal manner."[51]

Even these more nuanced positions, though, finally are exhortative rather than seriously prescriptive: that is, these writers, in their efforts to create a perfect society and ideal justice, speak to the state, not to its citizens, warning those in power to enact justice for the citizens, or else. They do not realistically confront what should occur if the state actually does nothing. They do not envisage a weak, impotent state that cannot judge and punish. They imagine an ideal strong state that has the capacity to be vigilant in exacting punishment. Because they seemingly cannot conceive of a state that cannot or will not act, they naturally do not provide any alternative to violence if the state does so fail.

Perhaps the best portrayal of this ambivalent feeling about revenge and the failure of the state can be seen in Shakespeare's play, *Hamlet*, in which he dramatizes the complex nature of revenge and the conflicted, if underground, attitude toward it. Like other playwrights of his time, Shakespeare was obsessed by revenge, his representations evolving from the barbaric excesses of *Titus Andronicus* (1594) to Prospero's abandonment of revenge in favor of reconciliation in *The Tempest* (1623). In *Hamlet*, his greatest and most complex play, Shakespeare depicts his intellectual prince as hesitant to take revenge yet obsessed with the need to do so. Using the conventional Senecan symbols of revenge tragedy—a ghost, madness, delay, hesitation, a play-within-a-play, the failure of the law, uncertainty, multiple murders, and the avenger's death[52]—Shakespeare creates a complicated hero whose inner psyche contains both the ancient duty to take revenge and the modern repulsion toward it.[53]

In the characters of the ghost and Laertes, Shakespeare represents, in different ways, the idea central to heroic societies that taking revenge is requisite to a loving relationship. The ghost of Hamlet's father demands, "If thou didst ever thy dear father love . . . / Revenge his foul and most unnatural murder."[54] The naturalness and even appropriateness of revenge is woven throughout the play in that line and others such as, "If thou hast nature in thee, bear it [the murder] not."[55] King Hamlet, a good and noble man unjustly betrayed and murdered (we "shall not look upon his like again")[56] speaks these lines, not a murderous villain in a Kydian treatment. Because they are spoken by someone we are supposed to admire, we are instructed to take this sentiment seriously and, like Hamlet, to turn it over in our mind. This ghost does not demand the excess characteristic to contemporaneous dramatic versions of revenge that left the stages littered with corpses of the innocent and guilty alike. Instead he admonishes Hamlet to restrain himself ("Taint not thy mind"),[57] and limit his bloody revenge to Claudius alone. Speaking of Gertrude, he advises, "Leave her to heaven."[58] The convention of the ghost demanding revenge, borrowed from Seneca[59] and familiar to revenge dramas of Shakespeare's time, is a variation of the Furies of Aeschylus, creatures from another world insisting that the unjustly murdered be avenged. The dignified and honorable ghost of King Hamlet approaches the image sought by Aeschylus of the Furies at Wisdom's side, a far more complex and ambiguous image than the polarized revenge and justice, passion and reason, of lesser plays. As Charles and Elaine Hallett note, "The Ghost in *Hamlet* . . . symbolizes that justice which is naturally intuited by the individual psyche."[60]

In Laertes, Shakespeare personifies the ancient, uncomplicated response to a wrong committed against a family; Laertes sees his course clearly. Hamlet has killed Laertes's father, Polonius, and driven his sister, Ophelia, to madness and suicide; Laertes will have his revenge. His course is so direct that he is easily used by Claudius for Claudius's own, less nobly inspired, ends. Claudius pointedly questions, even goads, Laertes: "Laertes, was your father dear to you? / Or are you like a painting of a sorrow, / A face without a heart?"[61] If Laertes really loved his father, in Claudius's schemed version, he must act. If he does not act, it is evidence he did not love his father. In the understanding of the old dispensation, love for a slain family member requires bloody revenge. Moreover, in Claudius's view (which aligns him with the revenge-seeking villains of contemporaneous plays), "Revenge should have no bounds."[62]

On the other hand, Shakespeare, influenced by Elizabethan ethical teaching that insistently condemned revenge,[63] endows Hamlet with a more modern resistance to private revenge.[64] At first Hamlet reacts to his father's demand for revenge with predictable emotion: "I, with wings as swift / As meditation or the thoughts of love, / May sweep to my revenge."[65] He hesitates to sweep, of course, and his hesitance causes him to despise himself: "O, vengeance! / Why, what an ass am I! This most brave, / That I, the son of a dear father murdered, / Prompted to my revenge by heaven and hell, / Must, like a whore, unpack my heart with words."[66] Hamlet believes that replacing action with ruminating language is weak and unmanly. Despite his private eloquence in the famous soliloquies, Hamlet is suspicious of language. He cannot unpack his heart with words to anyone (except the audience); when he speaks to other characters in the play, he feigns madness and dissembles. He actually disavows the possibility of speaking and requires the others who have seen the ghost also to be silent, to "still your fingers on your lips."[67]

Hamlet, educated at a German university, embodies the competing drives: the ancient impulse to avenge a loved one's murder and the more civilized realization that private revenge-seeking destroys a society. Hamlet's rational Wittenberg-student self wars against his more instinctive and passionate Danish self. He desires fully the appropriate and measured familial revenge his father demands: an eye for an eye, a death for a death. At the same time, he has the more modern understanding of the destructiveness of private revenge and the threat it poses to the stability of the state. Like Orestes, he is trapped between conflicting impulses, between two "goods," but no Athena, no *dea ex machina*, appears to resolve his dilemma. Instead, for him, "Denmark's a prison."[68]

Like some scenes in the *Iliad* and the conclusion of the *Oresteia*, *Hamlet* portrays the internal contradictions of the human psyche: the need to avenge a loved one and the knowledge that such vengeance leads to destruction and suffering. If Hamlet acts as his father desires, Denmark is threatened. And he cannot turn to the state to enact his revenge, because Claudius, the murderer, *is* the state. The central authority cannot play its assigned role, and when such a failure occurs, even the most civilized and educated among us may be driven to private revenge: "Man seems to take justice into his own hands when God or secular authorities fail."[69] The ghost of Hamlet's father, like the Furies of the *Oresteia*, has been driven underground only to emerge when he has no vengeance.

It is the ghost's parting words, "Remember me,"[70] that most obsess Hamlet. After the ghost departs, Hamlet repeats the words until they become a kind of litany:

> Remember thee?
> Ay, thou poor ghost, while memory holds a seat
> In this distracted globe. Remember thee?
> Yea from the table of my memory
> I'll wipe away all trivial fond records,
> All saws of books, all forms, all pressures past
> That youth and observation copied there,
> And thy commandment all alone will live
> Within the book and volume of my brain,
> Unmixed with baser matter. Yes, by heaven!. . . .
> "Remember me."
> I have sworn't.[71]

Violent revenge collapses into "remember." How is Hamlet to remember his father? His Wittenberg education has told him that violent revenge is wrong but has given him nothing to take its place if the state cannot or will not act for him. Hamlet struggles to imagine an alternative, and he fails.

Yet it seems to me that the play itself provides an overlooked alternative in its final act. Like *The Spanish Tragedy* and other similar but lesser plays, in the final scene of *Hamlet* the stage is covered with bodies of the guilty and innocent alike. Eight deaths occur—Polonius, Ophelia, Rosencrantz, Guildenstern, Gertrude, Claudius, Laertes, and Hamlet are all dead by the time the play ends. But before he dies, Hamlet entreats his friend Horatio "To tell my story":

O God, Horatio, what a wounded name,
Things standing thus unknown, shall live behind me!
If thou didst ever hold me in thy heart,
Absent thee from felicity for awhile,
And in this harsh world draw thy breath in pain,
To tell my story.[72]

Hamlet has never spoken truth to power; he has instead "put an antic disposition on."[73] He has forgone any opportunity to remember his father with language. And he has been unable to react with the comparable violence demanded by the old order; he never does decide to take revenge. The multiple killings at the end of the play occur only because Hamlet agrees to a contest with Laertes. It is Laertes's undifferentiated need for bloody revenge that causes the stage to be littered with bodies and the state destroyed, in true revenge drama style. Indeed, Claudius, the crafty goader, and Laertes, the hot-headed revenge seeker, are stock revenge drama characters. Only at the end of the play, with the new state present in the character of Fortinbras, will the true story be told. Hamlet's final words give his "dying voice"[74] to Fortinbras, and Horatio asks that he may "speak to th' yet unknowing world / How these things came about."[75] Hamlet does not ask Horatio for revenge; he asks him to tell the story.

In this final scene (too often cut from performances), this great play suggests that telling the story can end the cycle of revenge and bring a stop to the senseless deaths that we, the audience, have witnessed. Within the play, the words "if thou didst ever thy dear father love— / Revenge his foul and most unnatural murder" become transformed into "If thou didst ever hold me in thy heart . . . tell my story." Once the story is told (as indeed it has been told to us as we watch the play), the new state, embodied in Fortinbras, can move forward. But that progress requires a witness, a Horatio, to tell the misdeeds of the corrupt state under Claudius. It is not an easy task: "in this *harsh* world draw thy breath in *pain*" (italics added).

Is, then, this kind of storytelling an alternative for contemporary democracies that also "fail" to enact retribution in traditional ways, Denmark-like states in which, for one reason or another, violence for violence is not a suitable response? Can a new state effectively remember the past without violence? Can it "speak to th' yet unknowing world how these things came about"?

Chapter Three
Language, Violence, and Oppression

It did not matter that they might die along the way; what really mattered was that they should not tell their story.
—Primo Levi, *The Drowned and the Saved*

Physical pain . . . is language destroying.
—Elaine Scarry, *The Body in Pain*

The literary and philosophical traditions of many cultures reveal that the urge for revenge is an ancient, deep-rooted human need that has only tentatively been transferred to central authority in the form of state-sponsored retribution. If that need for revenge is not acknowledged by being in some way incorporated into formal systems of justice, as are the Furies by Athena in the *Oresteia*, it reemerges as private vengeance, as it does with Paulina in *Death and the Maiden*. It has the potentiality of "dripping poison over all the land," as Athena fears the unsatisfied Furies will do in the *Oresteia*. If a state fails to enact retribution that is emotionally satisfying to victims, the victims will eventually take justice into their own hands in an attempt to reestablish a psychologically necessary balance. Like Paulina, those seeking revenge are not driven by *ressentiment* or by political expediency, but by personal passion, "from an elementary sense of injustice."[1] Revenge-seekers do not see themselves as evil or cruel; they see themselves as setting the world back into its proper order. The original quest for revenge was less about excess (although excess certainly sometimes occurred) and more about balancing and reciprocity. The victims' passion is not directed at getting something new or extra for themselves, but for getting something *back*. Any legal forum that enacts retribution should take this passion and this need for balancing into account. Criminal sanctions against revenge seekers, moral or religious pleas to turn the other cheek, or state-ordered "forgiveness" cannot quell this deeply rooted need and can be futile and dangerous.[2] In countries that "attempt to induce a national amnesia . . . [victims'] unanswered calls for retribution develop into hate,"[3] often escalating into violence that perpetuates revenge cycles.

At the same time, violence for violence has not always been the norm, and the notion of what retribution means has not always focused exclusively on what the perpetrator deserves ("has coming"). People have been seemingly satisfied (as "satisfied" as one can be under such circumstances) by a payment of money (or even a parade)[4]. While there seems to be a human drive for getting something back, what that "something" is may not be self-evident. What, then, constitutes appropriate retribution that is emotionally satisfying to the victims, fair to the perpetrators, and not destructive to the society that enacts it in situations in which violent retribution by the state is not possible or wise? What does it mean to say "I don't want revenge, I want justice." What is wanted? Is justice necessarily a proportional act of violence? What is Paulina's "good"? The importance of this question should by now be clear, as should its difficulty.

This chapter examines the role that language plays in initial harms in an attempt to discover whether the recent plethora of truth commissions that substitute language for state violence have any chance for long-term success as adequate retribution. Leaving aside the distracting question of what perpetrators deserve, I want instead to analyze whether truth commissions can give something adequate back to the victims. I will proceed by examining the misuse, manipulation, and perversion of language that occurs with initial harms on three levels: personal, familial, and societal. If one of the significant things that victims lose in oppression is the ability to use language, then language as retribution begins to make sense.

Language and Violence

The harms that may be visited upon a population by an oppressive regime and the victims such a regime can create are limited only by the regime's creativity and malice. For the purposes of this study, however, I want to focus on three kinds of victims: (1) victims such as Paulina who were kidnapped and tortured and desire personal retribution; (2) relatives, such as Orestes, Electra, and Hamlet, of victims who have disappeared or been murdered; (3) society itself, which has been terrorized and "polluted" by the activities of the oppressors. And my primary interest resides in the way that language functions in the harms perpetrated against these victims.

Personal Harms

In her brilliant study of torture and war, Elaine Scarry establishes several principles about the relationship of language and pain that can help in the quest to understand the role that language plays in a situation involving a surviving victim. Scarry first lays bare the inarticulability of physical pain: when in pain we cannot accurately describe it to another nor can we fully understand another's pain. The closest we can get to communicating the reality of pain is metaphor: the pain feels *like* a burning, a piercing, a hammering, a vice. A primary attribute of pain is its ultimate unsharability because it cannot accurately be represented in language. Eventually, physical pain can become so extreme that its ceases to be articulable even as metaphor. The ability to speak words disappears: "Physical pain does not simply resist language but actively destroys it; bringing about an immediate reversion to the sounds and cries a human being makes before language is learned."[5]

The language-destroying nature of pain is linked to the political use of pain in torture: "physical pain is difficult to express, and . . . this inexpressibility has political consequences."[6] The torture victim is reduced to prelanguage screams and moans that are not heard or acknowledged by anyone.[7] Torture becomes the visible manifestation of power; it shatters the person's voice and makes language itself ineffective. Scarry's theories are buttressed by the testimony of actual victims. In describing his imprisonment and torture, Jacobo Timerman writes that the pain a tortured person experiences "is a pain without points of reference, revelatory symbols, or clues to serve as indicators. . . . It is impossible to shout—you howl."[8] Other Argentinian victims remember pain "so excruciating that one couldn't even scream or groan or move"[9] and the use of a high voltage device that caused the tongue to contract and thus prevented screaming.[10]

The political consequences of pain's ultimate inexpressibility can explain, at least in part, why the gratuitous infliction of pain is such a common and effective political tool, particularly for new and unstable political regimes.[11] The intense physical suffering that torture produces makes the invisible regime visible; it "converts the vision of suffering into the wholly illusory but, to the torturers and the regime they represent, wholly convincing spectacle of power."[12] The writers of *Nunca Más*, the Argentinian truth report, in apologizing for the "encyclopedia of horror" that the section on torture becomes, assert that avoiding the horror was impossible: "After all, what else were these tortures but an immense display of the most degrading and indescribable acts of degradation, which the military government, lacking all legitimacy in power, used to secure power over a whole nation?"[13]

Interrogation often accompanies torture even when, as is often the case, the prisoner has no meaningful knowledge to communicate to the torturers. The purpose of torture and its concomitant interrogation is not the elicitation of confessions or information from the victims, but to "deconstruct the prisoner's voice. . . . The prolonged interrogation . . . graphically objectifies the step-by-step backward movement along the path by which language comes into being and which here is being reversed or uncreated or deconstructed."[14] The intense pain the prisoners experience destroys their connection to their world and makes both questions and answers insignificant because links to friends, family, and country disappear in the all-encompassing world-destroying presence of pain. Torture is a primary means of "destroying . . . [any] sense of solidarity with an organization or community."[15] Pain annihilates everything but itself:

World, self, and voice are lost, or nearly lost, through the intense pain of torture and not through the confession as is wrongly suggested by its connotation of betrayal. The prisoner's confession merely objectifies the fact of their being almost lost, makes their invisible absence, or nearly absence, visible to the torturers. To assent to words through the thick agony of the body can only be dimly heard, or to reach aimlessly for the name of a person or place that has barely enough cohesion to hold its shape as a word and none to bond it to its worldly referent, is a way of saying, yes, all is almost gone now, there is nothing left now, even this voice, the sounds I am making, no longer form my words but the words of another.[16]

The forced betrayal serves to degrade the victim, and the very degradation (making into "filth") of the enemy serves the state: "Torturers humiliate the victim, exploit his human weakness through the mechanism of pain, until he does take on the role of filth, confessing his lowliness and betraying cause, comrades, family, and friends."[17]

The victim's ability to speak is first, through the device of interrogation, appropriated by the regime: "The victims are made to speak the words of the regime, to replace their own reality with that of the state, to double the voice of the state."[18] The victim's voice is then destroyed as the pain intensifies and the victim reverts to a prelanguage state of being. Torture reduces the victim to a voiceless body as the torturer becomes a disembodied voice. "Although the torturer dominates the prisoner both in physical and verbal acts, ultimate domination requires that the prisoner's ground become increasingly physical and the torturer's increasingly verbal, that the prisoner become a colossal body with no voice, and the torturer a colossal voice . . . with no body."[19] Torture, perhaps more than any other wrong, is designed to denote superiority over the victim, a superiority that becomes an essential insignia of the corrupt regime: "They [the torturers] would say: 'You're dirt. . . . You don't exist. . . . We are everything for you. We are justice. We are God.' "[20]

In addition to the inversion of a victim's language, other ordinary meanings become appropriated into the structure of torture. In the same way that words become a "confession" and a "betrayal" that manifest only the destruction of the victim's world and become appropriated by the enemy to objectify this destruction, commonplace objects associated with normal living frequently are used as instruments of torture and death—bathtubs, beds, chairs, refrigerators, brown bags, ovens, showers, radiators.[21] The infamous wet bag used in torture reenacted during the South African Truth and Reconciliation Commission hearings was not an instrument devised for this diabolical purpose, but instead an ordinary police evidence bag. Even if a victim can struggle to retain the ability to form thoughts in language, commonplace meanings have changed. The ordinary has become the horrible. The story that a victim has constructed about his or her own life is systematically destroyed, and the oppressors' story becomes the dominant and only narrative.[22] The writers of *Nunca Más* echo this disintegration as they describe the function of the secret detention centers: "To be admitted to these centres meant to cease to exist. In order to achieve this end, attempts were made to break down the captives' identity; their spatio-temporal points of reference were disrupted, and their minds and bodies tortured beyond imagination."[23]

We can isolate these elements and perhaps better understand them if we reflect for a moment on Paulina's situation. The purpose of Paulina's torture and interrogation was to unmake her world. The play provides only later accounts of the torture itself, but it is clear that Paulina has lost the ability to articulate her pain. She doesn't like to talk about what happened to her, and she has told her husband Gerardo only sketchy details about it. Meaning was inverted in that her favorite piece of music, Schubert's Quartet in D Minor, became background music for her pain. An agent of healing, a doctor, became an agent of torture and pain.[24] Her world became appropriated into the torturer's arsenal of weapons: her medicine (she was a medical student) and her music. Not only is Paulina's voice destroyed, the content of her world and eventually her self likewise disintegrate.

The "wild and fearless" Paulina who assisted in smuggling people out of the country has been destroyed or nearly destroyed. The student activist has become the woman who gave up her studies, who cries out "they're coming for me" more than a decade after her kidnapping, and who huddles in a fetal-like position when she hears voices or sees strange cars outside her house.[25] Through the technology of torture, the prior Paulina's world, self, and voice are unmade and the new disempowered

Paulina is transformed into the insignia of the regime. And this transformation does not cease with Paulina's release or even with the downfall of her oppressors. Years later she remains disconnected to the world. She has been unable to reclaim the things that were appropriated into her torturer's arsenal, and she cannot listen to her beloved Schubert. No rebalancing has occurred.

In addition to Scarry's compelling delineation of the language transference intrinsic in pain and torture, political injuries have a symbolic and communicative dimension that can help to explain why torture victims such as Paulina cannot heal themselves after their release. In a theory that extends Scarry's sense of pain and injury beyond the physical, Jeffrie Murphy argues that "One reason we so deeply resent moral injuries done to us is not simply that they hurt us in some tangible or sensible way; it is because such injuries are also *messages*—symbolic communications. They are ways a wrongdoer has of saying to us, 'I count but you do not,' 'I can use you for my purposes'" (original italics).[26] Political philosopher Jean Hampton puts forth an "expressive" theory of retribution that argues that "Those who commit such crimes essentially reason, 'I will hurt you in order to establish that your worth is less than mine,'"[27] thus making a "false moral claim."[28] Hampton maintains that some kinds of wrongs are moral injuries that affect a person's realization of his or her value. These wrongs "carry meanings that effect injuries to a person's value in one of two ways: either they can damage . . . that person's 'realization of his value,' or they can damage 'the acknowledgement of his value.'"[29] The person is diminished and treated as an object rather than as a person with, in the Kantian sense, intrinsic moral worth. Argentinian victims claim: "We were objects. And useless, troublesome objects at that."[30]

The wrongs are committed in such a way as to denote the superiority of the wrongdoer over the victim, and our fury at the wrongdoer in part results from his posture of superiority over the victim, his treatment of the victim as worthless, less than human.[31] He symbolizes "through his actions that he had the power as well as the authority to recognize their [the victims'] worthlessness and to decide their fate to the point of destroying them."[32] Or, as in Paulina's case, letting them survive: "This bitch can take a bit more."[33] The wrongful action, therefore, affects not only the victim's sense of worth but also the community's sense of the inherent value of all its citizens: "We care about what people say by their actions because we care about whether our own value, and the value of others, will continue to be respected in our society. The misrepresentation of value implicit in moral injuries not only violates the entitlements generated by their value, but also threatens to reinforce belief in the wrong theory of value by the community."[34] If a state does nothing, it tacitly acquiesces to the mistreatment,[35] by joining in the communication of superiority that says that the victim is worth little.[36]

Paulina's revenge in *Death and the Maiden* might be seen as a rebalancing of the language void created in her by her torture. Her voice and self were shattered, and a false moral claim about her worth was made by her torture, her treatment as an object. Her self was deconstructed and used for the symbolic purposes of the regime. If adequate revenge or retribution require a rebalancing, Paulina's discovery that she did not want eye-for-eye revenge, that she did not want to inflict pain on Roberto Miranda, is not entirely surprising. But she needed something both to balance her loss of language and to correct the falsehoods that Miranda's acts communicated. She discovered that she wanted a retelling of the story that would give her back her self, her voice, her worth, her Schubert. "The punisher who inflicts retribution on . . . a wrongdoer . . . wants to reassert . . . facts and vindicate the value of the victim."[37] The critical ingredient of the rebalancing, then, is not pain or violence, but a retold story, a reconstruction of the shattered voice. Scarry writes that "to be present when the person in pain rediscovers speech and so regains his powers of self-objectification is almost to be present at the birth, or rebirth, of language. . . . To describe one's hurt in an image of agency is to project it into an object which . . . by its very separability from the body becomes an image that can be lifted away, carrying some of the attributes of pain with it."[38]

We can actively observe this process of reconstruction, projection, and even rebirth at the beginning of Act Two of *Death and the Maiden* as Paulina babbles on to the bound and gagged Miranda, saying at last things she has not dared to say: "Isn't this bizarre, that I should be telling you all this as if you were my confessor, when there are things I've never told Gerardo, or my sister, certainly not my mother. . . . Whereas I can tell you exactly what I feel."[39] Paulina begins to use words to claim her own meaning for her experience.[40] The scene may be interpreted as the rebirth of Paulina's ability to speak. Paulina, in fact, uses some of the very vulgarities used against her, prompting Gerardo to exclaim, "she has never spoken like this in her life."[41] And she is cognizant that a rebirth is occurring: "And I can speak—It's been so long since I as much whispered a word, even a breath of what I'm thinking, years living in terror of my own . . . but I'm not dead, I thought I was but I'm not and I can speak."[42] Paulina's student/activist language was deconstructed by her torture and the language of the military regime replaced it. Newly empowered, she reconstructs her own language, she "makes a 'new language' but not out of nothing; [she] makes it out of an old language, reconstituting its terms of description and feeling, of fact and value, into new patterns of significance, new movements of the mind."[43] In the play's final scene, Paulina has reconnected with her world: she is attending a concert at which Schubert is being played.

The effects of such a process have been documented in a program used in Chile in which torture victims of the former military regime gave testimony—that is, told the story of their experience—to therapists who tape recorded the stories. The therapists encouraged the victims to tell their stories in their own words and asked questions only to help the victim clarify or expand on significant details. The tape was transcribed and reviewed by the victim and the therapist, who together edited it into a final document that acts "as a sort of 'memory' that can be shared, reviewed, rewritten and analyzed. . . . It has the ability to preserve the past exactly as remembered and experienced."[44] The testimony "allows the individual to transform past experience and personal identity, creating a new present and enhancing the future."[45] And the South African report maintains that "In order to heal, trauma victims must ultimately put words to their experience and thereby integrate the traumatic experience in order to find new meanings for themselves and their place in the world."[46]

On two levels, victims of torture experience a loss of their "story." First, their own personal narratives that make sense of their lives are silenced and appropriated; second, a false message about their worth is communicated. For just retribution, for the world to be put back into its proper order, both must be corrected and rebalanced. For the first, it may be enough that victims have an opportunity to tell their stories and reshape their own experiences in their own words. The second, however, requires that the new state actively hear and acknowledge the story, thereby recognizing the worth of the victim.

Familial Harms

Familial retribution is a theme common to mythology and literature and seems to receive the most attention in philosophical discourse. Familial revenge-taking was recognized as a right and a sacred duty that was crucial for holding the social structure in place. If a family failed to take revenge for a slain loved one, the natural order was out of balance. The desire of a victim's family to balance the harm may not be an antisocial destructive impulse that should be repressed at all costs. This desire can be recognized and even respected as a natural human emotion without requiring or allowing action.[47] Nonetheless, families whose loved ones have been harmed need something back. Allowing their losses to go unacknowledged and in some cases requiring that their lack of knowledge about a loved one's fate continues ignore the necessity of balancing the harm in some way. But what, short of full knowledge and full prosecutions, can in any way satisfy a bereaved family? Can the collections of stories that comprise large portions of truth commission reports approximate this balancing? To answer this, we must look again at the way that language has functioned in these harms.

Several qualities involving the use and misuse of language characterize the activities of an oppressive regime. First, such regimes tend to operate in secret, concealing the truth about what they are doing; second, they construct their own narratives about their activities, thereby creating a "master narrative" about the country and its citizens; and third, they operate in ways that fragment social bodies, such as families, that might challenge that master narrative.[48] Each of these qualities results in the appropriation and subversion of language and requires restoration of language to effect an adequate rebalancing.

Nearly every oppressive regime has its version of the secret police who operate clandestinely, often at night, about whom the general populace knows little or nothing.[49] The secrecy generates fear in the citizens, who do not know who is or is not associated with the secret police or when and where the police will strike next. Many oppressive societies are also characterized by the presence of death squads, which, while not secret, are covert.[50] They are not secret in that their activities are meant to be seen and feared; they are designed to spread terror among the citizenry. But they are covert in that no one knows the identity of their members or their sponsors. The government typically disavows knowledge of them, although death squads may well be on the government payroll.

Everyone is a potential conspirator and a potential victim. Families become fragmented, dismembered both figuratively and literally. Family members may come to distrust each other. The deliberate destruction of the institution of the family can even be one of the goals of an oppressive regime. In South Africa, for example, the policies of apartheid were designed to pull families apart with "ruinous consequences at the level of the local community."[51] If all else fails, family members are pulled out of the family unit and disappear.

If the family dares to question the disappearance of one of its members, the regime constructs a false narrative. A woman is told that her husband was not kidnapped but that he tired of her and left.[52] A mother is told that her son has joined an illegal guerrilla group.[53] A daughter is alleged to have committed crimes and been justly arrested and detained.[54] In one case, in an effort to deceive those involved in a campaign to compel the government to produce her alive, a kidnapped Argentinian woman who was secretary of the Commission of Families of those Disappeared and Imprisoned for Political Reasons was forced to write letters which were posted from Uruguay in which she denied her abduction and claimed she had fled the country.[55] In multiple and creative ways, a regime creates a framework of false narratives, a "fog of disinformation,"[56] that conceals and justifies its activities. Its victims are not acknowledged as victims at all; the harms visited upon the family remain invisible and unnamed. False moral claims are made that deny the worth of the lost family member and devalue the family connections. Family affairs cannot be settled because the regime denies that any deaths have occurred.

Official accounts blame victims,[57] and "[f]ew make inquiries for fear of meeting the same fate."[58] In El Salvador, when the mother of twenty-year-old Sara Christina Chan Chan Medina searches for her daughter who has been arrested, she is told, "Don't come back unless you want this to happen to you."[59] Officials even deny that disappearances occur. An army colonel in Chile tells a journalist: "A neighbor of mine was crying about a disappeared person and two weeks later he [the person] arrived from Argentina. There are a lot of myths about this disappearance thing."[60]

The regime surrounds the disappearance with silence and reacts if this silence is broken. In response to a mother's plea that his newspaper write a story about the disappearance of her two children, Jacobo Timerman thinks: "How can I tell this woman that if I published a story about her children, it would amount to a death sentence? How can I tell her that the government will never tolerate the assumption that a newspaper article can save a life? To permit this would mean losing the power of oppression, the utilization of Fear and Silence."[61] The widespread silencing is a crucial component of the technology of oppression.

The Chilean Report opens the section on the impact on families with this paragraph:

> The loss of a loved one is always painful—especially when that loss was deliberately inflicted and is perceived as a punishment meted out to adversaries, an irrational violence inflicted as a punishment. Families are at a loss to explain it. They were unable to experience the grief that goes along with death, because the fate of their loved ones who disappear after arrest remains unclear.[62]

This enforced silence disallows grieving, compassion, and normal human emotions that require external expression. Unlike normal situations in which a loved one is lost, family ties cannot be named and made visible. People cannot grieve openly in well-established public rituals that can give solace and closure. "In the face of official denials, the death becomes the family's own invention. . . . It disturbs the normal processes of grief and mourning."[63] Families may hold on to hopes that the missing loved one is "in transit, alive in a refugee camp, safely living abroad, or in unacknowledged detention" and therefore cannot "initiate or complete the mourning process."[64] The strategy of disappearances denies the family even the presence of the corpse of the loved one over which to grieve. "The families, especially the mothers, of the disappeared, even in relative certainty that their loved ones have been killed, search tirelessly, year after year, for their remains."[65] At a South African amnesty hearing, the mother of a fifteen-year-old victim, hoping to hear the truth about the murder from Jerry Richardson, says: "We just want to be able to take the bones home. It's our way."[66]

The writers of *Nunca Más* describe the unknowing state into which families are forced as a result of a disappearance as a "bottomless pit of horror":

There was something more, which had to do with the methodology of disappearance. First it was the people, their absence giving hope to the relatives that the kidnap victim would be freed and return; then the concealment and destruction of documentation, which undoubtedly existed in every case, prolonging the uncertainty about what happened; and finally, the nameless bodies, without identity, driving people distraught at the impossibility of knowing the specific fate of their loved one. It was a bottomless pit of horror.[67]

An oppressive regime silences and fragments the people. In the midst of that silence, it constructs its own narrative about what has happened to family members and about the worth of those who have disappeared—about the worth of family at all. For justice to be achieved and families to be re-membered, the true story must be told and acknowledged. Above all, families need to know the truth. And the revelation of this truth necessarily destroys the false master narrative that the regime has created. Its activities become known and acknowledged, and a space appears in which the new regime has the opportunity to rewrite the story.

Societal Harms

The harms of torture, kidnapping, and murder transcend the injury they inflict upon the victims and their families; they injure society as well. As early societies recognized in the evolution from revenge to retribution, harms against individuals "pollute the land." Under the pollution doctrine the land is infertile and lies waste after the shedding of innocent blood and cannot be restored until the family or the ruler obtains revenge for the slain. In the *Oresteia*, Orestes is instructed that he must avenge his father's murder in order to heal the "Swarming infection that boils within"[68] the land. A wrong was seen as being committed against the community, and settlements were not private matters but concerns of the state, although the actual avenger might still be a family member.

In our contemporary world, we might ask what forms this metaphoric pollution takes. How is a society or a nation as a whole affected by a corrupt and violent regime? In two important ways: the people are silenced and become alienated from each other, and in this silence, a new national narrative is created by the oppressors. The oppressors symbolically "have the microphone" and construct the dominant story, the master narrative, about the country and its citizens. Torture extends beyond the individual victim and becomes a visible and false symbol of the corrupt regime. Torture "creates a discourse of its own . . . [and] plays out a dream of a certain kind of state, the production of a type of power/knowledge . . . [that is] the *imagination* of the state"(original italics).[69] Nazi Germany, for example, constructed the narrative of Aryan supremacy and the relative worthlessness of its Jewish citizens. South Africa under apartheid rule constructed a narrative about the necessity of separation of the races, with the white race as the ruling class and nonwhites relegated to inferior zones. Chile under Pinochet told a story of a critical fight against the forces of Communism that threatened to take over the country, a fight that required draconian measures to insure the security of the state. The military dictatorship described itself as saving Western civilization in Chile. In South Africa, as the truth report acknowledged, language constructs reality: "Language, discourse, rhetoric does things: it constructs social categories, it gives orders, it persuades us, it justifies, explains, gives reasons, excuses. . . . It moves certain people against other people."[70] With any opposition opinions silenced, the master narrative takes hold and becomes the country's "history."

At the same time, torture (and the oppression and fear that result from it) is an "assault on social bodies" and is used not only to deconstruct individuals' relationships with their worlds but also to "fragment and disarticulate all social bodies which would rival its [the regime's] power."[71] In Argentina, during the "dirty war," the "culture of fear" imposed by the military regime "was conducive to an extreme individualization and privatization of human beings. People tried to isolate themselves from their social environment and emotional attachments in order to attain that state of detachment necessary to ignore the shouts for help and the cries of despair of their neighbors as they were abducted."[72] The goal of the oppressors was precisely this kind of social fragmentation and its attendant passivity and learned helplessness that "reduced society to a set of separate individuals living their atomized lives under the supervision of all-powerful authorities."[73] With rare exceptions, churches, political organizations, social groups, and all other signs of collectivity and unity disappeared. In Guatemala, the military made it a point to launch assaults on communities: "The army's fear was that the people were united; they knew how to share, to live together in their own village."[74]

The result of this fragmentation of social units into atomized individuals[75] is a silence that not only makes any opposition powerless and voiceless, but also forces a tacit complicity in the oppression. Timerman describes this situation as he observed it in Argentina: "What there was, from the start, was the great silence, which appears in every civilized country that passively accepts the inevitability of violence, and then the fear that suddenly befalls it. That silence which can transform any nation into an accomplice."[76] In South Africa, the report likewise notes the necessity of secrecy and silence for an oppressive regime to flourish: "Secrecy was particularly characteristic of apartheid rule. The massive curtailment of press freedom, restrictions on academic freedom, a considerable increase in censorship, the banning of organizations—all these went hand in hand with secrecy. . . . Along with secrecy went silence, and much of the country's populace was silent through fear, apathy, indifference, or genuine lack of information."[77]

Secrecy has the further effect of making any opposition invisible: "the strategy of oppression employed by the Pinochet regime in Chile [was] not the production of martyrs but rather the denial of martyrs."[78] There were no victims, in that the regime in Chile (as in Argentina, South Africa, and elsewhere) denied any responsibility for the fate of those who suddenly disappeared. When the West German Minister of Labor confronted him about human rights abuses in Chile, Pinochet said, "These [accusations of torture] are lies invented by the communists. I am a committed Christian and I pray every day. We must combat communism."[79]

In multiple ways, an oppressive regime appropriates and manipulates language to shatter the voices of victims and any unified voice of opposition. It uses the appropriated language to create itself as a state, to deny the worth of any who dare to oppose it, and to silence the populace. This misuse of language pollutes the land. Thus, for a "polluted" nation to give justice to its citizens, to cleanse itself, and to move forward without oppression, it must take back for itself and its citizens the ability to use language. It must allow the victims, even empower them, to tell their own stories, to re-member by remembering. And the state must shape a new story, but not just any new story. The form this new story takes is critical. To replace one oppressive master narrative with a different one does not empower the victims and, worse, it threatens to perpetuate the oppression, only in another, perhaps more benign, form. A single authoritative master narrative that functions to silence and to shut down dissenters, to curtail an ongoing struggle to discover whatever truth may be possible, repeats the sins of the oppressors. Somehow the voices of the victims—individuals, families, and the country—must be heard and acknowledged. Most of all, the victims must be given a space in which they may speak for themselves.

Chapter Four
What Can Stories Do?

Certainly all historical experience confirms the truth—that man would not have attained the possible unless time and time again he had not reached out for the impossible.
—Max Weber, *Essays in Sociology*

Ah, but a man's reach should exceed his grasp,
        Or what's a heaven for?
—Robert Browning, "Andrea del Sarto"

If a state cannot enact traditional retribution for its citizens who were victimized by the former government, is there any point in the gathering and publishing of these victims' stories? While the story of the evolution from revenge to retribution shows us that a state must do something, must take responsibility to effect a rebalancing for the victims or risk a reversion to personal revenge, our collective imagination has given us little in the way of alternatives to state violence. The pendulum of possible responses swings without pausing from the extreme of traditional retributive justice—requiring investigations, trials, and punishment well beyond the means of new and fragile democracies—to the extreme of doing nothing, putting the past behind, asking people to forget and forgive in a spirit of misplaced and premature goodwill. Or a country may espouse consequentialist approaches, such as that embraced by Gerardo in *Death and the Maiden*, which look only to remedies that promise to further the good of the country as a whole. The needs of the individual victims become buried under the avalanche of public goods, a practice that can endanger a country's future.

Recently, however, countries have begun to explore other possibilities for state action that recognize the practicalities without sacrificing the good of the victims. The encouraging, collecting, acknowledging, and publishing of victims' personal accounts is becoming a common approach that seeks to find this elusive middle ground.[1] The principles that can inform this search for a middle ground are well articulated by José Zalaquett, a member of the Chilean truth commission. Using a distinction first set forth by Max Weber, Zalaquett differentiates between an ethics of conviction, which entails acting on conviction regardless of outcome, and an ethics of responsibility, which entails incorporating a realization of the likely consequences of actions based on conviction.[2] Politicians, in Weber's view, should always be guided by an ethics of responsibility, and Zalaquett lays out two considerations that politicians entrusted with transitional democracies must balance: "the ethical principles that ought to be pursued, and actual political opportunities and constraints that ought to be taken into account."[3] The opportunities and constraints may vary widely from country to country, and responses possible in one place may be impossible or unwise in others. The storytelling that results from the establishing of truth commissions, according to Zalaquett, can justifiably grow out of an ethics of responsibility in which principles have been weighed against circumstances and consequences of action.

In fact, the idea of a truth commission and a report has captured the imagination, and much has been written about the many commissions that have appeared in the last two decades. They have spawned an industry of secondary literature, some written by those who participated in the processes. These writers investigate interesting and significant questions about the legal, political, and psychological implications of this work. Several claims are made as to what goods truth reports accomplish, claims that fall into two broad, overlapping categories: goods for the individuals and goods for the state.

The commissions and their reports also have their critics. Although typically the commissions are created and the reports issued in situations in which another official course of action—investigations and trials, for example—would be unworkable and unwise, some critics insist that these reports are an unsatisfactory alternative to *justice*. They use the term to mean, I think, retribution enacted by the state—investigations, trials, imprisonments, and executions—actions typically considered retributive justice. For the critics, the stories represent a trade-off between truth and justice. Or perhaps a prologue to justice: first truth, then justice. In other words, the stories are not justice; they are something other than justice. A cynical view holds that the truth commissions are, in fact, *unjust*, that they "preserve statehood at the expense of human rights."[4] According to this view, a state with a weak infrastructure that might collapse under the weight of traditional retributive justice chooses its own survival and well-being over the rights of the victims.[5]

Some commentators, however, use a more expansive understanding of justice. Richard Goldstone, a former chief prosecutor at the International Criminal Tribunal for the Former Yugoslavia and now a judge on the South African Constitutional Court, defines justice as finding out the truth, whether achieved by trials or truth commissions. He offers a more open-ended question: "what do we mean by justice, and what is the most effective mechanism for the implementation of such justice?"[6] Unlike many who see justice as taking a particular form, usually that of state-sponsored violence (classic retribution), Goldstone allows that the discovery of truth is also a form of justice, not a poor substitute for it: "Criminal prosecution is the most common form of justice. Prosecution is, however, not the only form, nor necessarily the most appropriate form in every case. The public and official exposure of the truth is itself a form of justice."[7] Legal philosopher/rhetorician Peter Goodrich makes an even stronger claim, asserting that the activity of the South African Truth and Reconciliation Commission (TRC) was "not an exercise simply in recollecting or condemning injustice; it was itself most powerfully understood as a radical and unique staging of justice."[8] Goodrich refers in particular to an event that occurred during the showing of a police video that depicted the killing of seven young men. The mother of one of the slain men shrieked and threw her shoe at one of the accused policemen. Goodrich maintains that with events such as that, the TRC provided "a forum in which the victims of violence could have their experiences of trauma publically validated,"[9] and that "justice is best understood as an imperfect and flawed practice of virtue . . . [and] is in this sense an endeavor; it is an always-failed attempt to actualize an ethical commitment and accounting of the past."[10]

In this chapter, I want to take up Goldstone's question and Goodrich's provocative redefinition of justice in the context of the storytelling activities engaged in by truth commissions. I analyze the potential worth of storytelling from various angles and put forth theories by which truth commission reports might be seen as a useful kind of justice. I hope to establish that collecting and publishing victims' stories can accomplish significant ends, some obvious, some less so. My approach, however, looks not at the requirements of international law or usual conceptions of justice. Instead, I want to regard these reports first of all as *stories* and to think about what stories do and how they operate in our lives. In so doing, I discuss seven ways in which the activities of truth commissions may provide justice—imperfect, perhaps, as justice always is—to victims and to their countries.[11] The first three can best be understood from the perspective of the victims,[12] in that the victims get something for themselves that helps to heal them and make them whole.

The first of these potential benefits is foundational: making stories of our lives is what we humans *do*. It is the fundamental means by which we assert and describe our humanity. While it is well documented in psychological literature and elsewhere that telling the story of a traumatic experience can be therapeutic for victims, the value of shaping one's experience into story form extends far beyond the therapeutic. Storytelling is an essentially human act that enables all of us to make sense of our lives and to feel integrated as members of a community. Through the recovery of language, a victim can constitute the story of his or her identity, tell a personal history that locates him or her in time and space.

Second, the appropriation and manipulation of language and of people's ability to speak words for themselves in their own voices are major weapons in an oppressive regime's arsenal. The retrieving of language and the restoration of the ability to speak in one's own voice can therefore go a significant way in balancing the harm done. Allowing people to tell their stories and to regain power over language is a critical component of a broader and classical sense of *re-tribuere*, a giving back, not of injury to the perpetrator but of something lost to the victim. The retrieval of language puts the world back into some kind of order.

Third, encouraging people to come forward and tell stories of what happened to them or their family members and, in the case of South Africa at least, encouraging perpetrators to come forward and tell the truth provide means by which the truth can be uncovered and people can receive information about what actually happened to loved ones and even where bodies may be found. Moreover, the truth enables people to be vindicated, in that the false stories told about them or their loved ones can be corrected.

The next group of benefits can be seen more clearly from the perspective of the social fabric, the state in which the victim is claiming a voice, an identity, and the power to speak the truth. Fourth, then, stories can communicate the experience of pain and suffering between people who normally cannot understand each other. Stories can "translate" events and emotions in a way that other forms of discourse cannot, can overcome the *différend* (the lack of a shared language in which a person can express an injury) that bars both justice and understanding, Fifth, the enactment of storytelling, in a display akin to Bakhtin's sense of *carnival* that overturns and disrupts an oppressive social order, can restore victims' dignity. As their pain is acknowledged by an official body in a setting that is not constrained or controlled by the official state, the victims have a space in which to celebrate their freedom and newly acknowledged equality. Sixth, the telling of stories, re-membering in a sacramental way, can put back together shattered selves, families, and societies. Each of these benefits—the communicative, the ritualistic, and the sacramental—can serve to create an empathetic and responsive community, which, it seems to me, should be the goal of justice-seeking mechanisms.

Finally, the stories collected and the larger narrative that contains them (the report) can actualize a radically new kind of constitutive history for an emerging democracy. The choices that the writers make about the form of the report define the kind of country that the report is constituting. I will explore this understanding of the reports in detail in the next chapter.

These seven categories cannot remain discrete. Clearly, they overlap and run into each other. The categories, however, provide an analytical tool by which we can discuss these attributes of stories that go to our sense of justice. Although truth commissions have been widely discussed and analyzed, these areas are largely undiscussed and can dramatically extend our understanding of the worth of truth commission reports.

Before turning to these benefits, however, we need to take note of the several levels on which the stories operate. First, and most obviously, there are the stories themselves, the personal narratives that people who have suffered first remember and then relate. Second, there is the process by which the stories are told, gathered, and published. Is it public or private? Who listens to the stories? Who else is present? Who counts as a victim? How much latitude is given to the storyteller? Third, there is the publication of the stories. Who transcribes them and how? What other story or stories are told with them? How are they used within the larger master narrative that is the report itself? How do they finally appear in print? How are they published and disseminated? Each of these levels—story, process, and publication—constitutes a critical component of what we mean by "stories" in the context of international truth commissions. And the entire process, from remembering to distribution, constitutes a social phenomenon with marked effects on a culture.

Storytelling as an Essential Human Act

Psychological studies have shown that victims of loss and violence are helped in their recovery by telling a story about what happened to them, that so doing engenders a transformation from *victim* to *survivor*.[13] This basic therapeutic method, familiar at least since Freud, holds true among those who have suffered human rights abuses at the hands of an oppressive government. Giving testimony about the horrific events they have undergone facilitates their recovery. "Testimony is the most critical component of therapy for survivors of traumatic human rights abuses."[14] Cienfuegos and Monelli, who worked with survivors in Chile, urge in particular that survivors be allowed and encouraged to tell their stories in their own words and in their own ways. They permitted people to tell their stories in this way, and they, the therapists, recorded them: "The experience narrated through the testimony includes fragmented chronological and affective sequences that are then integrated in the written transcript of the recording. It is through this whole picture that the patient can identify, understand, and integrate the meaning of their political commitment and suffering."[15] Richard Mollica, who founded the Indochinese Psychiatric Clinic to work with victims of violence, calls the trauma story the "centerpiece of therapy."[16]

Susan Brison, a victim of rape, gives a vivid description of the process by which the shattered pieces of the self are reconnected in the telling of the story:

> The undoing of self in trauma involves a radical disruption of memory, a severing of past from present, and typically, an inability to envision a future. And yet trauma survivors often eventually find ways to reconstruct themselves and carry on reconfigured lives. In this reconstruction, trauma narratives—what might be called "speech acts of memory"—play an important role. Working through, or remastering, traumatic memory (in the case of human-inflicted trauma) involves a shift from being the object or medium of someone else's (the perpetrator's) speech to being the subject of one's own. The act of bearing witness to the trauma facilitates this shift, not only by transforming traumatic memory into a more or less coherent narrative, which can then be worked into the survivor's sense of self and view of the world, but also by reintegrating the survivor into a community, reestablishing connections essential to selfhood.[17]

Throughout Brison's description, we see the metaphor of being broken apart and of being put back together using language in a speech act that effects a kind of healing. Several events occur in this healing: the "severed" past and present are reconnected; the victim "reconstructs" herself as an actor in a "reconfigured" life; the victim changes from object of violence to a subject in her own articulated story; traumatic memory is transformed into a "coherent narrative"; and the victim is "reintegrated" into the world. These reconnections are achieved through "speech acts of memory,"[18] which need not be public, of course. They may be entirely private, written in a journal or spoken into a tape recorder. Or they may be confidential, told to a therapist in a privileged relationship or told to a friend or family member. Or, as is the case with many truth commissions, they may be told to an official representative of the state in a public or private setting. In each case, the turning of inchoate pain and grief into a narrative gives the victim control and distance from the traumatic event and empowers the victim to get on with his or her life. "Survivors need to resurrect their personalities, memories, values, and dreams from before their trauma, integrate that past with the trauma experience, and move beyond that experience so that they can better enjoy their lives in the present and look forward to the future."[19] The stories told attempt to recover the self that existed before, a self that is, nonetheless, forever changed by the traumatic event. Stories bring about a connection between radically split selves—the self before and the self after the violence.

But we must not be tempted to think that conceiving one's life as a coherent narrative is a therapeutic necessity only for those who have been traumatized. So doing places this urge toward story in an overly medical context. Making stories of our lives is, according to many philosophers, what we humans *do*: "Life can be regarded as a constant *effort*, even a struggle, to maintain or restore narrative coherence in the face of a ever-threatening, impending chaos at all levels" (original italics).[20] Paul Ricoeur (following Aristotle) defines a story as a "verbal experience where concordance mends discordance."[21] At a basic level, humankind is "homo narrans,"[22] that is, we understand our lives in terms of narrative. Narrative is "our primary way of organizing and giving coherence to our experience."[23] Hayden White maintains that the storytelling impulse is a ubiquitous mark of our humanity: "So natural is the impulse to narrate, so inevitable is the form of narrative for any report on the ways things really happened, that narrativity could appear problematical only in a culture in which it was absent or . . . programmatically refused."[24] Narrative is "international, transhistorical, transcultural . . . simply there like life itself."[25]

Yet even as we narrate our individual stories, these stories we tell about ourselves and our lives are not autonomous, disconnected units. As we shape the discordant events of our lives into a coherent narrative, we also discover our "place" in larger units: in our families, communities, and nations. Our identity depends upon our place in relation to others and to our community. Alasdair MacIntyre explains this process:

Every society enacts its own history as a more or less coherent dramatic narrative, a story in which each of us has to find his or her own place as a character, in order to know how to participate in it and how to continue it further. This is why the initiation of children into the lives of their family, their tribe, their city, their country, in almost all cultures is one in which children learn a stock of stories and so encounter the magical and the religious, the historical and the contemporary, the familiar and the heroic in narrative forms. It is through narrative that they learn to hope and to fear, to love and to hate, to dream and to want, to understand and to identify.[26]

During years of oppression, violence, fear, and silence, many people lose not only their personal voices but also their "place." The "dramatic narrative" fostered by an oppressive regime that has taken hold as the country's history has either excluded many people or appropriated and rewritten their stories. People are personally "storyless," isolated and alienated from the state and from other social structures that define them. By encouraging them to come forward and tell their stories and by providing an official (state-sponsored) setting in which their stories are heard and acknowledged, a renewed state invites them back in and incorporates their stories as part of a new national narrative.

When one's more or less coherent life story has been radically interrupted by the random violence and chaos wreaked by an oppressive government, the integration of that story—the interruption—into a narrative of one's own is more than healing; it is a human necessity. While it may sound strange to speak of *coherence* in the aftermath of atrocity, it is this very making of coherence through story that gives life meaning and order. Without a story, the violence takes on an uncontrolled life of its own. A person remains acted upon rather than acting, experiencing events as mere sequence, which is "the fragmentation or dissolution of self."[27] "While I may not *write* the story, I *choose* the story in which I am cast as a character" (original italics)[28] The storyteller moves from passive victimization to being a morally responsible agent capable of choosing the shape of the narrative in which he or she is cast.

Such restoration in cases of widespread atrocities that have afflicted many people within a nation can transcend the healing that an individual may experience.[29] It can help to achieve the renewal that a damaged country may require to proceed with the work of building a new moral community, a community that must encompass both victims and perpetrators. For a country to enable and encourage its citizens to come forward and tell stories reflects an attitude that the country desires its citizens to be responsible moral agents and no longer passive victims. Thus the country itself benefits from having better citizens, and the stories help to bridge the chasm between the past, in which people were enemies to each other, and the present, in which former adversaries coexist as fellow citizens: the country before and the new country that is forever changed by the events of the past.

For this wider healing to occur, the country must participate in the process; the storytelling cannot be private or confidential. The stories must be heard by official representatives of the state and publicly acknowledged. "The goal is not exorcism but acknowledgment."[30] The public nature of the storytelling allows the individual victims to see their story as part of a larger narrative about violence and "to know that one's suffering is not solely a private experience, best forgotten, but instead an indictment of a social cataclysm."[31] It can transform individual victims into a community of survivors.[32]

If the stories are told publicly, they have the potentiality to construct meaning for individuals and also for nations. The stories are remembered and told in a present in which not only a reconstructed self is possible, but also in which a new community necessarily exists, a community that can hear and acknowledge the stories. The task of interpreting and making meaning of the collected stories of violence and pain, and of integrating the individual stories into a larger narrative that evidences that community becomes the vital work of a truth commission. And, as I will discuss more fully later, the stories themselves serve to reconstruct that very community.

Stories as Balancing

The historical surveys of Chapters 1 and 2 demonstrate that the need for balancing a harm was central to notions of both revenge and retribution, seen most obviously in the widely misunderstood mandate of *lex talionis* and in the many metaphors used about revenge, such as "getting even," "settling accounts," and "getting my own back." No perfect balancing can occur, of course, no real "getting even." Your eye in return for my lost eye does not get my eye back; the death of another in no way balances the loss of my loved one. There can be no perfect balancing either for the individual or for the society; in the wake of massive atrocity, there can be no "tidy endings," as Martha Minow points out.[33] The question nonetheless remains: what approximates a balancing, what will count in the "accounting"?

In the last chapter, I argued that political violence and oppression are characterized by the appropriation, manipulation, misuse, and finally silencing of language. In torture, for example, the victim's ability to make meaningful language, to speak words that belong to herself or himself, is entirely appropriated by the torturer as the torture victim, through the technology of pain, is reduced to prelanguage moans and screams. The widespread use of torture by an oppressive regime is not accidental or just sadism. The ultimate inexpressibility of physical pain has political consequences. Language becomes inverted, meaning changed, and "confessions" put into the mouths of victims, who have no language left but that constructed by the regime.

Additionally, the harms have an expressive function, as Jean Hampton and others have pointed out. Torture becomes the visible manifestation of power; it makes the invisible regime visible. The crimes affect not only the victim's own sense of worth, but also the community's sense of the inherent value of all its citizens. The harms are of the sort that communicate that the perpetrator is superior to the victim, a superiority that becomes the essential insignia of the regime. The victim's value and equality are denied. Patterns of harms misrepresent value and "reinforce belief in the wrong theory of value in the community."[34]

"Making whole" and "balancing," then, the central metaphors used in revenge and retribution that are critical to any sense of justice, natural or otherwise, require a restoration of the language that has been taken away, or a refilling of the void left when the ability to use language was appropriated. The opportunity to tell one's own story in one's own words, with no restrictions on what may be said, is not something other than justice; it is an essential component of justice.[35] The necessity of correcting the false message about the victims' worth is likewise requisite to a society that seeks to demonstrate its commitment to the inherent value of all its citizens. The victims regain dignity and autonomy by correcting for themselves the false message about their worth, which seems far superior to the state's doing so. The victims themselves, with the support and acknowledgment of the state, repudiate the misrepresentation that the regime's violence fostered. If, as Hampton convincingly maintains, "retribution is response to a wrong that is intended to vindicate the value of the victim denied by the wrongdoers' action through the construction of an event that not only repudiates the action's message of superiority over the victim but does so in a way that confirms them as equal by virtue of their humanity,"[36] allowing victims to tell their stories in a state-sponsored setting is indeed retribution and a critical form of justice.

Stories as Ways of Discovering the Truth

On a visit to South Africa, I asked the attorney George Bizos what he thought about the Truth and Reconciliation Commission. Bizos represented the Biko family in its suit against the South African government over the constitutionality of giving amnesty to those who had killed Stephen Biko.[37] Given that he had been the Bikos's advocate in their attack against the TRC's mandate, I expected that he would be tentative at best in his response. Surprisingly, he was a strong supporter of the TRC's work and the story gathering it had accomplished. His reason was simple: in his opinion the Truth and Reconciliation Commission was able to uncover far more truth than trials would have done.

Bizos went on to say that the trial of Magnus Malan and his fifteen codefendants helped to shape his opinion about the truth and justice capabilities of trials versus truth commissions. Malan and the other defendants were all acquitted on charges related to the 1987 KwaMakutha massacre. In such a trial, Bizos maintained, witnesses with anything to hide, and this would include many of those in the apartheid government and military, have no real incentive to come forward with the truth. Even those with nothing to hide may hesitate to come forward for fear of the revictimization possible with rigorous cross-examination in a defense lawyer's all-out effort to cast doubt on a witness's credibility. In the Malan trial, not only was the truth obscured but the already financially hard-pressed Mandela government also had to pay nine million rand (about $1.5 million) for the defense lawyers, and the acquittal caused the struggling South African judiciary to be viewed with great skepticism. In the minds of many, this high-profile trial did more harm than good.[38]

While I maintain that it is unnecessary to create a false dichotomy between trials and truth commissions, that both can serve crucial roles in a transitional democracy, Bizos's remarks deserve some scrutiny, especially if establishing the truth is essential to our sense of justice. What are the relative merits of trials and truth commissions in establishing truth and justice?

For many, the idea of a trial is equated with the overall notion of justice. When we say "we don't want revenge, we want justice," we are saying, it seems to me, that we are willing to give over our passionate feeling that some act is required in response to a wrong to a dispassionate, orderly, state legal system—that is, we want a trial. We have been carefully (and necessarily) taught to channel our need for revenge into lawful procedures enacted by the state. These procedures have, for a long time, been centered around trials. Thus "justice" has come to mean a trial. When someone is "brought to justice," he or she is brought to trial. And if justice includes, as I think it does, a sense that the truth will be revealed, a trial provides a dramatic enactment by which we are led to believe that indeed we will or should learn the truth. The witnesses at least, if not all the actors in the trial, purport to tell "the truth, the whole truth, and nothing but the truth." And we do not proceed naively: everything that is said by a witness is subject to challenge (cross-examination) and some lies are uncovered. After some trials, we may have at least a credible version of a story that we are willing to believe; after some trials, the perpetrator is subject to punishment that seems, if not commensurate, at least appropriate.

Yet because of the very procedures put in place to attempt to uncover the truth and at the same time to protect the rights of the accused, even in situations that leave us satisfied with the story and the punishment, we have at best what South African Justice Albie Sachs calls "microscopic truth," which is "factual, verifiable and can be documented."[39] Another kind of truth, which Sachs calls "dialogical truth," which "is social truth, truth of experience that is established through interaction, discussion, and debate,"[40] may be given short shrift because of rigid procedures and a false sense of closure after a trial. *That* perpetrator and *those* victims may have something akin to traditional notions of justice. But in situations faced by transitional democracies after massive oppression, many perpetrators and victims will never enter a courtroom, will never have an opportunity to tell or hear the truth. While a trial can name some specific conduct as wrong and to some extent educate the citizenry about the nature and extent of prior wrongdoing, it is focused in such a way so that the individual wrongdoing may not be adequately put into the context of the practices and ideologies of the oppressive regime. Many victims may have no official space in which to tell the stories of the harms that befell them and no master narrative of oppression emerges.

Rules of procedure, strictly observed, can impede open storytelling that might reveal some larger more inclusive truth. What a witness or victim may say is constrained. Most testimony about feelings, personal impact, or harms not entirely relevant to the matter at hand is impermissible, and thereby goes unsaid. Under diligent cross-examination, doubt may be cast on even a truthful witness's story. If a trial does reveal the truth about a perpetrator, it may not set the record straight about other individuals who were hurt by the prior government; it will not get to those stories at all.

I say all this not to malign trials as such but to chase down Bizos's insight, which challenges the often uncritical position that justice, truth, and trials go naturally together. I do not want to suggest that trials can never uncover the truth effectively. Certainly the Nuremberg trials and the Eichmann trial went a long way in broadcasting the truth of what occurred during the Holocaust and in rewriting the German national narrative. In fact, the stories told during the relentless testimony in those trials are one of the trials' major legacies.[41] But those trials were not, particularly at the time, seen as traditional retributive justice procedures. They were widely criticized as being illegal or extralegal. The procedures allowed much more victim testimony and more latitude in that testimony than is typical in a trial.[42] Juan Enrique Vargas, a member of the Chilean commission, maintains that trials alone are not adequate in any event because they reach conclusions in particular cases but do not connect the individual isolated cases into any larger scheme. "Truth . . . includes objectives that cannot be realized through the ordinary functioning of the established judicial process."[43]

The Magnus Malan trial in South Africa offers an easy example of the failure of a trial in achieving justice, in both its truth and punishment forms. The trials that occurred in Argentina after the fall of the military regime offer a more balanced instance of the successes and failures that may result from trials. In Argentina, newly elected President Alfonsín was committed to bring those responsible for human rights abuses to trial in "exemplary" trials to "prevent episodes of violence and authoritarianism from recurring."[44] Alfonsín navigated a minefield of problems: among them, the self-amnesty that the military junta had passed; the objections from both the right and the left that the scope and time frame of the trials was too broad or too narrow; and jurisdictional issues.[45] In the end, a limited number of defendants were tried and convicted.

On the one hand, much good was accomplished in that the public became engaged in the process. The 1985 trials of the leaders of the former military juntas were avidly followed by the Argentinian public. The journal of the trial sold 200,000 copies each week, and the events of the trial were widely discussed. "Through this discussion, a public space was reappropriated, a voice rediscovered."[46] The Argentine "big trial," in the eyes of some, deeply affected the moral consciousness of society and "made a perceptible impact on the minds of the people."[47]

Some individual stories did get told as the trial focused on crimes against individual victims and the "survivors took the stage one by one to describe their suffering at the hands of their captors."[48] On the other hand, despite the opportunity for individuals to tell their stories, the strict legalistic structure of the junta trials allowed no master narrative to emerge: "There was no place in this narrative for the common people who had not been imprisoned, disappeared, and tortured. There was no designated time to mourn the loss of a certain dimension of collective innocence. There was no site where common people could come to grips with the idea that they also had been victims of the system of terror. The trial failed to provide an outlet for the feelings of personal inadequacy, anger, and frustration repressed during the years of extreme individualization."[49]

Overall in Argentina, although trials accomplished much good in terms of public discussion about democracy and the role of the military, they were largely unsuccessful both in resultant convictions and in uncovering the complete truth. There were a variety of reasons for this failure, including acts of disobedience by the military and the passage of the Punto Final Law and the Due Obedience Law, which severely curtailed prosecutions.[50] As an ultimate affront to the justice sought by the trials, in the early days of his presidency, Carlos Menem issued pardons for almost four hundred people under trial and for most of those convicted in the 1985 trial. One of the architects of the trials writes that the trials were actually harmful because they reinforced the very authoritarianism they were meant to repudiate.[51]

Even some of the strongest advocates of trials for a transitional democracy recognize the critical nature of dialogue and storytelling and limit their enthusiasm for trials to situations in which stories can be told and open discussion flourish. Mark Osiel, whose work studies the role of criminal trials in democratic transitions, insists, and I agree, that the ways by which a country deals with transitional democracy should be evaluated by the level of public discussion the method fosters. "To this end, judges and prosecutors can profit from close attention to the 'poetics' of legal storytelling,"[52] and to achieve an appropriate level of dialogue and storytelling, "trials should be unabashedly designed as monumental spectacles."[53] Trials, he says, should be public enough and heeded and discussed by the citizenry enough that the trials create a collective memory. They should, in fact, be show trials, "where large questions of collective memory and even national identity are engaged."[54]

In her discussion of the controversies surrounding the trials at Nuremberg, Erna Paris provides some examples of the sort of trials Osiel advocates. She argues that some trials successfully tread the difficult line between what she terms an "exemplary show trial" and public extravaganzas used as vehicles for state propaganda designed to terrify a populace into submission. She cites as examples the trials of Adolph Eichmann, Klaus Barbie, and Maurice Papon, all of which led to broad discussions about complicity and the writing of false histories: "Although all these trials had educational 'show' purposes that stretched well beyond the realm of the law, they did settle down to the subject at hand: the guilt or innocence of one man."[55]

But that is not the nature of most trials, and Osiel carefully, but not convincingly, engages the many objections to such a use of trials. In addition to the problems of due process and fairness to the defendants and the general competency and role of courts, trials can be and often are unbearably tedious, and the public, although initially engaged, quickly loses interest.[56] A wrongdoer has been "brought to justice," but stories are not heard or heeded, no real dialogue ensues, and an artificial (and dangerous) sense of closure sets in. No narrative of the aspirations of the common people or the country emerges.

Truth commissions, despite the name, can no more guarantee complete truth than can trials. People can and will lie in both settings. In an amnesty hearing in South Africa, I listened to Eugene de Kock, in a desperate attempt to get a few years off his sentence through the amnesty process, as he told a patently untrue story about his involvement in the murder of an ANC activist. The victim's mother, hoping to discover who *had* killed her son, listened to the proceedings in pained disbelief that she should be put through such an ordeal.[57] In another hearing, I sat with the mothers of two teenaged victims who wanted only to find their children's bodies as Jerry Richardson clowned his way through false testimony about his involvement in their deaths.[58] Nonetheless, flawed as the amnesty process was, overall the testimony given by the perpetrators resulted in much being known that had been shrouded in secrecy and silence.

Victims as well as perpetrators can certainly lie to a truth commission, yet the storytelling settings can provide a different kind of truth than a mere recitation of facts. The testimony that a victim may give to a truth commission obviously differs significantly from that which would be given in a trial or before a tribunal. Truth commissions usually allow for far more breadth and freedom in the storytelling. Victims may talk about much that is legally irrelevant; feelings may be discussed and even displayed (the shoe throwing in South Africa, for example). These settings can reveal the truth about what oppression did to people—not just the recitation of events, but what oppression *felt* like, how it changed and destroyed lives, even lives not touched by a specific crime. Because so many stories can be told, a larger picture emerges in which individual victims can see their place in a community of survivors.

Many commissions have been scrupulous about inviting those named as wrongdoers to come forward and offer their own stories. In most instances, these invitations have been ignored, but that they were issued gives credence to the overall story that the commission finally publishes. Many commissions have also refrained from publishing specific accusations unless they have substantiated them with multiple overlapping stories and other kinds of evidence (such as military records or excavation of burial sites). Some commissions have refrained from naming names at all and have instead molded the stories into a larger narrative of violence and oppression, with accusations directed at institutions and policies rather than at individuals.

It may be that allowing people to tell their stories free from the necessary constraints of judicial process, in their own words with no threat of cross-examination, may yield far more universal truth than traditional retributive justice procedures. Stories can, as Michael Ignatief puts it, "reduce the number of lies,"[59] and the reputations of both the living and the dead can be salvaged when the true stories are revealed by multiple, even redundant, storytelling. José Zalaquett, a member of the Chilean commission, notes that the families he interviewed often maintained that what was most important to them was that the truth be revealed and that the memories of their loved ones cease to be vilified.[60] They believed that being able personally to set the record straight (a metaphoric balancing) vindicated the memories.

Perhaps in a perfect world, Osiel's vision of the trial as a setting for storytelling that could result in a shared memory would be a possibility: the truth and justice components of both trials and truth commissions could be combined.[61] To achieve that goal, emerging democracies would have to possess not only the will but also the infrastructure to pull off ambitious trials. Moreover, normal rules of procedure would have to be substantially altered to allow full stories to be told. Even at that, no system, state or international, can do much more than try a few of the perpetrators following a mass atrocity. At best, justice in a traditional sense is achieved for a few. As with Nuremberg, a few of the most visible leaders, who indeed bear great responsibility, can be tried and punished. Such trials provide a microscopic truth that is focused and limited. But the guard who raped and murdered someone's daughter, the low-level functionaries who ambushed and killed a group of peasants, these and many, many others, will never be "brought to justice." The stories of the harms that befell thousands of people are never heard or acknowledged—never even given a setting in which they might be heard. Thus even in Osiel's and Paris's perfect world of educational show trials that remain exemplary in terms of due process, truth commissions can provide additional settings that allow for fuller transformative and constitutive storytelling beyond the scope of any trials. They allow for other kinds of truths that trials cannot reveal.

Storytelling as Carnival

Russian literary theorist and philosopher, Mikhail Bakhtin, developed the concept of carnival in his studies of the work of Rabelais and Dostoevsky. Bakhtin's literary analysis takes seriously the celebration of the medieval carnival, which "celebrated temporary liberation from the prevailing truth and from the established order; it marked the suspension of all hierarchical rank, privileges, norms, and prohibitions."[62] Bakhtin saw the time of carnival in the Middle Ages and the Renaissance as the "people's second life,"[63] in which the common people could emerge from the routine of life and could temporarily be free from the existing social structure. In the space of carnival, "people were . . . reborn for new, purely human relations. . . . [which were] not only a fruit of imagination or abstract thought; they were experienced."[64] Unlike entertainment, carnival is not a spectacle that is performed by an elite few and observed by everyone else. Carnival provides an alternative social space that allows the participation of all. Carnival has the potentiality to open up and transform traditional, constrained spaces and to allow people to talk unguardedly and to be liberated from the forms and fears that might restrain them. It is a space of freedom, abundance, and equality.

In addition to universal participation, carnival encourages free and familiar contact among diverse people, a "special type of communication impossible in everyday life,"[65] in which physical and social distances between people are suspended, and constrained, coercive relations give way to ones based in freedom and equality. Discourse also changes into carnival abuse or *profanation*, not directed at persons but at practices and systems that oppress the people.

Bakhtin distinguishes carnival from official feasts, whether ecclesiastical, feudal, or state-sponsored, which reinforced the existing world order rather than leading people out of it: "the official feast looked back at the past and used the past to consecrate the present. . . . [It] asserted all that was stable, unchanging, perennial: the existing hierarchy, the existing religious, political, and moral values, norms, prohibitions. It was a triumph of a truth already established, the predominant truth that was put forward as eternal and indisputable."[66] Carnival, on the other hand, was "the feast of becoming, change, and renewal."[67] Official feasts were a "consecration of inequality,"[68] unlike carnival, which broke down the barriers of caste, property, profession, and age.

The freeing possibilities of carnival and this distinction that Bakhtin makes between carnival and official feasts are helpful in thinking about the kinds of settings in which the stories may be told. When the setting is a trial, as in an official feast, the state is in charge and the people are actors in the state drama. Rank is evident and celebrated as the judges are robed and sit above the people. In trials, dignity and reverence is accorded the court itself, and the victims are largely absent or unimportant. What the people say and when they say it are constrained and controlled by trial procedure and by the lawyers and judges.

Contrarily, some storytelling settings, particularly those in South Africa (which I discuss in detail in Chapter 5), can provide a carnivalesque healing of both storytellers and their audiences. In certain circumstances, the storytelling setting can restore dignity to the victims, and reverence may be accorded them. Storytelling settings, unlike trials, can invert the normal rules of formal judicial procedure, and in displays akin to Bakhtin's sense of carnival, the official established order can be temporarily obliterated, along with "all the forms of terror, reverence, piety, and etiquette"[69] connected to it.

Goodrich's example of the shoe-throwing event at the South African Truth and Reconciliation Commission hearing comes to mind as a precise example of the carnival possibilities in storytelling settings. The mother's shrieking and throwing of the shoe at her son's killer exemplifies the elevation of the profane in carnival, the bringing down to earth of the legalistic and abstract. The mother's anger, pain, and hatred become visible and acknowledged in a moment that would be impossible in formal trial-like settings. In her fictional rendition of a truth commission hearing in South Africa, Gillian Slovo searches for a paradigm that captures the otherness of a hearing: "That dusty dead-end Smitsrivier should be witness to the likes of this! This dance of the past, this baroque blending of court ceremonial, street party and revivalist meeting."[70] For Bakhtin, it would be carnival, which held out the promise of a renewal of society on a more egalitarian basis. Some storytelling settings, most notably those in South Africa, offer the hope of the destruction of the oppressive hierarchy and a renewal based upon a new society capable of embracing and seeing the pain and oppression of others.

Additionally, in his analysis of literary texts, Bakhtin looks to the influence of carnival on novels, on what he sees as the "dialogic line of development in novelistic prose,"[71] a development that comes to maturation in Dostoevsky's writing, which Bakhtin terms the *carnivalization* of literature. Carnivalization includes a "genuine polyphony of fully valid voices,"[72] a dialogic truth in which "*Truth is not born nor is it to be found inside the head of an individual person, it is born between people collectively searching for truth, in the process of their dialogic interaction*" (italics original).[73] The inclusion of personal stories in the master narratives that inevitably comprise truth commission reports allows for the *carnivalization* of history, an entirely new kind of history telling and nation making that encompasses a fuller dialogic truth. I explore this possibility in the next chapter when I turn to the reports themselves.

Stories as Translation and Communication

Stories enable citizens within a country to understand each other in ways that might not otherwise be possible. In countries that are deeply divided culturally, economically, politically, and otherwise, the sharing of personal narratives may be the only means by which such diverse people can begin to recognize the humanity of the other. An experience of pain or of the loss of a loved one crosses deep divides, and stories of pain and loss can bridge gaps in experience and lead to empathetic understanding. Stories solve "the problem of how to translate knowing into telling [footnote omitted], the problem of fashioning human experience into a form assimilable to structures of meaning that are generally human rather than culture-specific. We may not be able fully to comprehend specific thought patterns of another culture, but we have relatively less difficulty understanding a story coming from another culture, however exotic that culture may appear to us."[74] Events become translatable between and among people who normally do not understand each other: "narrative is a meta-code, a human universal on the basis of which transcultural messages about the nature of a shared reality can be transmitted."[75] When stories translate events into a shared language, they arouse our emotions. We do not respond only with our logical minds; stories move us to pity and compassion.[76]

Not only does narrative provide a means of translating from one culture to another, it also provides a way of speaking for the disempowered.

For those who have been outsiders to a country's power structure, narrative may be the only way that they can express themselves to the powerful other. This experience of being silenced by a power structure is what the philosopher Jean-Francois Lyotard calls the *différend*. If one has been disempowered and victimized by a system of justice, one experiences the *différend*, in which a common language does not exist by which one can express one's sense of injury. "A case of differend between two parties takes place when the 'regulation' of the conflict that opposes them is done in the idiom of one of the parties while the wrong suffered by the other is not signified in that idiom."[77] In practical terms, the *différend* arises when a victim of political oppression attempts to name the harm in the idiom of the oppressor, for whom it is not a harm at all. A victim of apartheid, for example, has no legal language to name the harm caused by that system. In the hegemonic legal language, there is no harm. It cannot be named. Normal logical and legal systems of discourse, which seem like foreign languages to many victims, fail. Stories, though, can break through the *différend* and provide a common language by which the less powerful can communicate with the powerful (or formerly powerful)[78] the nature of the harm that has befallen them. The sometimes useless language of the law is put aside, and one instead tells stories that capture and transmit common human emotions such as pain, loss, separation, desperation.

Storytelling as Sacramental

Terence Coonan defines sacramentality as "the belief that the visible, material elements of the world can in fact reveal what would otherwise be the invisible divine presence."[79] Without this tangible presence in the world, this view holds, humans would have no experience of an invisible God. Thus "it is of paramount importance that grace that is otherwise invisible become concrete and accessible."[80] The discovering of the truth, Coonan maintains, is a means for making the invisible visible: "that which was shrouded in secrecy and terror must be made concrete and rendered part of a country's collective memory."[81] In other words, the officially recognized truth (in the form of a truth commission report) becomes a visible sign of a country's new aspirational norms; it is grace made visible.

My claim for the sacramental nature of this kind of storytelling takes a slightly different form: something sacramental occurs in the reclaiming of language when a victim can remember and recite the story of what happened. The words take on a sacramental sense in that they are used to remember, an act fraught with psychological and historical consequences, and also to re-member, to pull together the pieces of a victim's symbolically dismembered self.

The metaphor of fragmentation, of being broken into pieces, of being *dismembered* permeates the discussion of pain, violence, torture, suffering, and oppression: "what is 'broken'—shattered—is the *experience* of life, the *construction of vitality*" (original italics).[82] With torture, an individual self is fragmented, one's voice is shattered and then silenced. With oppression, family members are separated from each other; the family unit is doubly dismembered. Other social units that could threaten the power structure, such as political organizations and churches, are likewise dismembered.

The symbolic and religious nature of dismemberment and re-membering is found in both mythology and Christian religious ritual. In Egyptian mythology, for example, after the body of Osiris was cut into pieces, his wife, Isis, undertook a long and tedious search to gather up the pieces of his body. When she found them, she re-membered the body and buried it at Philae, a place that thereafter took on great religious significance. A magnificent temple was erected at the place of re-membering, to which the faithful made pilgrimages.[83]

In Catholicism, the sacrament of the Eucharist is a re-membering of Christ, in which broken bread is transubstantiated into pieces of his body and wine into his blood, a ceremony initiated by Jesus at the Last Supper, in which "Jesus was indicating that his disciples were to share in his sacrifice."[84] The sacrament of the Eucharist repeats this ceremonial meal, "convinced that it [is doing] what Jesus intended when he said: 'Do this in remembrance of me.' "[85] The admonition "Do this in remembrance of me" in the eucharistic ceremony is followed by the *anamnesis* spoken by the people: "We remember, we do this to commemorate you."[86]

Remembering pain, violence, and oppression, then, has an unavoidable double meaning, in that the remembering and telling of the story carries with it the re-membering of that which was fragmented. The ritualistic retelling in a group in a space set aside for it symbolically allows for both sharing in the pain and putting the pieces of a broken life back together. Given an official space in which to speak and remember, shattered voices, lives, selves, families, communities and nations may be re-membered.

We can see that something sacramental occurs in the reclaiming of language in *Death and the Maiden* when Paulina projects her pain onto an agent, Roberto Miranda.[87] Paulina's torturer has been a ghostly unknown presence until she hears Miranda's voice in her house. Her inchoate anguish can now be projected onto him, and she assumes a strength that at last makes speech possible. She can move beyond the confines of her injured body back into the world of language. When she finally tells Gerardo all that happened to her and she hears these words re-said by Roberto Miranda, her torturer, the false moral claim that Paulina was worth less than Miranda and that Paulina was not an end in herself but existed for Miranda's and the regime's use is importantly set straight.[88] But more than that, the words take on a sacramental sense in that they are used to remember and also to re-member, to pull together the pieces of Paulina's symbolically dismembered self. In an act reminiscent of both the Roman Catholic Eucharist and many other religious rituals,[89] the retelling of a story is invoked to re-member and create a spiritual unity.

Let us pause for a moment and imagine how a truth commission would actualize these six benefits and achieve some justice for victims. What would such a truth commission look like? It would invite and encourage both victims and perpetrators to come forward to tell their stories. It would provide some official, public dedicated space in which the stories would be told, heard, and acknowledged by official representatives of the state as well as the citizenry at large. At the same time, it would turn this space over to the people and would allow great freedom in what could be said, how it could be said, and how people could behave. The processes by which truth commissions gather stories have great potential for creating a kind of justice that not only publicly exposes the truth and vindicates people, but also a kind of justice that is dynamic and ongoing, not perfect of course, but a visible manifestation of an ethical and political commitment that honors truth, individual worth, dignity, and equality. In this sense, justice is not a single event but a process that promises to create a nation in which the dignity and importance of individuals is maintained. Moreover, truth reports offer a new way to balance violence, a way of "getting even" that does not entail more violence. Our imaginations have strained at what possibilities there may be, and generally it has been believed that only another form of violence, personal or state, will suffice. Truth reports suggest another possibility.

But the process of story gathering is only part of what a truth commission does; it also writes a report. The form that this report takes can also constitute a kind of justice in the ways in which the report accounts for the past and the commitment it makes to the future. It matters who finally gets to tell the overall story, the master narrative, and it matters what form this narrative takes. The next chapter discusses the ramifications of the formal choices that report writers make, how their choices can contradict or complement the political claims they make. It also examines three reports from Latin America that appeared in the 1980s and early 1990s following the "dirty wars" in Argentina, Chile, and El

Salvador. The writers of these reports were, in many ways, inventing the form. Chapter 6 turns to the most famous report of all, the South African report, whose authors, having learned much from predecessor commissions and reports, pushed the possibilities for truth reports into new territory. This analysis of four truth commissions and reports strives to see what ways, if any, the potentiality for justice, which I have argued resides in storytelling, is realized.

Chapter Five
Telling Stories in a Search for Justice: The Argentinian, Chilean, and Salvadoran Truth Commissions

> Certain truths about human life can only be fittingly and accurately stated in the language and forms characteristic of the narrative artist.
>
> —Martha Nussbaum, *Love's Knowledge*

> To imagine a language means to imagine a form of life.
> —Ludwig Wittgenstein, *Philosophical Investigations*

The Return to Narrative

The rapid emergence of truth commissions and their collection and creation of narratives reflects, in part, the "return to narrative" that is prominent in diverse disciplines. Historians, philosophers, theologians, moralists, anthropologists, sociologists, psychologists, psychoanalysts, artists, and even legal scholars[1] have newly and increasingly embraced narrative as a valid and powerful mode of explanation and representation of reality.[2] This change is characterized as a "return to narrative" because narrative, once the primary mode of discourse, has been long devalued. From the time of the classical Greeks until recently, narrative was regarded as an inferior mode of discourse, frivolous and fanciful compared to logical argument. Even before the time of Plato, philosophers distinguished between modes of discourse with *logos*, carefully crafted logical arguments, seen as superior in form to *mythos* or *epos*, loosely crafted (if at all) traditional stories.[3] The discourse of logical argument was seen as the only appropriate way to convey serious, reflective thought. Martha Nussbaum describes the division as the "ancient quarrel" between the poets and the philosophers: those seeking answers to philosophical questions had no use for literary works as providing ways of answering them,[4] or for narratives as the appropriate form for conveying them.

Despite this theoretical stance that devalued narrative as a means of serious discourse, in practice narratives were always an important mode of expression and provided means by which people reflected on critical questions about their lives. The ancient Greeks attended dramatic performances, where they were moved and persuaded by the stories presented and their minds were engaged: "To attend a tragic drama was not to go to a distraction or a fantasy, in the course of which one suspended one's anxious practical questions. It was, instead, to engage in a communal process of inquiry, reflection and feeling with respect to important civic and personal ends."[5] This double engagement was possible because stories have the power to touch us emotionally as well as intellectually, to compel us to anger, grief, terror, pity, and, at their best, to force us to reflect on the social and political situation they present. They do not teach us, as many philosophical texts do, that "the good person is self-sufficient,"[6] best unmoved by the tragic events that occur, both to oneself and to others. Instead, stories draw us in, challenge our autonomy, and make us cognizant of our inevitable interconnectedness.

The form, then, that a text takes—whether abstract, philosophical discourse or a story, for example—can supplement or contradict the values it espouses. The formal choices a writer makes "entail ontological and epistemic choices with distinct ideological and even specifically political implications."[7] Accordingly, the formal choice that a country makes to collect personal stories and to publish them, perhaps as part of a larger, more general story, reflects a view of life, of politics, of what it means to be a government, of who citizens are and should be. Clearly, a country's examination of an oppressive past need not include personal stories at all. A country could employ political scientists and philosophers to write a general, abstract rendering of what occurred and why. If chosen, this abstract theoretical style would "make, like any other style, a statement about what is important and what is not, about what faculties of the reader are important for knowing and what are not."[8] It would say that political abstractions are paramount, that the particulars are less important, if at all. It would mean that it hopes to engage its readers' intellectual faculties, their minds, not their hearts.

On the other hand, the choice to include narratives says that individuals matter; such a text refuses to generalize or to allow its readers to ignore the particulars. It, frankly, rubs its readers' noses in the particulars, especially if it allows the personal stories to stand in the first person, thereby making the pain and misery unavoidable for a reader. The decision to include narratives in a truth report demonstrates that its writers want and require its readers to be moved, even horrified. Such a form disallows dispassionate distancing from the blood and gore of the past. By presenting the stories of victims as worth sharing and reading, it tells us that good citizens are not self-sufficient, autonomous individuals, but connected members of a community who can empathize with each other's pain.

The use of personal stories in a truth commission report, moreover, reflects a kind of language that differs vastly from the discourse typically used in describing acts of violence in war. In conventional war discourse, the individual human body disappears and is replaced by generalities: "*Berlin* is bombed" (not thousands of individual inhabitants of Berlin are killed and the structures in which they lived and worked are destroyed).[9] Instead of the usual depersonalized war rhetoric that shields us from the horrific realities, the inclusion of the verbatim stories as core parts of the historical record emphasizes the pain and deaths of individuals, of actual people who could be (perhaps were) our neighbors, our friends, our family.

The use of personal stories also can reflect a use of language that Mikhail Bakhtin describes as "polyphonic" in his analysis of the novels of Dostoevsky.[10] Instead of a "monological" text with a single, unified authorial voice, some truth reports, like Dostoevsky's novels, allow for the inexhaustible complexity of experience to be revealed in competing but "fully weighted" voices that the authorial voice does not subsume or silence. The reports can represent a "plurality of unmerged consciousnesses, a mixture of 'valid voices' not completely subordinate to authorial intent or the heavy hand of the authorial voice."[11]

Thus truth commission reports that include personal stories have captured the imagination for a multiplicity of reasons, and prominent among them is that stories capture the emotional complexity of a brutal past in a way that other forms of history may not. It may remain difficult and controversial to search for language to represent radical evil because we do not have a vocabulary or moral framework that can contain or even evaluate some kinds of evil actions. Nonetheless, we can allow accounts of them to be told by those who have endured them, and we can force ourselves to listen to and acknowledge them. Stories do not force historical closure upon the reality of pain and death; they account for but they do not justify or excuse.

In this chapter, I want to turn to a close analysis of three reports— *Nunca Más* (Argentina, 1984); the *Report of the Chilean National Commission on Truth and Reconciliation* (the Rettig Report, 1991); and *From Madness to Hope: The Twelve-Year War in El Salvador* (1993). These reports span nearly a decade and reveal certain things, including an evolution in understanding the potentiality of truth commission reports. I have selected these three not only because they are relatively well-known truth reports, but also because they are excellent exemplars of the possibilities and, in some cases, the failed potentiality of truth commissions and reports. No description, finally, captures or does justice to the reports. Nor is my analysis of their forms meant in any way to impugn the monumental effort and self-sacrifice of all those who worked on them or to denigrate the reports' importance. It may be that any report is better than none. People are given a space in which to speak, usually after a long period of enforced silence. People find out some truth about what happened to loved ones and what happened in their country. At the same time, the reports I examine tell their stories in quite different ways. And if we are seeking justice in these reports—as well as truth—it is worth thinking about what story is told by the process by which the stories are gathered and by the final forms of the reports themselves. What valuable stories do they tell and what dangerous ones? Thus my discussion of these reports will focus on three questions: First, what overall story—what master narrative—does the report tell? Second, how are the personal stories (of victims and sometimes perpetrators) used in the master narrative? And, finally, what community does the narrative imagine and create?

A Brief History of Truth Commissions

Truth commissions, with the task of writing reports, did not exist before the 1970s. Although atrocities committed both by external enemies and by states against their own citizens have occurred with unhappy constancy, the general practice following such events was to put the past behind, to engage in collective amnesia as a country moved on. Victims "forgot and forgave"; perpetrators escaped without punishment, except for an occasional act of private vengeance. "Silence and impunity have been the norm rather than the exception."[12] Often, nonetheless, hatred and resentment festered, and revenge was eventually enacted, even if generations later.[13] Following World War II, a consensus arose among the victors that some official action was required to deal with the crimes committed during that war, and much debate (and disagreement) led to the Nuremberg tribunals.[14] Indeed, truth commissions are sometimes seen as growing out of the Nuremberg trials, which reinvigorated discussions of the natural right of individuals against the immoral, unjust, and criminal acts of their governments.[15]

Nuremberg, however, is not easily repeatable. It is, in many ways, singular, and is certainly not a paradigm transferable to transitional democracies.[16] It was, first of all, a victors' trial: the winners were prosecuting and the losers were on trial. Most contemporary transitions to democracy do not have clear winners and losers. Second, at Nuremberg the opposing sides were not attempting to build a new political community together. They were separate sovereign states whose futures would be connected at arm's length.

When a country emerges from an oppressive past, despite the atrocities of that past, the opposing sides will necessarily be contained within a new moral and political community. A version of victors' justice with harsh retribution against those complicitous with the past regime threatens to deepen the divide. At the same time, a country needs to distinguish the new regime from the old one, and victims require some kind of balancing, or ancient urges towards revenge fester and break out.[17] Consequently, there is a growing trend toward seeking some kind of accounting, and the decisions about what measures are appropriate and workable are complicated. When full-blown trials are impracticable and unwise but people still desire some reckoning with the past, the idea of a truth commission and an official report emerges as one way to respond.[18]

To date there have been more than twenty truth commissions, and they are widely diverse. While they share some similarities, they differ in, among other things, who conducts the inquiry, the scope of the inquiry, the powers given to those who conduct the inquiry and write the report, the mechanisms by which the stories are found, how and where (and if) the results are published. Reports are usually written by commissions that are set up at the time of transition from a former regime, a military dictatorship, for example, to a new democracy. The creation of such a commission is often part of a negotiated settlement in which there is no clear winner or loser. Even if the transition occurred peacefully, there is nearly always a sharp discontinuity with the previous regime and a strong commitment to fundamental change in the governing structure and policies. The commission may be set up by a new president, by the legislature, or by an outside organization, such as the United Nations, or, as in Brazil, the story gathering may be done by private initiative. Although many commissions are official government organs, they are often staffed by private citizens rather than government officials; some (as in El Salvador) are staffed by noncitizen outsiders. They are designed to investigate the human rights violations committed in the recent past, are usually temporary in nature, and are charged with giving an official report of their findings, thus "Leaving an honest account of the [past] violence [that] prevents history from being lost or re-written, and allows a society to learn from its past in order to prevent a repetition of such violence in the future."[19] Their role is not to judge but to gather information and make it known.[20]

Each commission's mandate has its own peculiarities. Chile's commission was specifically limited to the "most serious human rights violations," that is, those that resulted in death; Uruguay's commission's mandate was to focus on reports of illegal detention and torture. The Salvadoran commission's mandate was wider and broader—to "report on serious acts of violence . . . whose impact on society urgently demands that the public should know the truth,"[21] and the commission chose to concentrate almost exclusively on discovering information about the disappeared. The resources and powers also vary. Some commissions have large staffs with investigative organs and legal powers; others have little or no staff and tiny budgets and must rely upon voluntary testimony. The Philippine commission set up in 1986 by the Corazon Aquino government had neither staff nor budget and shut down after a few months without issuing a report.

Commissions gather their information in a variety of ways. A commission may set up an office or offices and invite victims to come in and testify (tell their stories) before commission members or staff. Sometimes commission members go out and gather information on their own, not only testimony, but also physical evidence and information from jails, hospitals, morgues, and former secret holding centers. In some instances, the testimony is given privately; in others the testimony is given publicly in highly ritualized settings.

The role of the alleged perpetrators varies from denial and resistance (El Salvador, for example) to participation and actual telling of stories (South Africa). While most of the reports become public documents, they vary in how widely they are made available. The Argentinian report, *Nunca Más*, became a best-seller; the Chilean report was sent to each named victim's family; the Zimbabwean report was kept confidential.

Writing History—Truth Commission Reports as Constitutive Documents

Truth commission reports write what we traditionally regard as history, of course. They state a version of the facts as they occurred in a circumscribed past and also interpret those facts. That is, they provide a "plot"[22] that demonstrates (or argues) cause and effect, what Hayden White calls "emplotment."[23] The reports are thus themselves *master narratives*, that is, the reports impose a form of story on the circumscribed events that they are charged to uncover. The events are not only "registered within the chronological framework of their original occurrence, but . . . [also] revealed as possessing a structure, an order of meaning, that they do not possess as mere sequence."[24]

Certainly, historical inquiry has played an important role in the work of truth commissions. "Historical inquiry can be used in a particular investigation to reconstruct the circumstances and nature of the crimes and to ascertain the involvement of particular individuals," and it also "may be used to place an individual crime within the general context of wartime activities and wartime criminality."[25] Historical inquiry can also lay bare the kind of ideologies that gave rise to the crimes being investigated, and in so doing, make us alert to any renewed currents of similar ideologies that could, if we are not watchful, lead to similar crimes.[26] Many truth commission reports contain these aspects of historical inquiry and critically examine events and ideologies leading up to the violence and oppression that the personal narratives reveal.

But the history contained within a truth commission report is not just the story about *that* (former) state. It is also a constitutive history of *this* (emerging) state. The countries that emerge from a period of internal oppression and violence experience an identity crisis. Because the oppressors have "had the microphone," that is, have had complete control of language and have thus constructed the national master narrative, the new democratic state that emerges from the ashes of the old state needs ways to reconstruct and rewrite the master narrative. One way that this new narrative is written is through a truth report. As a transitional democracy negotiates its new identity, that identity is not only contained within the report but is constituted by the very form of the report. Who gets to tell the nation's story, write its history, is an essential component of power.

In other words, a state has a huge investment in controlling the kind of story that is written, in shaping the master narrative. In Hegel's view of history, any "history" presupposes a state in whose interest events are recorded and narrated; the state "creates [history] as it creates itself."[27] To have a full understanding of itself, a state (and for Hegel, a state becoming an ideal state) must have a complete understanding of its past. It must construct a master narrative because "the identity of a group, culture, people, or nation is not that of an immutable substance, nor that of a fixed structure, but that, rather, of a recounted story."[28] As we read the reports, which are inevitably master narratives, we must ask, what story is being told here? What is the master narrative? What kind of community is the report constituting? What does the form of the report tell us about the kind of new country that is being founded? About its ethical commitment to the future? About its vision of power?

The truth commission reports, then, represent an innovative kind of history. Many of them include personal stories as salient and illustrative parts of the larger story that comprises the truth commission report. The authoritative voice that one inevitably experiences in reading a history, the voice that shapes events into a single master narrative, is joined in these reports by the voices of the victims. The report is still, necessarily, a master narrative that looks to the past and speculates about reasons for the oppression and also looks to the future and promises change. But the inclusion of the personal stories can produce a radically new kind of historical document in two ways. First, the reports function as founding documents that reconstruct and even invent the new political community. Their publication is a constitutive, foundational moment in a nation's history. The reports become documents that are speech acts, bringing the new reformed state into being. Second, the reports provide a way of unifying widely diverse people who have become even more alienated from one another as a result of the violence and oppression. These people view the state, quite reasonably, with suspicion and fear instead of being able to see the state as a place where citizens together can aspire to higher things. As they tell the story of the past in an unprecedented way—privileging personal narratives—the reports invite people back into the community, people who have become fragmented individually and socially as well as alienated from the state.

The new (or renewed) state must not only rewrite the national narrative but also must find ways to reintegrate its alienated citizens. A new state in which one can tell one's story is allegedly present. But how are victims to know that? They know if the state announces itself by allowing these stories to be told, by making the victims' stories part and parcel of the new national narrative, much as Fortinbras does at the closing scene of *Hamlet*, when he promises to listen to Horatio tell the story of Hamlet to the unknowing world. Marina Geldenhuys, a victim of the Church Street bombing in South Africa, stated that "the new government is significant to me because now I can sit here and tell my story."[29] A commentator on the Argentinian report maintains that "A narrative of the past, with central premises and a general outline shared by the different groups in society is a powerful unifying force in any country. In the has-been countries, this narrative is even more significant, as much of people's sense of self-worth and identity depends on what is perceived as the countries' grand heritage and historical tradition."[30]

In a truth commission report, individuals tell personal stories, the commission uses them and constructs the *plot*, the inevitable master narrative, and the two together manifest a unique sharing of power reflecting the promise of democracy. That the personal stories comprise a notable portion of the new history connotes that the voices of the people are meaningful in the newly constituted country. A truth report, with its core personal narratives, announces, "we hold these truths to be self-evident"; it proclaims that it is published in a country in which such harms are unacceptable, in which these voices can be heard and valued, and in which these stories can be acknowledged. We hold *this* truth to be henceforth *self-evident*. By its very existence, such a report brings a new nation into being.

If a truth commission report exists as the sole or major remedy, have the victims forgone any opportunity for "justice"? In the preceding chapter, I suggested several ways in which victims and nations benefit from the truth-seeking and the storytelling process, ways that may approach a dynamic conception of justice. Here I want to look at the reports themselves, the end products of the storytelling process, and at the innovative ways in which these reports are both writing history and creating community. Each of these reports, while largely sharing methodology and purpose with the others, tells its story in a different way, tells its own unique story, using the victims' stories in diverse ways.

Argentina

Background

The first significant truth report appeared in 1984: *Nunca Más*, presented to the president of Argentina by the National Commission on the Disappeared.[31] At that time only two other truth commissions existed: the Commission of Inquiry into "Disappearances" of People in Uganda Since the 25th of January, 1971 and the National Commission of Inquiry into Disappearances in Bolivia. The former, created by Idi Amin to investigate his own government, is largely seen as a self-serving attempt to throw a sop to the critical international human rights community. Although the Commission took its task seriously, heard witnesses, documented cases, and made recommendations, Amin neither published the report nor implemented any of the Commission's recommendations. The second commission, the Bolivian Commission, disbanded without issuing a report.[32] The Argentinian report, then, is recognized as the first serious attempt to use a truth commission to reckon with the past.

In Argentina, the National Commission on the Disappeared (CONADEP) was created by President Raúl Alfonsín in 1983. The democratic election of Alfonsín followed seven years of repressive military rule, during which time an estimated 10,000 to 30,000 people were "disappeared" at the hands of the military. That is, people were kidnapped from the streets, their homes, or their places of work, detained, tortured, and never seen again, in the alleged cause of crushing "subversive activity." Most of the bodies of the disappeared were never found. Although the period of repression received much international condemnation and by 1980 "the military dictatorship began to lose steam"[33] and the economy to falter, only the misjudgment of entering into a war with Great Britain over the Falkland Islands, which ended in defeat and disgrace for Argentina, led to enough public outrage that the military was forced to relinquish its stranglehold on the country and allow democratic elections. Just five weeks before the elections, however, the president, General Reynaldo Benito Bignone, signed the "self-amnesty law," which granted a blanket amnesty for all subversive and counter-subversive acts and crimes that occurred between May 25, 1973, and June 17, 1982.

Alfonsín had made human rights and an investigation into abuses a priority during his presidential campaign, and by the end of the first week of his presidency, he created CONADEP by presidential decree. He appointed ten commissioners "chosen for their consistent stance in defence of human rights and their representation of different walks of life."[34] He also invited both chambers in Congress to send three representatives. Only the Chamber of Deputies complied. Ernesto Sabato, a respected author, was unanimously elected president of CONADEP.

Despite Alfonsín's election and resolve, the creation of CONADEP was not unopposed. In its report, CONADEP describes the political climate in which it began its work.

Embarking on something completely new to Argentina, the Commission started work in a climate charged with tension not only due to the nature of the task in hand but also because of incredulity shown in some quarters, disagreement in others and criticism in many more. We must also remember that the setting up of the Commission caused resentment among those who favoured other channels of investigation (e.g. parliamentary), or who saw the Commission as an attempt to circumvent any more profound clarification of the matter.[35]

CONADEP was given 180 days to interview, investigate, and write a report for President Alfonsín; it began its duties on December 29, 1983.

The Process

As indicated by its title, CONADEP's mandate was focused on and limited to investigating and reporting on the "disappeared." Although it was initially viewed with some distrust, human rights groups soon recognized the gravity with which CONADEP was working and began collaborating with it. It also received cooperation from the United Nations, the Organization of American States, and various countries. The Commission set up shop in the San Martín cultural complex in downtown Buenos Aires, quickly taking over the entire second floor. The Depositions Department, the Commission's largest, took depositions (stories) from people for eight hours a day from Monday to Friday.[36] Each deposition received a number, corresponding to a file of supporting material—newspaper clippings, letters, writs of habeas corpus, and anything else that would help the Commission verify and validate the details of the story told. In addition to seeing people in the central office, representatives from the Commission traveled to fifteen provinces, hearing stories in the provincial capitals. Representatives also went into the countryside to collect stories from people in remote regions. Over 1400 depositions were taken outside the central office. "CONADEP's arrival in a province was generally an important event. There were press conferences, interviews, round tables for information purposes at which the media were present."[37] Additionally, because so many Argentines were in exile as a result of the oppression, Commission representatives traveled abroad to collect stories. Their visits were well supported by the host countries and widely covered in the press. The telling and collecting of the stories, while publicly known, was done in private, victim and commission member alone, behind closed doors.

In addition to collecting stories, in its efforts to find out what happened to the disappeared, the Commission visited the secret detention centers, inquired at morgues about irregular admissions, checked prison and police records, and, in general, investigated and questioned wherever and whoever might have information that would shed light on the events following a disappearance. Each file was compiled and scrutinized: "With the primary objective of determining the fate and ultimate whereabouts of the disappeared always in mind, it [the Commission's legal department] organized, selected and linked the large number of depositions and evidence received, paying special attention to any relevant details which would point the investigation in a fruitful direction."[38] Consistent with its mandate, CONADEP sent over 1000 files to the judiciary. The report, accompanied by 50,000 pages of files, was presented in a ceremony to President Alfonsín on September 20, 1984. Alfonsín ordered publication of the report, and it became Argentina's biggest bestseller. In addition, before CONADEP disbanded, it sponsored a television program to publicize the report and give details of its findings. Despite ongoing resistance and controversy, CONADEP was considered successful: "CONADEP's efforts helped account for those who had disappeared, collected invaluable evidence for the trials,[39] created a haven in the state apparatus for the victims and their relatives, and fostered good relationships with human rights groups."[40]

The Report

Nunca Más has six sections, introduced by a Prologue written by the Commission chair, Ernesto Sabato. Sabato's six-page Prologue and the

four-page final section, "Recommendations," are the only sections of
the report that are not characterized by the dominance of personal victim narratives, mostly in the first person; in some sections, over half the
text is comprised of stories. We must remember that the writers of the
Argentinian report were inventing the form, and the choices that they
made for their report have significantly impacted the form of truth commission reports that followed. In light of the obvious community of dissent that would receive the report, it is not surprising that some stories
were used, if only to offer eyewitness testimony of that which the Commission characterized as "hard to believe." Indeed, one of the report's
obvious purposes is to confront and silence those who deny or excuse
the acts of the "dirty war." But the sheer volume of the text given over to
stories is both surprising and telling. The beginning of Part One, which
delineates the abductions and tortures that occurred, is at least half
given over to the voices of the victims and their relatives, these victims
speaking with and above the imposing din of the master narrative.

But before turning to the report proper, it is worth examining
Sabato's Prologue, which establishes the report's master narrative with
its unflinching and sometimes contentious tone. A prologue is always an
effort to control, to tell us how to read what follows and "an attempt to
guard against certain misreadings of the text."[41] Sabato's is no exception. Although it begins with the passive voice—"Argentina was torn by
terror"[42]— it quickly establishes the military as responsible: "The armed
forces responded to the terrorists' crimes with a terrorism far worse than
the one they were combating, and after 24 March 1976 they could count
on the power and impunity of an absolute state, which they misused to
abduct, torture and kill thousands of human beings."[43]

This misconduct is set against the example of Italy, which, like Argentina, "was torn by terror from both the extreme right and the far left,"[44]
but, which, unlike Argentina, did not "abandon the principles of law."[45]
In the first two paragraphs of the Prologue, Sabato sets the tone, establishes the stakes, and signals the primary resistance to the report that
follows. What the military did has no excuse; it *unnecessarily* abducted,
tortured and killed thousands of human beings. Argentina, the country,
was not to blame, was victimized (the passive voice); certain, but not all,
of the military were the criminal actors.

Sabato's audience includes both believers and disbelievers, silenced
victims and protesting perpetrators, all of whom will comprise the new
Argentina. Nonetheless, the Prologue and the report that follows it insistently refuse to be conciliatory in the face of denials and excuses. In vivid
and accusatory language, the Prologue describes what CONADEP
encountered as it worked on the report:

   In the course of our investigations we have been insulted and threatened by the very people who committed these crimes. Far from expressing any repentance, they continue to repeat the old excuses that they were engaged in a *dirty war,* or that they were saving the country and its Western, Christian values, when in reality they were responsible for dragging these values inside the bloody walls of the dungeons of repression. They accuse us of hindering national reconciliation, of stirring up hatred and resentment, of not allowing the past to be forgotten. This is not the case. We have not acted out of any feeling of vindictiveness or vengeance. All we are asking for is truth and justice.[46] (original italics)

What the report demands from its first pages, then, is acknowledgment from the Argentinian populace and, more critically, from those responsible that these events did in fact occur. At the same time, it also strives to vindicate not only Argentina but also the military as an institution, reclaiming for the military an honorable past: "Truth and justice . . . will allow the innocent members of the armed forces to live with honour; otherwise they risk being besmirched by an unjust, all-embracing condemnation. Truth and justice will permit the armed forces as a whole to see themselves once more as the true descendants of those armies which fought so heroically despite their lack of means to bring freedom to half a continent."[47]
   The report ultimately makes clear, however, that the crimes were not aberrations, the "excesses" of a few "sadists," as the military claimed. The amount of documentation in the report establishes, according to the Prologue, that the abductions, tortures, and murders were "part of a planned campaign of terror conceived by the military high command";[48] the crimes demonstrate a pattern revealing a "diabolical technology"[49] utilized by the military to terrify and subdue the opposition. Sabato is introducing a new master narrative that is intended to replace the old master narrative, and the producers of that old narrative, largely the military establishment that controlled the country, are meant to be silenced in their protests of innocence and in their ability to wield power. In the Prologue we see a harbinger of this otherwise fine report's major flaw. Set up by the Prologue, the report tells an us/them story. It puts forth a schematic—the good guys (the people of Argentina) against the bad guys (the military)—that problematically oversimplifies the nature of the conflict and the problems that had beset Argentina for several decades.[50] It depicts a black-and-white world populated by the completely innocent and the fully guilty, an authoritarian view that the world is split into allies and enemies, a view quite like that of the oppressors, who kidnapped and tortured all those suspected of being against them.
   The Prologue introduces the story of a new Argentina that has lost its innocence, and is, as the voices in the report evidence, a country that

now knows what evil can occur within its borders. It is a story, also, of return, return to a past of heroic armies and trustworthy public officials who serve, not terrorize and destroy, the citizenry. And, as repeated passages in the report reveal, the report encompasses a detailed story that is offered as evidence of the crimes of those who will continue to refuse, despite the demand in the Prologue, to take responsibility for the wrongdoing.

As we turn to Part One of the report, "The Repression," it becomes clear that the structure itself buttresses the major point of this master narrative: events that were experienced as random did not "just happen." They were set in motion and enacted by certain individuals who are responsible for what happened to Argentina and its citizens. In this lengthy section of the report (265 pages), subtitles and numbering (tabulation) are repeatedly used to group like horrors together. For the writers of the report, the ordering is essential because it implies agency and purpose. Abductions and tortures are revealed as part of a master plan devised by specific people, in this case the corrupt military:

> Month after month of listening to accusations, testimonies and confessions, of examining documents, inspecting places, and doing all in our power to throw light on these terrifying occurrences, has given us the right to assert that a system of repression was deliberately planned to produce the events and situations which are detailed in this report. . . . It is the sheer number of similar and interrelated cases which makes us absolutely convinced that a concerted plan of repression existed and was carried out.[51]

The organization of the report, structured around kinds of harms, thereby produces a "plot," which is characterized by temporality and causality.[52] The nearly 9000 disappearances (the "drama of disappearance"[53] as the Commission terms the phenomenon) that the Commission uncovered were not chaotic, random events, but crimes structured into component parts: "The typical sequence was: *abduction—disappearance—torture*" (italics original).[54] Perhaps most importantly, the imposition of a plot gives this story a beginning, an end, and meaning.[55] Although what occurred was a "concerted plan," it was a temporary one, an aberration that is not Argentina. The "true" Argentina, to which the report aspires the return, appears, like the ghost of Hamlet's father, behind the report itself.

Thus the new master narrative is twofold: a story that explicitly blames the members of the military for the crimes and a narrative of return to a mythic prelapsarian Argentina, a story still completely controlled by those in authority. Although the narrative that Sabato introduces in the Prologue is a far better one than that which it supplants, the report threatens to become, nonetheless, an authoritarian narrative in which the people are silenced in the presence of power. Worse, the victims' personal stories may well be put in service to the new master narrative.

The stories are clearly requisite to the argument of the master narrative: the protesting military is responsible for inconceivable events. Indeed the very first words of Part One—"Many of the events described in this report will be hard to believe"[56]—echoes the tone of the Prologue, that the report is offered to a populace that is in part protesting, disbelieving, and lacking in remorse: "those who insulted the history of our country . . . have yet to show by word or deed that they feel any remorse for what they have done."[57] A brief, half-page Authors' Note that precedes Part One (and follows the Prologue) explains that the stories ("cases") were selected to substantiate the arguments that the report makes, arguments that "were formed on the basis . . . of the evidence given by first-hand witnesses of the events described."[58] The stories, then, are supposed to frame the report itself. They first provide information for the report, and they then are used to support the claims that the report contains. And, although the Authors' Note allows for "occasional errors" in the stories, they are obviously given great weight as the buttresses that hold up the structure; they prove the accusations of responsibility for wrongdoing that the report puts forth.

In reading just this far, it becomes obvious that there is an "other" out there ready to repeat denials, not an imagined or expected other, but one that has already staked out its position of innocence. The accumulation of the stories allows the Commission credibly to make claims and attribute blame: "The evidence has now [in the report] reached proportions unimaginable a few years ago, when a few isolated instances created the illusion that such things could not be representative of a general practice. But now the evidence is with us."[59] The report also contains multiple verifications of the personal narratives. The long sections of Part One called "Secret Detention Centres" and "Description of Secret Detention Centres" (158 pages) begin provocatively with the military's protestations of innocence; "I categorically deny that there exist in Argentina any concentration camps or prisoners being held in military establishments. . . ."[60]; "There are no political prisoners in Argentina";[61] "La Perla, did it exist? Yes. It was a meeting place for prisoners, not a secret prison."[62] To refute these denials (the old master narrative), victims' stories of being taken to secret detention centres and hand-drawn detailed maps of the centres follow immediately. Importantly, the Commission, and the argument of the report, does not depend solely on victims' memories. The Commission members visited some sites and compared what they found with the former prisoners' descriptions: "At the end of the Commission's inspection, once our architect produced his plans, we could see that they concurred exactly with various rough sketches already in the Commission's possession, drawn by the witnesses themselves out of their most searing memories."[63] The report thus painstakingly builds its case, story after story, memory after memory. The personal stories of violence and pain threaten to become reduced to "evidence" that substantiates the new master narrative.

But that is not what entirely happens. After the report's contentious beginning, the voices of the victims take over just three pages into Part One, and the new master narrative is both undermined and enhanced by the choice to devote so much of the text to the victims. As the narrative of the report unwinds, the stories are indeed both explanatory and exemplary but they are also disruptive. The experience of reading the report is of power shared, of the controlling voice being willing to stop, listen, and give way. Despite the fact that the stories are intended to be in service to the new master narrative, they are in some ways aligned against it, interrupting, insisting that the master narrative not be controlled by those newly in power (Alfonsín's Commission), but that it give way to the voices of the powerless. While the first-person accounts are doubtless edited to some extent, names, personalities, irrelevancies are allowed to remain: "My other daughter, Graciela Mabel, arrived home at 11 p.m. from a friend's house where she had been studying for an exam she was due to take in the science faculty the following day."[64] These are not merely stories of atrocities committed; they are stories about *people*, with lives, jobs, friends, exams to take, ordinary people whose lives were interrupted or ended.

While the narrative of the report proposes a new order, authoritarian as all orders inevitably are, the dominance of the stories in the first person undercuts that order with a cacophony of individual voices. No amount of master narrative ordering—thirty pages given over to "Torture," for example—can contain this paragraph taken from a torture victim's personal narrative:

> There was a constant struggle in my mind. On the one hand: "I must remain lucid and get my ideas straight again": on the other: "Let them finish me off once and for all." I had the sensation of sliding toward nothingness down a huge slippery tube where I could get no grip. I felt that just one clear thought would be something solid for me to hold on to and prevent my fall into the void. My memory of that time is at once so concrete and so personal and private that the image I have of it is of an intestine existing both inside and outside my own body.[65]

The report does not need this paragraph to make its point; it offers no useful evidentiary details. Yet the report allows it to stand even though writers and readers alike cannot find a place for it, cannot categorize it, and definitely cannot dismiss it. Thus there is a constant tension between the stories themselves, which are stories of disorder and chaos, of a world in which nothing was predictable, of "voids" and phantasmagoric sensations and images, and the report, which explicitly puts the stories in an order—stories of abduction, of torture, of certain kinds of victims (children, pregnant women, clergy, etc.).

This first significant and widely publicized truth report, then, established an iconoclastic template. Although the stories serve the new master narrative, which is the story of the repression and those responsible for it, they are allowed to escape the chains of that servitude and tell their own story as well. Like Dostoevsky's novels, as they are viewed by Bakhtin, the report speaks with many diverse and uncensored voices, is polyphonic, and, in so doing, opposes all that threatens to be authoritarian. The community imagined by the report, the "new" Argentina, is one of shared authority, one in which voices are not punished, censored, or merely used to achieve centrally selected ends. In many ways, it is no surprise that *Nunca Más* became a best-seller, not just because it gave a version of the truth of what happened from 1976 to 1982 and went to great pains to substantiate its version as true. Intentionally or not, it told the citizens of Argentina that they would never again be silenced or invisible; by its very structure, it told them that they *mattered.*

The report thus reveals a creative tension between what appears to be the design of its writers—to focus on the perpetrators and to attribute blame—and the form of the report itself, which gives so much space and freedom to the victims. Justice is more importantly served when victims remain at the center of the process, when something important is returned to them, in this case the ability to use language for themselves and to shape for themselves the chaos of their experiences of violence into their own coherent stories. The Argentinian report teaches us that report writers need to be wary of the impulse to focus on accusations, that pointing the finger of blame at specific perpetrators might serve short-term political ends and might be a justifiable agenda of those newly in power, but it can problematically appropriate stories of pain and in so doing inadvertently perpetuate oppression. The Argentinian report avoids being fatally flawed by its political agenda because the single authoritative voice of the report is undercut by the inclusion of many, many individual stories, a polyphony of voices in search of an elusive truth.

I want to turn now to a discussion of two other Latin American truth reports that followed *Nunca Más*, the Chilean and Salvadoran reports, because they offer useful contrasts to the Argentinian report. While both of these reports, in part, are efforts, like *Nunca Más*, to attribute blame, their end results are quite different for reasons that can tell us much about the efficacy of truth reports in general.

Chile

Background

In 1973, during a period of political, social, and economic upheaval in Chile, President Salvador Allende's government was overthrown by a military junta led by Augusto Pinochet, the commander in chief of the Chilean army.[66] Under Pinochet's rule, political dissent was handled by police brutality, exile, extrajudicial executions, kidnapping, and torture. The Chilean people were silenced and terrified. In 1980 the military government approved a new constitution which allowed Pinochet to remain as president for eight more years, from 1981 to 1989, when a new election would occur. Since the regime completely controlled the country, mainly through violence and threats of violence, it was fully expected that Pinochet would be reelected to another eight-year term. But, surprisingly, in October 1988 the military government was voted out of power, and Patricio Aylwin was elected president.

During the presidential campaign, the issue of how to handle human rights violations that had occurred during the Pinochet regime was key; nonetheless, the new government faced significant obstacles. The Pinochet government had passed an amnesty law in 1978 that blocked the prosecution of any crimes against persons that had been committed by the government between 1973 and 1978. The Chilean courts had been notoriously lax during the regime. And Pinochet, who remained as commander in chief of the army, announced that "if even one of his men were touched, the rule of law would end."[67] As the Aylwin government did not control the senate, amending the amnesty law would have been impossible.

Thus, in an effort to discover some truth and to achieve some measure of closure, the Chilean National Commission on Truth and Reconciliation was created by presidential decree in April 1990.[68] The new government under President Patricio Aylwin had been influenced by transition experiences in Argentina and Uruguay, in which trials had been attempted and had largely failed. Given the politically restricted circumstances in Chile and the experiences of other transitional democracies, the government believed that its obligations could be met through an official disclosure of the truth. The Commission came into being on August 24, 1990, comprised of eight people from across the political spectrum and led by Raul Rettig, a lawyer. "Its mandate was four-fold. First the Commission was to describe how the repressive system operated and what role the press, the Church and the judiciary had taken on in reaction to it. Second, the Commission was to account for every person who had been killed or had disappeared. Third, it was to submit a proposition for measures of reparation. Finally, it was asked to present measures of prevention."[69] Additionally, its mandate was limited to investigating and disclosing details of events that ended in death or the presumption of death.

The Process

Much of what occurred in Chile during the seventeen years of the military regime was already known. The United Nations had issued reports about the human rights violations occurring during the dictatorship, Amnesty International's annual report had detailed many violations, the Vicaria de la Solidaridad had documented thousands of cases and had compiled complete files, and best-selling popular books had been published and sold, both legally and illegally.[70]

The Commission and its staff of sixty drew from all these sources and also conducted interviews and investigations of its own during its nine months of operation.[71] It "examined more than 4,000 individual complaints nationwide, hearing every family and countless witnesses."[72] Like the Argentinian Commission, the Chilean Commission sought out those living abroad, receiving affidavits through its foreign embassies.

An individual meeting lasted for about an hour, and, ideally, a lawyer, a law student assistant, and a social worker were present. Those testifying were encouraged to tell not only *what* had happened, but also to tell how they felt—"the impact of these events on the family so that this aspect of the truth could be made known."[73] One of the commissioners, José Zalaquett, has written eloquently about his experience:

I traveled through Chile. I heard hundreds of cases. The contact with so many families of victims convinced me of the paramount importance and cathartic power of seeking to establish the truth. It was a very personal experience to ask what happened to the victims' families, and not just what happened to the victims. The families had refused to allow the previous government authorities to see them cry as they searched for their loved ones. But now they were being received with respect and offered a seat and a cup of coffee. The Chilean flag was on the desk as befits an official commission. They often broke down, because now they could allow themselves that measure of relief.[74]

The Commission self-consciously operated under the aegis of the state; the Chilean flag hung at the entrance to the Commission's building and stood on each desk where a victim testified.[75] At the same time, the formality and authority of the state was set aside in favor of the dignity of those testifying. They, not the state officials, were the ones accorded respect. In the regional capitals, the families met together in small groups "so that they could express what they had suffered"[76] with others who had also suffered. Those whose names were mentioned as committing the crimes were invited to give their versions of events; most chose not to testify.

A single copy of the report was delivered to President Aylwin on February 9, 1991, and on March 4, he made the report public in a television address during which, as head of state, he apologized for the crimes committed by state agents and asked the military to acknowledge its role in the oppression and the crimes. The report was fully published in the newspaper the next day. Many reprints were sold, and thereafter a three-volume book that became a best-seller was available in bookstores.[77] All the political parties acknowledged that the report contained the truth, but the military rejected it.[78] In February 1992, the government created the National Corporation for Reparation and Reconciliation, as the report recommended. The corporation implemented reparations and investigated cases unresolved by the Commission, in particular, searching for clandestine graves of the disappeared. When the Aylwin administration ended, "'closure' was officially announced"; the legacies of the past had been handled and the transition to democratic rule was complete.[79]

The Report

The two-volume, 893-page Chilean report is twice the length of *Nunca Más* and operates on several levels of storytelling: it tells the story of itself, how the Commission came into being, how it saw its role, and how it operated; it sets up a master story, written by the Commission, about the political situation in Chile before and during the regime, including the actions and reactions of social and political sectors of society such as the press and the judiciary; it provides individual stories, detailed accounts in the third person, of over two thousand cases in which victims died or disappeared; and it concludes with an ongoing story—the voices of survivors, relatives of the victims, who relate in their own words what they suffered and continue to suffer. This final section—just twenty-two pages long—is the only part of the report in which anyone speaks in the first person, and these are sentence-long excerpts grouped generically, for example, "Grief Disturbed" and "Looking for the Disappeared." The Commission's limited mandate, the investigation of cases that resulted in death or the presumption of death, gave it no living victims. The victims' stories necessarily are told by the writers of the report and become subsumed into the master narrative, except for this brief section when we hear the voices of their relatives.

Because the stories about the victims are told in the third person, the impact of reading the Chilean report differs significantly from that of its closest counterpart in method and ambition, the Argentinian report,

Nunca Más. The tone throughout is less passionate and more legalistic than in *Nunca Más.* From its first paragraph, which calls for reconciliation from a "profound division between Chileans, and a violation of human rights that affected many people and disrupted our traditional observance of the norms of the rule of law,"[80] it is apparent that this narrative is about a return to the rule of law, under which these divisions and violations cannot occur. The renewed nation that the report envisions, its intended audience, is not the cacophonous pluralism of the Argentinian report, but a nation of laws. Its tone is more formal, abstract, and legalistic. For example, the Introduction, unsigned, is written in the first person plural—"We"—representing the unified voice of the commissioners. This point of view is maintained throughout the report; the authoritative voice of the Commission speaks repeatedly in sentences that begin, "The Commission has come to the conviction."[81] The Introduction then concludes with the "utter conviction that full democracy and the rule of law are the only dikes that can contain violence, render it useless, and banish it forever."[82] As evidence of this conviction, wedged between the Introduction and the first chapter, is Supreme Decree No. 355, the decree that established the Commission.

The first two parts, comprising 126 pages, relate the Commission's methodology and its version of the political context after and during which the human rights violations occurred. This section is overtly establishing a new legal order, operating self-consciously under the new laws that brought it, the Commission, into being and the laws of the international community from which it derives its definitions of human rights violations. Maintaining that emphasis upon the new law, the report then immediately turns to a discussion of past failures and abuses of the law, found in the war tribunals and in the courts. Of the war tribunals, it states:

> Nevertheless, in violation of fundamental legal norms and essential ethical principles, the war tribunals and other military tribunals, acting during the "state or time of war" in accordance with this new legislation, applied the new sanctions to events that had taken place prior to their entering into effect. They were thereby explicitly contravening the provisions of Article 11 of the 1925 Constitution, which was then in effect, and Article 18 of the Criminal Code, which enshrines the universally accepted principle that criminal law is not retroactive.
>
> In submitting its report, the Commission expresses its condemnation of these violations of the law.[83]

Of the courts, it concludes:

> Nevertheless, what it has observed of these situations as a whole during the period that began on September 11, 1973, has led the Commission to the convic-

tion that the judiciary's inability to halt the grave human rights violations in Chile was partly due to serious shortcomings in the legal system as well as to the weakness and lack of vigor on the part of many judges in fully carrying out their obligation to assure that the essential rights of persons are truly respected.[84]

These passages, and the many others like them, are not only condemnations; they are also prescriptions that describe how the courts and judges should behave in the country the report is constituting: they should strictly observe principles of law and they are obliged to protect essential rights. The battle waged in the discourse of the Chilean report is between a good legal system, the one from which the report derives its authority, and a bad one, Pinochet's.

The discussion of the individual cases in the Chilean report also takes a form quite different from that in *Nunca Más*. After an overview section, the report states that "We will now present in chronological order all the cases throughout this region from September 11, 1973 to the end of that year in which the Commission concluded that human rights were gravely violated and that the result was the death or disappearance of the victim."[85] The report lists names (in bold print), ages, political affiliations, and brief (usually) synopses of what the Commission discovered about what happened to the victim and who was responsible. A few deaths are agentless and are described as being the result of "political violence"; others are described as a result of "human rights violations at the hands of government agents." The human rights violations are arranged by chronology (this volume discussing cases from September through December 1973), by agents, and by kind of harm. The decision to group as to time makes clear that many harms occurred in the first few months of the new regime; grouping as to agent lays bare the dominance of state agents in perpetrating the violations. The section focused on government agents is 323 pages long; the section on "Human Rights Violations Committed by Private Citizens for Political Reasons" is eight pages.

Volume 2 repeats the structure and methodology established in Volume 1, dividing the remaining mandate years into two periods: 1974 through August 1977 (the years in which the DINA, the National Intelligence Directorate created in 1974, was active) and August 1977 through March 1990. Again, the vast majority of cases were perpetrated by government agents, in particular the DINA, which "engaged in repression against those whom it perceived as political enemies."[86] Again, the law is invoked as the stabilizing power whose misuse resulted in human rights violations: "Although it cannot be said that the DINA was created expressly for unlawful repression, in practice it was an unlawful organization."[87] To make its illegal activities apparent, the report devotes over thirty pages to a discussion of the organization and operation of the DINA. The section concludes by assigning responsibility for the DINA's work: "we must not forget . . . that this whole series of grave violations is not the work of an abstract entity. Like any other institution, the DINA was conceived and set in motion by human beings who had to plan it."[88] The next 120 pages chronicle the cases, with the names of the victims appearing in bold print. Chapter 2 concludes with a discussion of the reactions of major sectors of society (churches, media, political parties, etc.). Chapter 3 repeats this pattern for the post-DINA years, assigning the blame to the CNI (National Center for Information), with another 110 pages given over to victim stories.

In Chapter 4 of Volume 2, on page 777 of the report, the voices of the relatives of the victims are heard. The report explains the Commission's decision to include these stories that are technically outside of its mandate:

> The Commission believes the truth would remain incomplete if the relatives of these victims were not allowed to testify on what they have suffered as a result of these grave human rights violations. . . . As a rule family members felt free to express their emotions and feelings, and they reclaimed the good name and dignity of their relatives by telling of their life and personal qualities.[89]

The Commission states that it decided to allow these personal accounts to remain in the first person and that it could not publish them all and thus selected a few that "present as faithfully as possible the overall message we heard in thousands of interviews."[90] The Commission explains that it has refrained from interpreting, although it does organize the selected testimony into kinds of harms and introduces them with short overview paragraphs that generalize about the pain. For example, under "Grief Disturbed," which deals with situations in which bodies were never found, the Commission writes:

> Family members were denied not only the possibility of finding out why their loved ones had been killed, but even of seeing their bodies, giving their remains a decent burial, and expressing and sharing their grief. Since they were prevented from participating in any funeral rites, since this death was associated with horror and then they had to survive for years in fear, loneliness, and poverty, these families could not let themselves feel the pain of death.[91]

The report also has organized the testimony so that it moves from despair to hope, from "I cannot find any meaning to give this unjust death"[92] to "I don't want revenge. I only want peace."[93]

The controlling voice of the master narrative is everywhere apparent, disallowing the polyphony of *Nunca Más*. The story it strives to tell about the law is one critical to Chilean political life, in that Pinochet continued, even after Alfonsín's election, to use the law to perpetuate his power. For example, he had himself declared "senator for life" to give himself an additional layer of immunity from possible prosecution. It is not surprising then that the writers of the report were concerned with giving the message that Chilean law must be based in higher principles of human rights law and that people—judges, as well as citizens—must have the tools to discern between good laws and bad ones. Much of the text is devoted to this argument.

This report poses a very real danger that the political aspirations of the report writers, however noble, will submerge the stories of the victims. Yet on balance, although the beginning of the report threatens to result in a document bogged down in legalistic detail and although the victims' stories are (necessarily) told by the Commission, the report nonetheless succeeds largely because of the attention to detail, sometimes seemingly trivial, in the accounts told about the disappeared and murdered. Although they are told in the third person, the stories dominate the report, filling over half its pages, and they are not devoid of personal detail or passion. The deaths are often attributed (most often to government agents), but the focus remains on the stories of the victims, and it is clear that the Commission saw its most critical task to be establishing what happened to those who died and disappeared and clearing up mysteries and misinformation.[94] This impulse toward allowing the stories finally to dominate over the story of the law, of the new good order supplanting the old order, gives the Chilean report its force. Its purpose is to tell the truth to the people. Although it is the report itself that tells the truth and not the people, as in *Nunca Más*, the report nonetheless holds forth a promise of a future, established by a good legal system, in which the people will be told the truth.

The final Latin American report discussed here, the Salvadoran report, tells a far different story than its predecessors, largely for political reasons. Its successes and failures demonstrate the critical nature of the political climate in which a report is written.

El Salvador

Background

Unlike the Chilean and Argentinian Commissions, which were established by presidential decrees following transitions to democratically elected governments, the Salvadoran Commission came into existence as the result of a negotiated peace between the existing government and the insurgent Frente Farabundo Marti para la Liberación Nacional (FMLN), and it operated under the sponsorship and supervision of the

United Nations.[95] The Salvadoran government and the FMLN had begun peace negotiations under UN auspices in April 1990; each side accused the other of crimes and called for investigations and prosecutions. Consequently, the UN proposed dealing with issues of accountability and impunity by means of a truth commission. After much debate, it was decided that a panel of foreigners would best serve the needs of El Salvador.[96] A formal agreement was signed in Mexico City on April 27, 1991, as part of an interim peace accord.[97] On December 10, 1991, UN Secretary General Boutros Boutros-Ghali named the three commissioners: Belisario Betancur, former president of Colombia; Reinaldo Figueredo, former foreign minister of Venezuela; and Thomas Buergenthal, an American professor of law and former president of the Inter-American Court for Human Rights of the Organization of American States. The Commission was charged with writing a report and making recommendations "destined to prevent the repetition"[98] of crimes and to foster "national reconciliation." [99] Furthermore, the mandate that grew out of the peace accord required the Commission, and, seemingly, the judicial system, to end the impunity that had attached to officers in the armed forces; according to the mandate, "acts of this nature [serious acts of violence], regardless of the sector to which their perpetrators belong, must be the object of exemplary action by the law courts so that the punishment prescribed by law is meted out to those found responsible."[100]

The Process

The Commission on the Truth worked with a $2.5 million budget, all of which came from international sources. It had a six-month time period in which to complete its work and was staffed entirely by non-Salvadorans. It began its work on July 13, 1992, by inviting all Salvadorans who knew about acts of violence to make them known to the Commission, guaranteeing anyone who came forward both discretion and confidentiality. During a preliminary phase, the Commission advertised in newspapers and on television and radio about its "open door" policy in an effort to encourage people to tell their stories. At first, in spite of a promise of confidentiality,[101] very few people came forward, largely for fear of reprisals in the "climate of terror" that persisted in El Salvador even after the peace agreement.[102] The Commission summoned anyone who might have been involved to testify, often in secret locations or outside of El Salvador, in an effort to protect witnesses. To increase participation, the Commission opened offices in various parts of the country. Commission members and staff talked to government and military officials, as well as representatives from the FMLN, churches, the media, and labor and rural community organizations. They also examined court records and military personnel files that covered the time period under scrutiny, 1980–91. In the words of one commissioner, "we wanted to hear what people had to say, what their hopes and aspirations were, and what they expected from the Commission."[103] The Commission took direct testimony from over 2000 Salvadorans, which involved 7,312 victims. This preliminary work enabled the Commission to select, as mandated, the "most serious" cases about which the public should know the truth, cases that were "paradigmatic of a practice of violence that terrorized the country."[104] The Commission was viewed distrustfully until after the elections in the United States in November 1992 and after another body, the Ad Hoc Commission (a government- approved panel composed of Salvadorans), published a report implicating officers in the military.[105]

The next stage of the process involved a thorough investigation of the selected cases, interviewing victims and alleged perpetrators and sifting through documents. Despite widespread intimidation and the conceal-ment and destruction of documents, the Commission was able to gather sufficient evidence in specific cases, which was recorded in detail, including the names of the guilty parties, in the face of ongoing pressure not to name names. All information not subject to confidentiality was sent to the courts.

The Report

The slim Salvadoran report is divided into six major sections: Introduc-tion, Mandate, Chronology of the Violence, Cases and Patterns of Vio-lence, Recommendations, and Epilogue; and two appendixlike sections: Instruments Establishing the Commission's Mandate, and Persons Work-ing on the Commission on the Truth. The Introduction and Epilogue serve as frames around the collected narratives, which are used as illus-trations of the kinds and patterns of violence that occurred in El Salva-dor from 1980 until 1991, when the peace accords were signed. Beginning with the epigraph—a piece from a Mayan poem, "all these things happened among us"—the report makes a valiant attempt to speak in the voice of all the people of El Salvador, despite the inescap-able reality that it could only be written by outsiders.

Once again I want to begin by focusing on the eight-page Introduc-tion to the report, as it instructs us how we should read what follows. The Introduction begins (in a section puzzlingly called "Institutions and Names") by circumscribing the time of violence, making it a kind of black hole of "madness" that afflicted the country. After this time— from 1980 to 1991—the warring parties signed a peace agreement that "brought back the light and the chance to re-emerge from madness to hope."[106] The language also depersonalizes violence, describing it as a force of nature, like a tornado, tidal wave, or uncontrolled fire:

Violence was a fire which swept over the fields of El Salvador; it burst into villages, cut off roads and destroyed highways and bridges, energy sources and transmission lines; it reached the cities and entered families, sacred areas and educational centres; it struck at justice and filled the public administration with victims; it singled out as an enemy anyone who was not on the list of friends. . . . [I]n its blind cruelty violence leaves everyone equally defenceless.[107]

This "violence" is characterized as some sort of natural force that has intruded on the people and places of El Salvador. The unsigned Introduction is characterized throughout by eloquent, metaphoric, passionate use of language that begins by accusing carefully and evenhandedly: "repeated human rights violations had been committed by members of the armed forces; these same rights had also been violated by members of the guerilla forces."[108] Its language unifies the people of El Salvador: "When there came pause for thought, Salvadorans put their hands to their hearts and felt them pound with joy"[109] and let out a "unanimous outcry"[110] for an end to the conflict. It describes El Salvador as a "country . . . although small . . . made great by the creativity of its people."[111] In a few dozen lines, the initial language of the report erases the divisions of the prior decade, distances and depersonalizes the acts of violence that occurred in those years, and creates a polarity: the violence against the unified, creative people of El Salvador.

At the same time, the Introduction, grappling with the phenomenon of violence, does not flinch from laying most of the blame for it on individuals in the armed services. Facing up to great pressure that it implies the Commission has endured, the report specifically disallows institutional blame—"The Commission on the Truth did not fall into that temptation"—[112]and insists that individuals, the "criminals," are the ones responsible for acts of violence, despite their institutional affiliation. Thus the Introduction deftly serves both as an aspirational prologue to the unified people of El Salvador for all that is to follow in the report and, in direct contradiction to its impersonal and unifying tone, prepares the reader for the naming of specific names of wrongdoers. It reflects, to be sure, a certain tension between the united community that is its imagined audience and the resistance to its work that it anticipates.

The final lines of the Introduction return to the tone of the initial lines and introduce a language of rebirth and resurrection: El Salvador will "lift itself out of the ruins," "a new people is rising from the ashes," the dead are "watching . . . from the great beyond."[113] The problem with the voice in this impassioned Introduction, however, is that it speaks *to* the Salvadoran community rather than out of it. It is, finally, the voice of the international community, not of El Salvador.

The second section, "The Mandate," in an admirable and necessary show of transparency, lays out the legal basis for the Commission's existence and its interpretation of its mandate and the international bodies of law on which it relied. It also delineates its methodology. Truth commissions in general operate in a nebulous legal area; they are not judicial bodies with well defined standards and due process requirements. At the same time, their work, although not resulting in legal penalties, can cause significant consequences, especially if the wrongdoers are named, as they are in this report. Without transparency, commissions can easily be viewed as quasi star chambers, bending rules of law to get information that condemns people to calumny and ostracism. This truth commission, in particular, comprised of non-Salvadorans, had to tell its own story—how it came into existence and how it did its work—openly and clearly or it could have been easily dismissed as the work of meddlesome outsiders. This seven-page section, then, attempts to provide the writers of this master narrative for El Salvador with both authority and credibility.

Part III, "Chronology of Violence," strives to enclose the chaotic violence in a grid or pattern, using time as its primary organizing device. It explains that "the Commission, for methodological reasons, divided the years 1980–1991 [covered by the mandate] into four periods . . . corresponding to political changes in the country."[114] After a graph showing the frequency of reports in the Salvadoran press concerning acts of violence over the eleven-year time span, the report does a year-by-year history, focusing on the political changes that occurred in that year and the most notorious acts of violence that seemed to accompany, or even result from, these political changes. Each of the four periods receives a title and an introductory section giving the main characteristics of the period. The narrative of each year concludes with an identical terse, single-sentence paragraph giving the numbers of victims that were made known to the Commission; for example: "The Commission on the Truth received direct complaints concerning 2,597 victims of serious acts of violence occurring in 1980."[115] The wording for each year (except for 1991, which varies slightly in that it covers only the first six months of the year, signaling an end to the violence) is exactly the same, save for the numbers, which at first diminish dramatically and then hold steady: 2,597; 1,633; 1,145; 513; 290; 141; 155; 136; 138; 292; 107; 28. This repetition serves as a kind of litany, making clear the ongoing nature of the violence and also laying bare which periods, accompanied by what political changes in power, were the worst.

Over half (129 pages) the report, which is only 252 pages (including footnotes), is given to the fourth section, "Cases and Patterns of Violence," which uses narratives as illustrations. As the title indicates, it is organized around patterns or kinds of violence, according to the identity of the perpetrators. The choice to organize around perpetrators carries enormous significance and reflects the thrust of this master narrative that was hinted at in the preceding sections. The cases of violence could be organized in many ways: according to geography or kind of victim or kind of harm, for example. The focus on perpetrators makes clear that this narrative has a point to make that is not neutral and detached. Although both agents of the state and adherents of the FMLN are named as perpetrators, this organization throws a spotlight on the dominance of agents of the state in the commission of harms against the people of El Salvador. The introductory overview states that "Those giving testimony attributed almost 85 percent of cases to agents of the State, paramilitary groups allied to them, and the death squads. . . . The complaints registered accused FLMN in approximately 5 percent of cases."[116] The evenhanded tone of the beginning of the Introduction has completely given way. There is a definite story being told here, and it is a story that damns the state, and particularly the armed forces. Although both state agents and the FMLN are specifically named as perpetrators and have parts of this section devoted to their activities, this organization highlights the differences in numbers, strategies, and purposes.[117]

Nearly all the stories told in the section were already well known, even outside of El Salvador: the murders of the Jesuit priests, the massacres at the San Francisco Guajoyo cooperative, the murders of the four American churchwomen, and the murders of four Dutch journalists.[118] These and other stories are told in the third person, beginning with a summary that includes the Commission's findings, followed by a detailed description of the facts—the truth of what happened—and a final section entitled "Findings" that essentially repeats the findings in the summary. The language is dispassionate and official; the victims are named and the murders described, but in many ways the horror and pain are obliterated. The story being selected to be told here concerns the perpetrators, not the victims; the goal is to assign blame. In pointed sentences—subject, active verb, direct object—the findings name names and acts: "Deputy Sergeant Tomas Zarpete Castillo shot Julia Elva Ramos . . . and her 16-year old daughter. . . . Private José Alberto Sierra Ascencio shot them again. . . ."[119] Additionally, this pointed structure is not limited to the crimes themselves but is extended to assign blame to those who ordered the crimes or knew about them: "Colonel Oscar Alberto Leon Linares, Commander of the Atlacatl Battalion, knew of the murder and concealed incriminating evidence"; "Rodolfo Antonio Parker Soto, a lawyer and member of the Special Honour Commission, altered statements in order to conceal the responsibility of senior officers for the murder."[120] The report's focus is riveted on the perpetrators, and the victims' stories become blurred and used as evidence in assigning blame.

After the report was made public, President Cristiani told the nation that "the Truth Commission report does not respond to the wishes of the majority of Salvadorans who seek to forgive and forget everything having to do with that sorrowful past," and he reiterated his appeal for a general amnesty.[121] The military responded with a long televised statement by the defense minister calling the Commission's actions illegal and beyond its mandate. Within five days, the legislature passed a general amnesty for anyone charged with political and related crimes, whether named in the report or not. Despite this legal protection, all the military officers named in the report retired shortly after it was made public.

In political terms, the report has been described as both a stunning success and a major disappointment. The report was generally well received by human rights activists and by the people of El Salvador, who finally had an official rendering of what had occurred in their country.[122] In terms of narrative theory, however, the potential balancing that might have occurred was probably not possible from the outset and was certainly scuttled for good with Cristiani's hostile public reaction to the report. The wonderfully eloquent report began by imagining a unified community that did not and could not exist. The form of the report mirrored and solidified the adversarial nature of Salvadoran political life. The situation in El Salvador remained "us," the people, opposed to "them," the government and the military. Although the people of El Salvador received, from outsiders, detailed accounts of what happened, those accounts were in no way acknowledged by the state. In a way, it is heartbreaking and so clearly reveals that language, however eloquent, alone cannot provide justice. The words must be received, officially acknowledged, and incorporated into the history of the renewed state, or, despite lofty and well-intentioned goals, no renewal occurs.[123]

What we saw in the evolution from revenge to retribution was that the people, for whom revenge taking was once a sacred duty, gave over that duty to the state. People trust their governments to act in their behalf when they are injured. Citizens' trust in the state depends, in large part, on the state's efficacy in pursuing justice for them. In El Salvador, the government not only did not act, it defiantly refuted the actions of those who did. Although people were able to tell their stories and although perpetrators were named, adequate balancing did not, could not, occur.

In each of these countries, the process by which the report was written provided an opportunity for people to regain their voices and take back the ability to use language. In each report the inexplicable chaos of the years of violence and oppression was shaped into a story, different stories (master narratives) to be sure, with the crucial assistance of the victims themselves. The stories give the chaos a beginning, an end, and a significance. And in each case the people learned the truth, sometimes a truth they already knew, but, nonetheless, the truth that was rumored or part of folklore took on official significance.

Each report has its strengths and each its weaknesses. Report writers will always have their own agendas. As long as reports are written by humans, they will inevitably reflect points of view. What the analysis of these three reports has shown so far is that the inclusion of victims' stories has the valuable potential to undercut a totalizing point of view, to disallow the "primacy of a particular moral perspective," even if the stories are meant to serve the master narrative.[124] Furthermore, the truth reports that are the most effective keep the focus on the victims, rather than the perpetrators.

The final truth report I will analyze is the most famous of all, the South African report. But, in actuality, the report itself is not so widely read or known. The South African report is famous because of the hearings that preceded it—highly publicized hearings that drew the world's attention. The innovative nature of the hearings added another dimension to the storytelling that engages a truth commission; the process itself is another kind of "story," and one that I will argue is a rare example of the carnivalesque in modern political life. Additionally, a primary focus of the South African Commission was on forgiveness. After a seemingly universal legacy of violence repaying violence being all we humans knew about balancing, some South Africans suggested something shockingly new: forgiveness.

Chapter Six
Telling Stories in a Search for More Than Justice: The South African Truth and Reconciliation Commission

> So hope for a great sea-change
> On the far side of revenge.
> Believe that a farther shore
> Is reached from here.
> Believe in miracles
> And cures and healing wells.
> —Seamus Heaney,
> "The Cure at Troy"

From the outset, the South African Truth and Reconciliation Commission faced a formidable task. Unlike the Latin American commissions, which were rebuilding moral and political communities that had at least in theory preexisted the periods of oppression, the South African commission was creating an entirely new and hitherto inconceivable state that had never existed on the southern cape of Africa. The postapartheid South African government was committed to building a bridge between the past and the present, a link that fully acknowledged the harms that had occurred during the reign of apartheid and the new society that embraced equality. The interim Constitution of 1993 described this link as "between the past of a deeply divided society characterized by strife, conflict, untold suffering and injustice, and a future founded on the recognition of human rights, democracy and peaceful coexistence and development opportunities for all South Africans, irrespective of colour, race, class, belief, or sex."[1] A truth commission, with a large budget and unprecedented powers, and a report were proposed as a means of achieving this link.

The unique public process by which the stories were told and acknowledged caught the world's attention. A photograph and many cartoons of a weeping Archbishop Desmond Tutu listening to a witness at the first hearing hit the international wire services. Probably sensitive to the fact that pressure from the international community had been instrumental in bringing down apartheid, the truth commission played to this audience. But its primary audience was the people of South Africa: white, black, and all the now-uncategoried hues in between who would for the first time live, vote, work, and aspire together. The hearings created monumental spectacle wed to solemn quasi-religious ritual, an entirely new kind of political event that was widely attended, watched, and read about. The report itself, though, despite many attempts to reach a broad audience, is not widely read at all.[2] In an effort to be all things to all people, it bursts from the seams, at once both problematic and brilliant, and decidedly different in form from the hearings.

Background

Apartheid, the legal system that required the separation of the races and gave societal and legal preferences to whites, was in force in South Africa from 1948, when the National Party, which represented Afrikaner political views, came into power, until 1993.[3] To ensure the continuation of white power in view of a huge black majority in the country, blacks and other people of color were denied the vote, and numerous laws were enacted that deprived nonwhites of land and opportunity. In those years, many human rights violations were committed against ordinary citizens and against and by those who joined organizations such as the African National Congress (ANC) that were determined to bring an end to apartheid. The turning point crisis occurred in March 1960 in Sharpeville, when blacks marched against the pass system, a legal device that kept blacks in rural areas and effectively banned them from good jobs. Police confronted the marchers, and many were shot. When protests erupted across the country, the government declared a state of emergency and outlawed the ANC and the Pan-Africanist Congress, another black political party. The next thirty years brought many infamous misdeeds: the jailing of Nelson Mandela, the death of Steven Biko in police custody, the killings that resulted from the march in Soweto, to name just a few that received international attention and condemnation.

In 1990, under increasing international pressure (which included economic and social boycotts of South Africa), the newly elected president, F. W. de Klerk, began the process of dismantling apartheid. He granted Mandela and other jailed ANC activists amnesty and began a dialogue with them that resulted in 1993 in an interim constitution, the product of much political and racial compromise. The discussions that led to the establishing of the interim constitution included negotiations concerning amnesties, both for the outgoing government and its agents and for the anti-apartheid activists, who had fought against the government for decades. The interim constitution provided for the first fully democratic, multiracial elections in 1994. In 1994, Nelson Mandela was elected president and the ANC took over the government.

Once the idea of a truth report was introduced, South Africans embarked on a process of discovery. Delegates traveled to eastern European countries that had undergone a political transition from totalitarianism to democracy. South Africans also hosted two preparatory conferences to which representatives from eleven countries were invited.[4] The South African Commission was thus able to benefit from the experiences of the nearly twenty other commissions that had preceded it.

In response to the commitment to build a bridge to the past, the newly elected Parliament enacted the Promotion of National Unity and Reconciliation Act, No. 34, 1995, which established the Truth and Reconciliation Commission, with the mandate to investigate the violations that occurred between 1960 (the Sharpeville massacre) and 1994. One innovative, even iconoclastic, feature of this act, which was required by the interim constitution and was the result of the difficult negotiations and political compromises between the de Klerk government and the ANC, was that amnesty would be granted for certain acts to those "persons who make full disclosure of all the relevant facts relating to acts associated with a political objective."[5]

After a public nomination process, seventeen commissioners were selected, with Archbishop Desmond Tutu as chair, and the commission was inaugurated in December 1995. It was organized around three committees: the Human Rights Violations Committee, which would collect witness statements; the Amnesty Committee, which would process amnesty applications and decide individual cases; and the Reparations and Rehabilitation Committee, which would design and put in place a reparations program. Additionally, an Investigative Unit, also mandated by the act, conducted inquiries into allegations made by both victims and perpetrators in order to lend validity to the testimony. The commission was given a large staff (300 people), a substantial budget ($18 million a year for two and one-half years), and wide powers, including the powers to search and seize property, to subpoena witnesses, and to grant individual amnesty.[6] It also differed from earlier commissions in its decision to take the testimony in public and in its ability to offer a witness protection program.

Like other truth commissions, from its inception the South African

Truth and Reconciliation Commission met with opposition from many quarters: from the Afrikaner right wing, which saw the hearings as a witch hunt; from families of victims who believed that the giving of amnesty denied them justice (and their civil right to sue); and from many who saw the very idea of amnesty as repugnant.[7]

The Process

The Human Rights Violations (HRV) Committee of the TRC first received written statements from over 21,000 victims. In April 1996, the HRV Committee embarked on a series of public hearings at various sites in South Africa that attracted national and international attention; it publicly heard and acknowledged some of the 21,000 stories of victimization and suffering. Over the next two years, South Africans faced a nearly daily exposure to testimony and discussion about the country's violent past.[8] The hearings were both televised and broadcast over the radio, and they were translated into the eleven official languages spoken by South Africans. Each Sunday evening a television program broadcast a summary of the previous week's events and offered a preview of what was to occur in the new week. Short, nearly unavoidable, "news bulletins" punctuated each day with quotable witness statements, often focused on a horrific event or a victim's ongoing trauma, or, occasionally, on a victim's public forgiveness of a perpetrator. Excerpts were printed in the daily newspapers. The public nature of the hearings and the widespread attention they received was a new phase in the evolution of truth commissions[9].

The hearings spawned many articles and entire books, thereby creating another level of storytelling: the stories that were told about the process and about the people who observed or underwent the process.[10] Among the most notable of these books is Antjie Krog's *Country of My Skull*, a curious hybrid work, often more poetry than prose, as much fiction as fact, that tells the story of her reporting of the hearings for the South African Broadcasting Company (SABC). Krog describes the first hearing, which set the ritualistic tone for all that would follow:

> Commissioner Bongani Finca starts with the well-known Xhosa hymn: *Lizalise idinga lakho.* "The forgiveness of sins makes a person whole." As the song carries, the victims file into the hall and take their seats at the front. Through ritual they are physically separated from the rest of the audience.
>
> Archbishop Tutu prays. But untypically he sounds as if he is praying from a piece of paper: "We long to put behind us the pain and division of Apartheid, together with all the violence which ravaged our communities in its name. And so we ask you to bless this Truth and Reconciliation Commission with your wisdom and guidance as a body which seeks to redress the wounds in the minds and the bodies of those who suffered."

Everyone stands with their heads bowed while the names of the deceased and disappeared who will come under the spotlight today are read out. A big white candle emblazoned with a red cross is lit. Then all the Commissioners go over to the row of victims to greet and welcome them, while the audience stays standing.[11]

Two thousand people attended this hearing, which was held in the city hall in East London, the section of the Eastern Cape that had seen some of the heaviest resistance to apartheid and hence the heaviest oppression.

Despite the formal quasi-Christian ritualistic quality that introduced the hearings, the hearings belonged to the people, who often crowded the accessible public halls in which they were held. Efforts were made to make the hearings inclusive, and, most notably, the victims who testified were invariably treated with dignity and compassion. Witnesses took "pride of place and there was to be no suggestion of their being 'in the dock' as in a court."[12] One observer wrote:

Each hearing is opened with a prayer—sometimes Christian, sometimes Muslim, sometimes Jewish—and a large, white candle representing truth is solemnly lit. The audience is then asked to rise out of respect for the victims and their families when they file in. . . . The seven commissioners in attendance then came down from their white linen-clad tables to welcome the victims—by shaking hands, embracing, kissing. Many of the victims were already sobbing, overcome by the mere fact that an official government representative was showing them respect . . . .

As each victim, often accompanied by two or three family members, went to testify, a psychotherapist sat by his or her side. Before the testimony began, one commissioner asked about the victim's family—parents, spouse, children, siblings—their names, ages, where they lived, how they were employed. This was more than a strategic ploy to put the victim at ease; rather, this ritual grounded or located the victim as a person in the fullest African sense—with a family, a community, a place.[13]

As they testified, victims were permitted to ramble, cry, and scream. Although commissioners did ask occasional clarifying questions, sometimes attempting to elicit names of perpetrators and corroborating witnesses, the witnesses were not subject to cross-examination.[14] The commissioners constantly made it apparent that they represented the state and that they, and thus the state, heard and sympathized with the victims. Archbishop Tutu, in a widely reported and photographed event, bowed his head and wept as he listened to the stories of torture and death. He told a white Afrikaner who had lost an eight-year-old son in an ANC attack, "The reason why we still hope that reconciliation will triumph is because of people like you."[15] Witnesses and their friends wept, commissioners thanked those testifying for their "rich stories"[16] and sometimes hugged the witnesses.[17] "The public sat silent and spellbound during the testimony, but was occasionally moved to angry murmuring."[18] Traditional music was played, and many witnesses testified in their mother tongues. When a victim finished testifying, one commissioner responded by summing up the story, affirming and thanking the witness. Witnesses were also asked what reparations they desired.[19]

The Commission's twin goals of forgiveness and reconciliation were highly controversial. Tutu defended them as constituting restorative rather than retributive justice and as related to the African idea of *ubuntu*, which emphasizes the interdependence of humanity. He maintained that the Commission's goals went beyond traditional notions of retributive justice that are embodied in criminal prosecutions. For my purposes, I recognize in it an overdue alternative to violence for violence. In our civic (as opposed to religious) imagination, we define justice as receiving harm for harm, whether enacted by ourselves and our families (as it was long ago) or by the state. After this centuries-old legacy, the TRC offered another alternative—forgiveness. People could take it up or not; certainly forgiving is deeply personal. But forgoing retributive violence was presented as another *choice*, rather than a failure. Importantly, though, the surrender of violence did not exist in a void; it was accompanied by the opportunity to put the harmful experience into words, to shape it into a story, and thus to receive retribution in a different sense, getting back control over the telling and shaping of one's own story. Krog relates an observation made by her friend, Professor Kondlo, "the Xhosa intellectual from Grahamstown":

It's significant that she [the witness] began to cry when she remembered how Nyameka Goniwe was crying when she arrived at the Goniwes' house. The academics say pain destroys language and this brings about an immediate reversion to a pre-linguistic state—and to witness that cry was to witness the destruction of language . . . was to realize that to remember the past of this country is to be thrown back into a time before language. And to get that memory back, to fix it in words, to capture it with the precise image, is to be present at the birth of language itself. But more practically, this particular memory at last captured in words can no longer haunt you, push you around, bewilder you, because you have taken control of it—you can move it wherever you want to. So maybe this is what the Commission is all about—finding words for that cry of Nomonde Calata.[17]

The hearings were variously described as "exemplary civic theatre, a public hearing of private griefs which are absorbed into the body politic"[21] and a "secular Eucharist" that "require[d] a faith in the *mysterium* of the event, a faith in the rite of reconciliation, a belief in the rituals of confession, rather than an expectation in the outcome of the process."[22]

For many, though, the hearings were a disappointment, perhaps because the rhetoric surrounding the Commission's formation and work promised too much. Those hoping for widespread forgiveness and reconciliation had to content themselves with inspiring but isolated instances, like the response of the parents of slain Fulbright scholar Amy Biehl toward the four young men who killed her. Not only did the Biehls openly forgive the killers and engage in acts of reconciliation like visiting their families, the young men also demonstrated clear remorse. Those who expected widespread remorse from all perpetrators, however, were faced with former President P. W. Botha's snub of the Commission, with Winnie Mandela's "things went horribly wrong"[23] nonresponse to the accusations against her, with stony, even arrogant countenances on former police and defense force operatives.[24] Whether one approves or disapproves of the Commission and the hearings, one can find an exemplary anecdote: forgiveness here, lack of forgiveness there; remorse here, lack of remorse there. And the country itself, the new South Africa, continues to struggle with crime, with ongoing economic injustice, with unemployment, and with discontent among many of its citizens.

Despite their imperfections, though, the hearings were a public enactment of a radical kind of justice, justice that returns dignity to those who have been victimized; justice that gives back the power to speak in one's own words and to shape the experience of violence into a coherent story of one's own, thereby allowing for a renewed (or new) sense of autonomy and sense of control; justice that allows victims, in hearing stories from other victims, to locate their personal stories in a larger cultural story; justice that corrects the erroneous message communicated by the system of apartheid—that these people of color are unworthy—the message corrected not in the official language and setting of the legal system, but in public space that belongs to the people. The victims were given the opportunity and the public venue to "speak to th' yet unknowing world how these things came about."[25]

Additionally, the state benefited in that widely diverse people heard the human experiences embedded in the stories—the shared experiences of loss, pain, and hopelessness. The stories began to bridge the gap between the vast differences in the people who had been legally separated in the past. Even skeptical white South Africans were compelled to acknowledge that these things had, in fact, occurred. The atomized individuals and groups were publicly invited back into the body politic. The individuals, families, communities, and the country were ritualistically re-membered in this public remembering. In that communal and sacramental space in which the ability to speak was regained, it was possible to believe the impossible—that the chance of forgiveness might emerge.

An example of the manifestation of many of these benefits may be seen in a story related by Alex Borain, deputy chair of the TRC, about the response of a woman who had listened to the testimony of her husband's killer.

After learning for the first time how her husband had died, she was asked if she could forgive the man who did it. Speaking slowly, in one of the native languages, her message came back through the interpreters: "No government can forgive." Pause. "No commission can forgive." Pause. "Only I can forgive." Pause. "And I am not ready to forgive."[26]

In this setting, this woman, a victim of apartheid violence, may speak in her own voice, in fact in her own language. She can speak her mind and take her stand as an included member of the renewed body politic. Her words reveal her recognition of this. In this space, she is given the opportunity to forgive, forgiveness is offered as an option. She freely turns it down—she cannot forgive—not yet. But this moment manifests a state in which her dignity is acknowledged, her voice counts, her opinion matters, her mind and heart are free.

When the victim hearings ended (the amnesty hearings continued), the Commission turned to the perhaps impossible task of writing a report that could somehow meet the Commission's mandate *and* contain the testimony given at the hearings. The messy, celebratory and very public nature of the hearings made this task especially formidable. Given the high expectations aroused by the attention to the hearings, pleasing everyone was not going to happen. The Commission was faced with the dilemma of "how to construct a narrative of human-rights violations that does not oversimplify, nor reduce pain to a cipher, yet that remains true to the experiences of those who testify."[27] The Commission had to find "words for that cry of Nomonde Calata."[28]

The Report

The *Truth and Reconciliation Commission of South Africa Report* weighs in at a staggering 2,739 pages contained in five volumes, perhaps not surprising in length in light of the Commission's mandate, which included covering nearly four decades and many kinds of violations.[29] The South African report dwarfs the slight 252-page Salvadoran report and triples its closest counterpart, the Chilean report, a relatively modest 893 pages. Decorated with collages of pictures—of commissioners, witnesses, victims, perpetrators, as well as some words in the form of posters and banners—the covers of the five volumes echo the populist stance taken in the hearings and the messiness inherent in the process. Yet within the covers a different story emerges from that which resulted from the daily inundation of victim and perpetrator stories that had rained on the people of South Africa for nearly two years. The hearings, despite their highly ritualized nature, had let loose a riot of emotion. The hearings had been *carnival*, temporarily releasing the people from the strictures of the state. The report, on the other hand, is a monumental effort to control the chaos, to reintroduce the state with its orderliness and discipline; this time, to be sure, a new state that values equality and compassion. Nonetheless, the tone of the report is largely formal and bureaucratic, a startling contrast to the hearings.

Within the volumes a compelling story unfolds slowly and with many interruptions—a story self-consciously described as a "long journey through these volumes."[30] But it is less a story of what happened to the individuals (although individual testimony intersperses all the volumes, particularly Volumes 2 and 3), and more a story about South Africa—its horrendous past, the troubled transition, and the new effort at building a just and inclusive community. The journey begins, as do many other such reports, with an introduction by its chairperson, in this case the high-profile Archbishop Desmond Tutu. This part, Chapter 1, commences with a kind of benediction, a large, two-page picture of Tutu kissing an ornate cross that hangs around his neck. Tutu's language is conciliatory and explanatory, using words of unity for the people and words of distancing and depersonalizing for the violence: "All South Africans know that our recent history is littered with some horrendous occurrences."[31] Tutu's choice of words and syntax characteristically avoids pointing a finger of blame; instead, it seemingly says to the diverse people of South Africa, "we are all one and bad things happened to all of us." After establishing this tone, the rest of the introduction explains why the truth report exists and preemptively deals with the major objections to it and the major controversies surrounding the Commission's work, in particular the blanket amnesty granted to thirty-seven ANC leaders and the amnesties given to the perpetrators of the St. James Church killings and to the killers of American activist Amy Biehl. It also clarifies that the report does not (could not) contain all of the material discovered and heard by the Commission; instead it should be seen as a "window" into the National Archive material.[32] It thereby acknowledges both the Commission's and the report's shortcomings and importantly takes the position that the report should not be seen as the Truth and as closing the discussion, but rather should be read and regarded as part of an ongoing process of discovering the truth. Despite its scope, therefore, the report begins with a warning against the danger of closure, a danger inherent in all narratives.

In short declarative and injunctive sentences that are uttered as great truths, Tutu's introduction concludes with even stronger language of unity directed at and including all the people of South Africa: "Ours is a remarkable country. Let us celebrate our diversity, our differences. God wants us as we are."[33] And, in direct contrast to its beginning warnings about closure, it twice asks its readers to "shut the door on the past,"[34] "close the chapter on our past."[35] Thus, at first blush, South African readers are asked to hold two conflicting ideas in their heads at once: this report is not to be taken as closure but they should close this chapter on their past. Yet the ideas do not conflict if we can understand that the report does not close the door on the past, does not and cannot forgive and move forward in a spirit of reconciliation. It is only the people of South Africa, its readers, who can decide to do that. The report, carefully read, may be seen as an offering—a means by which the people may find reconciliation and closure. But the report is not itself that reconciliation and closure.

Chapter 2 is introduced by a picture (all the chapters in all the volumes are introduced by a picture) of a policeman walking away from a dead body in the street. Without reading a word, we know that the tone has changed and that the "horrendous occurrences" warned of in the report's first lines are due. But we are pulled up sharply; starting on the "long journey through these volumes," we must understand two things. First, the report covers a limited amount of time; and second, and relatedly, it tells just a small part of a much larger story of human rights abuse in South Africa. Violence was a "well established tradition" in South Africa, in comparison to the stories of violence in the Argentinian, Chilean, and Salvadoran reports that make clear that the violence that they narrate was part of a temporary and aberrational time. There is no prelapsarian South Africa to which this report aspires to return. The report is not *retrieving* something; it is *creating* something.

The report then proceeds to tell a short version of this larger story, demonstrating that not all the evil can be laid at the feet of the National Party, that violence and racism preceded 1948. The report moves back and forth from broad strokes to fine points, retelling, for example, the story of the squatter, Kgobadi, who lost his land under the 1913 Land Act. At the same time, the report does not flinch from what becomes one of its primary tasks—showing that "the apartheid state that was constructed after 1948 [by the National Party] had dimensions that made it different [and worse] from the discriminatory order that preceded it."[36] These initial pages begin with a broad history and then narrow the focus to apartheid, the system, which is named as a human rights violation. The Commission's limited, mandated focus on specific acts of violence must not obscure, the report repeatedly emphasizes, the larger, overarching crime—the very system of apartheid. To emphasize this point further, it then provides a detailed history of the racist legislation enacted under apartheid.

The subsequent eleven chapters of Volume 1 extend the pause begun in the first words of Chapter 2 and become the story of the Commission itself: its setting up, its interpretation of its mandate and the decisions it subsequently made, its definition of truth and its view of the relationship between truth and justice, its understanding of what justice requires, its methodology, the legal challenges brought against it, the reprehensible destruction of records by the former government that hindered its work, and reports from various arms of the Commission. In an extensive effort at admirable transparency, the report delays in getting to its real purpose: the uncovering of the truth of the past.

Volumes 2 and 3 take up this mission, the first focusing on the perpetrators and the second on the victims, organizing the chaotic violence by time and space.[37] In both instances, the report informs its readers that the information on which it relies was culled from multiple sources: the testimonies of over 21,000 victims; over 7000 applications for amnesty; court records and police reports; and applications from groups such as the South African Police and the South African Defence Force. Both volumes are self-conscious attempts to understand patterns of abuse. They reveal an effort to contain the uncontainable in charts, statistics, graphs. What kinds of people (age, political affiliation, homeland) were killed, tortured, or banished? In what time periods? The report seems to say, gazing on forty years of violence and oppression, "There is something in all this we can comprehend."

Each of these volumes uses three typefaces to indicate which of three voices it is using at a given time: regular typeface for the basic ordering master narrative, italics for the first-person victim or perpetrator stories, and boldface for the Commission's official findings. The reader is thereby compelled to hear each part differently, to adjust when the text moves into italics to the cacophony of voices heard in the hearings, to adjust when the text moves into boldface to the somewhat stentorious official voice of the Commission, the mouthpiece here of the new state.

Volume 4 moves from individuals to institutions and special hearings. Individuals fade into the background as the master narrative takes up once again the overarching story of apartheid. What roles did business, labor, the faith community, the legal community, the health sector, the media, prisons, and military service play in the system of apartheid? Were these institutions complicitous or victimized? Just two type faces are used, regular and italics, and the italicized individual voices are rarely identified. They are instead the voices of people who represent institutions. The Commission makes findings about each institution from which it took testimony, findings that largely announce active and passive complicity on the part of the institutions. It is as if the Commission believes that by writing and preserving all these details it can prevent these occurrences in the future. For example, it finds that "The mining industry not only benefited from migratory labour and the payment of low wages to black employees; it also failed to give sufficient attention to the health and safety concerns of its employees";[38] "Christianity, as the dominant religion in South Africa, promoted the ideology of apartheid";[39] and "the courts and the organised legal profession generally and subconsciously or unwittingly connived in the legislative and executive pursuit of injustice."[40] No institution escapes these damning findings that read both as indictments of past behavior and, perhaps more critically, as prescriptions for future behavior, actions, and attitudes against which these institutions must guard. These parts of the report seem explicitly to describe the roles that institutions must play in the new South Africa.

Volume 5 is a catchall mainly of details and unfinished business, providing a description and listing of the hearings; an incomplete list of those who, the Commission has concluded thus far, suffered a gross violation of human rights (over 18,000 names alphabetized in small print taking up eighty pages of text); an interim report of the Amnesty Committee, including a list of the amnesties granted. Chapter 4 of this final volume, however, which focuses on the consequences of gross violations of human rights, perhaps best captures the spirit of the hearings and redeems this unwieldy (and perhaps unreadable) report. In the italics that dominate this forty-four-page chapter, the unforgettable voices of the victims give us unimaginable details. Here is one torture victim's description of his first view of his cell:

When dawn eventually broke, I had the first opportunity of looking around my cell. What I saw still haunts me to this day. The wall on one side of my cell was smeared with faeces. The spot where the night soil bucket stood was a pool of urine. . . . The blankets were old, threadbare, smelly, dusty, coarse, with tell tale signs of perverse sexual acts. I tried walking toward the door, but I staggered about sick to the bottom of my gut. . . . I remembered tactics about killing someone without laying a finger on them.[41]

Another describes his psychological state after friends with whom he was abducted were killed: "I am a living zombie; psychologically and emotionally, I am dead."[42] The chapter relentlessly chronicles the psychological and physical consequences of abuse, as well as the effects on shattered families and communities. The photograph that appropriately concludes the chapter is of a woman in African dress, weeping.

Chapter 5 recommends reparations and rehabilitation; Chapter 6 summarizes the Commission's findings; Chapter 7 gathers together the perspectives of the perpetrators, allowing them also to tell their views. For example, a Koevoet operative explains police training: "Pride and patriotism. By the end of our training we were fully indoctrinated in the functions of the established system . . . they strip away your individuality and they make you a man, kind of thing."[43] Chapter 8 makes recommendations, both broad and specific. The final chapter of the report,[44] in keeping with the teleology that underpinned the Commission from its inception, is entitled "Reconciliation." Again, the first-person italics dominate the text, the apologies and testimonials coming from judges, businessmen, victims, and perpetrators.

The very form of the report exposes the master narrative of the new country. Tutu's Prologue: South Africa is a unified nation of people; Volume 1: *but* it has a long and painful history of racism culminating in the regime of the National Party for the last half of the twentieth century, which has now changed legally with the new Constitution and the creation of the TRC; Volumes 2 and 3: specific, horrific events occurred between 1960 and the recent election in 1994, events that were purposeful, have a pattern we can discern, and created thousands of victims whose needs have been, until now, ignored; Volume 4: the rest of the country and its citizens, although not actively involved in the oppression that was apartheid, nonetheless were either complicitous and benefited from apartheid, or, at best, passively allowed it to occur; Volume 5: we continue to suffer, some of the suffering will never end, but the new country will do all it can for the victims (reparations, more symbolic than real), and many of the victims can forgive those who injured them in the past and will move forward together in a spirit of reconciliation. The opportunity to forgive and to participate in nation building is offered and the report returns, full circle, to the Prologue. The hearings and report dared to imagine something on the "far side of revenge." The act of imagination alone is worth the effort.

The report was delivered to President Nelson Mandela on October 29, 1998, amid attempts from both former National Party President F. W. de Klerk and the ruling party, the ANC, to block its publication. Since then, numerous conferences, articles, and books have analyzed and deconstructed both the hearings and the report itself, subjecting the South African process to intense domestic and international scrutiny.[45] Lauded, lamented, ceaselessly dissected, and largely unread—at least in its entirety—the TRC report launched, for good or ill, a culture of truth reports.

Chapter Seven
The Truth Must Dazzle Gradually

> The symmetry of form attainable in pure fiction cannot so readily be achieved in a narration essentially having less to do with fable than with fact. Truth uncompromisingly told will always have its ragged edges.
>
> —Herman Melville, *Billy Budd, Sailor*

My ongoing project is to explore the question as to whether there is any reason to think, indeed hope, that the collecting and publishing of victims' stories—the activities that surround writing a truth report—can bring an end to the cycle of revenge that threatens the stability of an emerging democracy. Is it sensible to suppose that language can carry such a burden? By examining some of the history of revenge and our troubled and ambivalent relationship to it, the early chapters have provided, I hope, a clearer understanding of what a victim such as Paulina might mean when she asks, "What about my good?" If we recognize the central role that language plays in political oppression, how the use of language is appropriated from an oppressive regime's victims, then our traditional ways of thinking about revenge and retribution might be expanded. If a victim wants a balancing—an "accounting," to "get her own back," to "settle the score"—getting back the ability to use language for oneself might indeed be seen as a significant kind of retribution. Thus for a state to provide an opportunity for victims to tell their stories and for the state officially to acknowledge them seems to be a sensible response to redressing the harms of the past regime. It is a response that keeps the focus of retribution on the victims, allows the victims to express emotion, and in so doing reincorporates the Furies into a dynamic understanding of justice.

Truth reports in theory can achieve significant ends, all of which should be part of any understanding of justice. Truth reports in actuality achieve some of these ends and fail to achieve others. Our understanding of what a truth report is, what it can do, and what form it should take continues to evolve. In this final chapter, I hope to raise some questions and suggest some strategies. Before the world is awash in truth reports that can do harm as well as good, truth reports proposed and implemented for wrong reasons, it is wise to consider what can be learned from the reports that we already have, especially if we are to hope that truth reports can deliver, or be a significant part of, justice. In so doing, it is important that we look not to what the commissions promised or claim to have done, but rather to the phenomena—what they actually did. Writers of truth reports might well be advised by Thomas in T. S. Eliot's *Murder in the Cathedral* when he is confronted by his last and most insidious tempter: "The last temptation is the greatest treason / To do the right deed for the wrong reason."[1]

Although we continue to harbor many misconceptions of what truth reports accomplish, they have become the thing to do. One commentator writes that since (and because of) the South African Truth and Reconciliation Commission, "the international community has become blindly besotted with truth commissions."[2] The creation of a truth commission indeed seems to have become one of the first things a new leader does. On taking office in October 2000, Yugoslavia's new president, Vojislav Kostunica, announced the creation of a truth commission to investigate crimes that occurred during the interethnic wars. In 2001, Peru's new president, Alejandro Toledo, made a similar promise to create a truth commission. Some are currently advocating the creation of a permanent international truth commission, like the international criminal tribunal that will replace the ad hoc tribunals created in response to the crimes in the former Yugoslavia and in Rwanda.[3] Between Yugoslavia's and Peru's commitments, ten other commissions were created, from Bosnia to Sierra Leone. "Unthinkable a short time ago, such gestures now accompany practically every transition . . . [and have] become a popular way for newly minted leaders to show their democratic bona fides and curry favor with the international community."[4] The international community has become so enamored with truth reports that they are being seen as the sole requisite remedy in reckoning with the past. Money for other efforts is refused because of the existence of a truth commission.[5] This impulse reflects perhaps the major misconception about truth reports—that they alone are the appropriate measure for accounting for the past. Despite the sudden popularity of truth commission reports, none of them have delivered instant gratifying results, nor have they brought about "closure," the word so often seen in relationship to them. When the aftermath of the reports is examined, we can see that truth reports are described with the wrong metaphors: instead of closing doors on the past, they open them; instead of burying the past, they help to exhume it. As it turned out, the stories that the commissions wrote were not the final words. They were a first, critical step in a process that may have no end: an inverse reflection of the revenge cycle—a truth-telling cycle.

In Argentina the struggle to discover what happened to *los desaparecidos* continues. Under the Menem government (the administration that followed Alfonsín's), the investigative work begun by CONADEP continued and the files CONADEP assembled quadrupled in number.[6] Some military officers began to tell their own stories of torture and murder, leading the way for the 1995 acknowledgement by General Martin Balza of the army's responsibility for systematic human rights violations. Scholars continue to be engaged in studies of the collective memory of the repression, discovering that "memory" is multifaceted and sometimes contradictory. Recently, several former leaders have been charged in cases involving the abduction and illegal adoption of children born in detention. "The return to democracy has unleashed a continuing flood of new evidence of crimes, lawsuits and reparation cases, and personal stories too horrific for most people to imagine."[7] On March 24, 2001, the twenty-fifth anniversary of the military coup, tens of thousands of Argentines marched to protest the atrocities committed during the military rule. The mothers of the Plaza de Mayo, although now split into two groups over differences concerning reparations and other issues, still gather for their weekly march. Plans abound for projects and memorials. In November 2001, a federal court in Buenos Aires nullified Argentina's Punto Final and Due Obedience laws, and the court allowed the first trial since 1987 of an officer for torture and disappearances committed during the oppression.[8] At the same time, courts are conducting highly controversial "truth trials," in which the court can subpoena military witnesses to appear and testify under oath, although the court lacks the power to charge or convict them, thus shifting truth commission work into the judicial realm. The new president, Nestor Kirchner, a full twenty years after the end of the "dirty war," has promised a reexamination of the criminal behavior of the army during that time. He is asking the supreme court to nullify the amnesty laws and pardons and is also purging the military.[9]

In Chile, General Augusto Pinochet remains under house arrest after being arrested in London on a Spanish warrant charging him with human rights abuses. A Spanish magistrate, Baltasar Garzon, issued the indictment and extradition request, accusing Pinochet of crimes against humanity—genocide, torture, and terrorism—committed against Spanish citizens in Chile. The world watched and waited as the British House of Lords debated whether Pinochet, as a former head of state, was immune from legal process in the United Kingdom. The Lords concluded that sovereign immunity did not extend to crimes against humanity, but Pinochet was not extradited to Spain. Instead he was returned to Chile because of his failing health. At the time of his return to Chile, he faced more than sixty domestic criminal complaints filed by the families of victims of his regime and by political parties, trade unions, and professional groups. In May 2001, the Santiago Appeals Court voted to remove his immunity from prosecution, although he has since been found too ill to stand trial because he is suffering from mild dementia.[10] In July 2001, a court sentenced two former military officers and a cadet to life imprisonment for a murder that occurred in 1982 under the Pinochet regime. The legislature has also passed various laws protecting freedom of expression and the rights of journalists.[11]

Along with these legal developments, the silence that followed the publication of the Chilean truth report has been broken in numerous ways. Pinochet's arrest catalyzed the emergence of many victims of torture under his regime—those people like Dorfman's Paulina whose harm was omitted from the investigative sweep of the Chilean truth commission. Newly invigorated human rights groups have sought out torture victims, looking for evidence to use in a trial against Pinochet and then urging them to seek counseling. Spurred by the arrest of Pinochet, a growing number of torture victims, who had remained frightened and silent even after the fall of the Pinochet government, are seeking help from doctors and psychologists. "Pinochet's arrest was a great catharsis that has begun to break the silence."[12] Pinochet's arrest also resulted in some of his former collaborators coming forward to reveal his role in covering up atrocities, "revelations that have had a snowball effect."[13] In July 2003, members of Pinochet's junta and retired military generals revealed that mass exhumations had taken place to prevent the discovery of bodies and hide evidence, a disclosure that, according to a human rights lawyer, would have been "unthinkable" previously.[14] The report of "closure" announced when President Aylwin left office in 1994 was clearly premature.

In El Salvador, the government has done nothing to investigate further the crimes revealed by the truth report or to bring the perpetrators to trial.[15] Outside of El Salvador, however, prosecutions are occurring. On July 23, 2002, a West Palm Beach, Florida, jury found two retired Salvadoran generals responsible for atrocities committed during the "dirty war" and ordered them to pay $54.6 million to three of their victims.[16] The victims had sued under the 1991 Torture Victim Protection Act, an American law that allows United States courts to assess damages against the perpetrators of atrocities, even though the atrocities were committed abroad.

In each of these three countries, the aftermath interestingly reflects the master narrative of the truth report. The community that the report imagined and helped to create has taken up the work of justice. In Argentina the ongoing activism stems largely from an empowered populace, mirroring the form of the Argentinian report that allowed the voices of the people to override the controlling voice of the state.[17] In Chile the ongoing activism and reforms are largely legal in nature, instigated in significant part by foreign judges but taken up by the Chilean courts and legislature, reflecting the master narrative of the Chilean report that emphasized the hegemony of the law. Legal action in turn has encouraged those who stayed silent even during and after the work of the Commission and the publication of the report to begin to speak. In El Salvador, the Salvadoran people continue to act unsupported by their own government; bringing perpetrators to trial occurs outside of the country.

In South Africa, not enough time has passed to assess intelligently the results of the TRC. Early responses are mixed.[18] A poll taken shortly after the TRC hearings showed that 74 percent of whites and 62 percent of blacks felt that the TRC hearings had stirred up racial resentments rather than settling them.[19] This perception may exist because the discussion about apartheid, the TRC, and reconciliation continues in venues such as community theaters, where actors engage in dramas with titles such as *Speak So That I May Speak*,[20] and in numerous conferences, articles, and books that analyze, praise, and criticize both the process and the publication. One of the chief architects of the report, Charles Villa-Vicencio, emphasizes the lack of closure, calling the TRC "a fragile foundation that needs to be reinforced by a range of other nation-building initiatives."[21] The work the truth report began continues, and discussions about previous and ongoing racial divides persist, a development that stands in sharp contrast to the enforced silence and false narratives of the apartheid years.

This dynamism suggests that justice is indeed an ongoing process and that truth reports are critical components of it. What might comprise this dynamic sense of justice? First, the process that has come to be seen as necessary for the making of a truth report — providing venues for people to come forward and tell their stories—gives back to victims the ability to use language, an ability that was appropriated and manipulated by the oppressive regime. Once the ability to use language is restored, people can use that language themselves to shape their experiences into coherent narratives, both personal and collective. That is, the story they tell shapes their own experience into a coherent part of their life story and their story becomes part of the larger national narrative (literally, in that it may be included in the constitutive master narrative). If part of justice is finding out the truth, as Goldstone and others avow—finding out what happened to one's loved ones, where bodies are buried, who did what to whom and perhaps even why—few deny that truth reports are at least as effective as trials and other posttransition responses in accomplishing this end. If the venues in which the state listens to the stories are public, ones in which the people are empowered, as was so often the case in the South African TRC hearings, then the oppressive state hierarchy is overturned and the people can publicly celebrate a newfound sense of place and equality that offers a promise of renewal. As diverse others listen to the stories that are told, they become emotionally engaged as experiences of pain, loss, and hopelessness are translated by means of story and become accessible in ways that abstract renderings of them cannot achieve. As we can see in the differences between the Salvadoran report and the other reports I have examined, acknowledgment of the stories by the international community is meaningful, but acknowledgment by the state importantly demonstrates that the state intends to actualize an ethical commitment. Truth reports sponsored by the state are a visible manifestation of a country's willingness to listen to its citizens and to incorporate their voices. In this way, the reports can be sacramental, in the sense that a sacrament is grace made visible. In these acts of storytelling, both public and private, something even more profound can occur. In remembering, we re-member. We put back together that which was broken apart—ourselves, our families, our communities, our countries. In this new space, which may be both carnivalesque and sacramental, the unimagined may occur.

But that is not enough: justice requires a balancing (an accounting), that something taken from the victim of the injustice must be restored, be given back. The balancing that truth reports afford victims begins to put the world back into order. The victims retrieve the ability to speak and shape their own stories. For some, their new story includes forgiveness and reconciliation; for others it requires the pursuit of trials and punishment. The stories are necessarily and inevitably varied—as different as the people who shape them. In circumstances in which the state has actively been involved in seeking out and encouraging the initial storytelling (Argentina, Chile, and South Africa), each person's story becomes a part of the story of the emerging country. In an atmosphere of enhanced human flourishing, other aspects of justice may begin to move forward. These countries, though fragile, thereby gather strength. The judiciary becomes newly determined and active; the legislature is emboldened to enact reforms; the people, if necessary, take to the streets in peaceful protest and engage in other activities that make a country fully democratic. Their storytelling and the countries' official acknowledgment of it has overcome the *différend* that had excluded and alienated many of them. Having the story told and acknowledged—what Paulina wanted in *Death and the Maiden*, what Horatio promises the dying Hamlet—opens the way for the state to move forward.

Although I have argued that the telling of stories has far-reaching power and that truth commission reports provide critical components of justice, at the same time their very popularity should give us pause. As truth commissions become pro forma for an emerging democracy after a period of violence and oppression, the number of serious critics grows along with the number of advocates. Some in the international human rights community who were once advocates of truth commissions are switching sides. The most persistent criticism is that a truth commission is a sop thrown to a country's victims, citizens, and the watchful international human rights community, a poor substitute for justice that diverts attention away from pursuing real justice, defined as criminal prosecutions. An emerging criticism argues that the conceptual basis for truth commissions—that they can put forth a unified version of the truth—is flawed from the start.[22] But even if I am right that truth reports are an indispensable aspect of justice, that they do not operate as closure but instead open the way for continuing justice, and that the best of them are polyphonic and put forth *truths* instead of truth, nonetheless, some dangers remain. Before we plunge headlong into a culture of truth commissions, it seems wise to reflect on their downside. In so doing, we can perhaps contribute to the evolution of the form. I want to engage three overlapping potential dangers that stem in particular from truth reports' nature as narratives: psychic numbing, premature closure, and the problematic ethics of appropriating stories of pain for political ends.

Psychic Numbing

Robert Jay Lifton popularized the term "psychic numbing" in his book on the effects of the bombing of Hiroshima. He initially applied it to survivors of the bombing and of concentration camps. He defines it as a "cessation of feeling . . . . that protects the survivor from a sense of complete helplessness" in the face of overwhelming death and disaster.[23] Lifton first applied the term to those who had actually suffered and witnessed devastating violence, but he later extended it to those who perpetrate the violence or hear about it from a distance, "where it serves the additional purpose of warding off potential feelings of guilt" and "prevents the mind from being overwhelmed and perhaps destroyed by the dreadful and unmanageable images confronting it."[24] Most of Lifton's work refers to actual images—either witnessing horrific events or seeing multiple pictorial representations of these events—but it seems that this theory might be logically extended to hearing or reading many, many victim stories; attending truth commission hearings, if public; or reading truth reports. In a kind of psychological self-protection, minds and hearts might symbolically shut down.

With the increasing popularity of truth commission reports with their numerous victims' stories of unimaginable violence, it is critical to reflect on whether these many stories, like repeated images, may actually have a reverse effect on their hearers and readers. Instead of arousing empathy and stirring people to political action to insure that such events cannot recur, they could by their very number and repetition make people numb to the violence, make them insensitive to acts of violence that occur around them. Those who take on the responsibility of writing truth reports should be sensitive to the fact that there is a line between presenting enough information to make us aware, an adequate number of personal stories so that we are empathetic and politically committed to change, and presenting so many stories of violence that we cease to feel anything at all.

Premature Closure

Truth reports are not mere collections of stories. They are themselves *stories*, master narratives that provide a grand design—what the past was and what the future should be. At their best, they are constitutive documents that create the renewed country in which they are written. They have, as do all stories, a beginning, a middle, and an end. They often contain a review of events leading to the time of violence that the report chronicles (the beginning), a detailed discussion of the circumscribed time that the commission has been mandated to examine (the middle), and the end of the violence and a vision of the renewed country (the end). We read them not only to discover truth but also to discover order, and the writers of the reports use various, but inevitable, means to impose order, not only on the beginning, middle, and end, but also to order the chaotic events being scrutinized. As we have seen, chronology, geography, kinds of harms, and kinds of perpetrators are among the most common ordering devices. Beyond this, most reports offer a teleology—from the breakdown of order to its reestablishment, from the misuse or obviation of law to its reinstatement, from fragmentation to union, from hatred and violence to forgiveness. These are satisfying structures. Not only do we want narratives to be coherent, we want them to give us a reassuring sense that problems are solved, crises are over. Not only are we storytelling creatures, we are also story-needing creatures, and the reports, if they are to succeed at all, provide us with a desired story and a happy ending. They point us toward an imaginary future in which all the country's ills are solved. No one is immune from wanting a master narrative, from wanting to be comforted by coherence.

The primary caution is this: narratives tempt us to a comforting sense of closure, to what Frank Kermode has famously called a "sense of an ending" that is necessary for our emotional well-being, but inappropriate for a transitional democracy.[25] The very nature of a report as a story reassures us that the problems have found a solution. In a transitional democracy, nothing could be further from the truth. We call these countries fragile democracies for good reason. It is naive to suppose that all victims feel satisfied by having had their stories told and acknowledged, just as it is naive to expect that reconciliation necessarily follows the revelation of the truth. Because reports can tempt us to closure, an adequate report must also warn us against it. It must insist that much more needs to be accomplished; in fact, the word *closure* and truth report are best seen as contradictory, and the post-report experiences of the four countries I have discussed lay bare this contradiction.

Appropriating Stories of Pain

In *Country of My Skull,* Antjie Krog creates an imaginary conversation in which someone says, referring to the TRC, that "one has no right to appropriate a story paid for with a lifetime of pain and destruction."[26] This admonition, directed specifically at the South African situation, has its roots in a much longer ongoing debate about the propriety of using stories of pain to achieve personal, political, or economic ends. Such utilization of images and stories of pain has become increasingly commonplace, resulting in the "mediatization of suffering."[27] Images of suffering are "infotainment" on the nightly news: "The existential appeal of human experiences, their potential to mobilize popular sentiment and collective action, and even their ability to witness or offer testimony are now available for gaining market share."[28] The mediatization of stories of suffering can, like the phenomenon of psychic numbing, make us respond cynically or not at all, rather than arouse empathy in us. Moreover, empathy alone may not be an appropriate response to stories of oppression. If we weep, but do not act to insure through social and political action that these events do not recur, then the stories have been used to bad ends. They exempt us from responsibility because we feel sorry for the victims. Feeling sorry cannot in itself be enough.

All these problems with appropriation of pain are inherent in the very nature of truth reports and perhaps especially in the kind of open, public hearings that occurred in South Africa. Are there precautions that can be taken by truth commissions so that such appropriation is minimized? Kleinman and Kleinman, among the most diligent critics of appropriations of suffering, maintain that, despite their critiques, to conclude all appropriations are invalid would "undermine any attempt to respond to human misery. It would be much more destructive than the problem; it would paralyze social action."[29] The use of stories of suffering in truth reports, then, is not in itself problematic, but careless, unreflective use of them might well be.

One of the dubious sides of the appropriation of images of human misery resides in the unstated message of many of these images and stories that the individual suffers alone; the images are not contextualized. In this respect, truth reports and hearings have a built-in safety measure. One of the basic purposes of truth reports is to fit individual stories into a larger picture, to take seemingly isolated instances of victimization and make them part of a larger pattern. But this use gives rise to an associated problem: "while there are many examples of the formation of a community of suffering through which individuals can transform their past hurts into visions of collective good, there are also examples of the manner in which the heterogeneity of individual experience of suffering can be homogenized into collective stereotypes."[30] The writers of truth reports confront this dilemma: how to contextualize the individual stories but not reduce them to "examples" or "evidence."

The best approach, it seems to me, is to allow for what Bakhtin calls the carnivalization of the reports, an approach that allows the individual voices to be fully weighted and to compete with the voice of the master narrative. *Nunca Más*, the Argentinian report, is the best example so far of how this may be achieved. The stories remain in the first person; they are allowed to be messy and slightly irrelevant at times. For some commentators on truth reports, the tensions that are created in the reports between the master narrative, the unified national account, and the multivoiced stories, some contradicting others, result in an "awkward methodological straddle,"[31] which undercuts the force and historical veracity of the reports. If, however, we can retain the negative capability to see the reports as an iconoclastic kind of history, both revelatory and constitutive, then the clashing narratives are epistemically appropriate: "The truth, uncompromisingly told, will always have its ragged edges."[32] We can only know the past through many competing narratives, and we can only envision the future by incorporating this polyphony into the new national story. Some critics of truth reports argue that this polyphony is a weakness, that the reports should speak with a unified voice. I want to suggest that just the opposite is true. Truth reports best serve the interests of justice if the victims' stories compete with the master narrative, supporting it at times, at other times interrupting and contradicting it. In this way, the stories both witness and contribute to the transformation of society. The victims are served and so is the good of the country.

These three pitfalls—psychic numbing, premature closure, and appropriation—are inherent in the nature of truth reports as stories. Hence they are to some extent unavoidable. But they can be minimized by awareness that they lurk wherever personal stories of suffering are used in a public way. As long as we remain cognizant of the potential harms of truth commissions and their reports, truth reports offer great promise. But we need continually to deconstruct old ways of thinking. What is the ultimate fulfillment of justice? Is it punishment of the perpetrator as we so quickly assume? Is it doing something and then putting the past behind? Or is justice best understood as something continually in the making? For Paulina, justice was having the story of what happened to her told and acknowledged. She wanted to get back what she had lost—the ability and freedom to use language to shape her own life story. Then the perpetrator lost power over her and became, for her at least, insignificant. So what is Paulina's "good"? Narrative theory has shown us that her intuition that she wanted her story of suffering told has a solid foundation.

If we are to continue to think—and it appears we are—that truth reports can somehow contribute to ending a cycle of violence, what should such a report look like? Can we design a process and report by which "revenge" collapses into "remember"? Importantly, we should not accept the template that calls for a certain kind of story, a certain kind of process. We should eschew any design that asks for seamlessness or for tightly organized narratives. If the conceptual basis for a truth commission is that it will find a single truth, that it will achieve closure, that it will automatically provide reconciliation, then I hope that I have undermined that basis. To capitalize on the justice-producing potential of truth reports, we must be brave enough to trust stories to be tools of disruption. We must allow reports to be incomplete, multivalent, heteroglossic.

If we must talk about burying the past, perhaps we should think of the past as seeds, rather than as corpses—not dead and forgotten but something from which a future can grow. In the midst of her own painful experience of reporting on the South African truth commission hearings, Antjie Krog found the poetry for it, words that eerily echo the closing sentiments of *Hamlet*:

Beloved, do not die. Do not dare die! I, the survivor, wrap you in words so that the future inherits you. I snatch you from the death of forgetfulness. I tell your story, complete your ending—you who once whispered beside me in the dark.[33]

Notes

Prologue for Paulina

1. Ariel Dorfman, *Death and the Maiden*, Act One, scene one (London: Duke of York Theatre, 1992). This text, which I purchased at the theater the night I saw the play, differs slightly from that published by Penguin Books in 1992.

2. Dorfman, Act One, scene one.

3. Dorfman, Act One, scene one.

4. The international legal community has officially named rape as torture. See Kelly Dawn Askin, *War Crimes Against Women: Prosecution in International War Crimes Tribunals* (The Hague: Nijhoff, 1997), 314–23. David Luban's excellent article, "On Dorfman's *Death and the Maiden*," analyzes the political use of rape in wartime and its significance to Dorfman's play. *Yale Journal of Law and the Humanities* 10 (1998): 123–33.

5. Dorfman, Act One, scene two. As Dorfman notes in his afterword to the play, this was, in fact, the situation in Chile: "My country was at the time . . . living an uneasy transition to democracy, with Pinochet no longer the President but still in command of the Armed Forces, still able to threaten another coup if people became unruly or, more specifically, if attempts were made to punish the human rights' violations of the outgoing regime."

6. Dorfman, Act One, scene four.

7. Elaine Scarry, *The Body in Pain: The Making and Unmaking of the World* (New York: Oxford University Press, 1985), 57. This polarization is developed more fully in Chapter 3, in which I discuss the relationships among violence, pain, and retribution.

8. Dorfman, Act One, scene four.

9. Dorfman, Act Two, scene one.

10. Dorfman, Act Two, scene one.

11. Dorfman, Act Two, scene one.

12. Dorfman, Act Three, scene one.

13. Dorfman, Act Two, scene one.

14. Dorfman, Act Two, scene one.

15. Dorfman, Act Two, scene two.

16. Dorfman, Act Three, scene one.

17. When the play was performed in Chile in 1991, former torturers, indistinguishable from the general population, would have had to look at their own reflections.

18. See Naomi Roht-Arriaza, ed., *Impunity and Human Rights in International Law and Practice* (New York: Oxford University Press, 1995), 8ff, which lays out the arguments for and against investigations, prosecutions, and reparations.

19. The play's ending is open to both interpretations. When I saw the play, it seemed clear to me that Paulina had spared Miranda and that the final scene was portraying reality rather than imagination. When I used the play as a text in my Law and Literature class, however, my students disabused me of the obviousness of my interpretation; the class split on whether she shot him or not. My purpose here is not to interpret the ending, which should, I think, remain ambivalent, but to take a point of view as to what can constitute Paulina's revenge.

20. Gary Jonathan Bass, "War Crimes and the Limits of Legalism," *Michigan Law Review* 97 (1999): 2103, 2116.

21. Some maintain that since World War II this duty has been imposed on states by international law. For specifics, see Roht-Arriaza; Diane F. Orentlicher, "Settling Accounts: The Duty to Prosecute Human Rights Violations of a Prior Regime," *Yale Law Journal* 100 (1991): 2537, 2553–55.

22. Roht-Arriaza lists the contextual differences as "The extent and severity of past violations, the prior history of democratic rule in the country, the number of victims, the extent of the complicity by the citizenry, cultural and historical traditions, the stability of the new government, and the press of other—especially economic—matters" (5). Tina Rosenberg in *The Haunted Land: Facing Europe's Ghosts After Communism* (New York: Random House, 1995), 400, also sees the eastern European and Latin American contexts as decidedly different, the former being "criminal regimes" and the latter being "regimes of criminals."

23. Martha Minow's *Between Vengeance and Forgiveness: Facing History After Genocide and Mass Violence* (Boston: Beacon Press, 1998) discusses the pros and cons of the various responses. In "Reconciling Order and Justice: New Institutional Solutions in Post-Conflict States," *Journal of International Affairs* 52 (1999): 758, Michelle Sieff and Leslie Vinjamuri attempt to delineate why a country chooses one response over another, arguing that "institutional design is a function of the balance of power, the role played by transnational advocacy networks and the goals of political leaders in post-conflict states. The outcome of conflict, specifically whether conflicts are resolved through military defeats or negotiated settlements, and its effect on the balance of power influence the range of options for transitional justice."

24. Carlos Santiago Nino, *Radical Evil on Trial* (New Haven, Conn.: Yale University Press, 1996), ix. This question is taken up in Saul Friedlander's *Probing the Limits of Representation: Nazism and the "Final Solution"* (Cambridge, Mass.: Harvard University Press, 1992), 2, in terms of the Holocaust: how narratives about the Holocaust and Nazism "test implicit boundaries and . . . raise not only aesthetic and intellectual problems, but moral issues as well."

25. Narrative theory in a narrow sense would include those semioticians and philosophers known specifically in this area: for example, Paul Ricoeur, Hayden White, Michel Foucault, Frederic Jameson. By a broad sense, I include the thinking of others, such as Martha Nussbaum and James Boyd White, who focus on the impact of stories in a larger way. Contemporary narratology has expanded the scope of study to include the multitude of narratives found in everyday life, such as films, music videos, advertisements, and jokes. "In more academic contexts, there has been a recognition that narrative is central to the representation of identity, in personal memory and self-representation or in collective identity groups such as regions, nations, race and gender." Mark Currie, *Postmodern Narrative Theory* (New York: St. Martin's Press, 1998), 2.

26. Kader Asmal, Louise Asmal, and Ronald Suresh Roberts, *Reconciliation Through Truth: A Reckoning of Apartheid's Criminal Governance*, 2nd ed. (New York: St. Martin's Press, 1997), 12.

27. See, for example, A. James McAdams, ed., *Transitional Justice and the Rule of Law in New Democracies* (Notre Dame, Ind.: University of Notre Dame Press, 1997); Nino; Rosenberg; Orentlicher; Richard Goldstone, "Exposing Human Rights Abuses—A Help or Hindrance to Reconciliation?" *Hastings Constitutional Law Quarterly* 22 (1995): 607; José Zalaquett, "Balancing Ethical Imperatives and Political Constraints: The Dilemma of New Democracies Confronting Past Human Rights Violations," *Hastings Law Journal* 43 (1992): 1425.

28. See, for example, Robert I. Rotberg and Dennis Thompson, eds., *Truth v. Justice: The Morality of Truth Commissions* (Princeton, N.J.: Princeton University Press, 2000); Wilmot James and Linda van de Vijver, eds., *After the TRC: Reflections on Truth and Reconciliation in South Africa* (Athens: Ohio University Press, 2001); Martin Meredith, *Coming to Terms: South Africa's Search for Truth* (New York: Public Affairs Press, 1999).

29. Harry Keyishian, *The Shapes of Revenge: Victimization, Vengeance, and Vindictiveness in Shakespeare* (Atlantic Highlands, N.J.: Humanities Press, 1995), 150.

Chapter One. The Demise of Paulina's Good: From Personal Revenge to State Punishment

1. Susan Jacoby, in her excellent discussion of this issue, describes the reaction to Holocaust victims and others who dare to voice a desire for revenge. One reporter described a witness as "unbalanced by the quest for revenge." *Wild Justice: The Evolution of Revenge* (New York: Harper and Row, 1983), 3.

2. Karen Horney, "The Value of Vindictiveness," in *The Unknown Karen Horney: Essays on Gender, Culture, and Psychoanalysis*, ed. Bernard J. Paris (New Haven, Conn.: Yale University Press, 2000), 3. Horney's 1965 article discusses the often overlooked distinction between a normal expression of vindictive anger and the neurotic repression or expression of it. More recently, Martha Minow also writes that feeling the urge for revenge is "entirely understandable." Martha Minow, "Institution and Emotions: Redressing Mass Violence," in *The Passions of Law*, ed. Susan Bandes (New York: New York University Press, 1999), 265.

3. There is much evidence of the idea of revenge for a wrongdoing being the responsibility and right of the victim's family in many societies: Aryan, Hindu, Greek, Roman, Teutonic, Russian, Icelandic, Welsh, etc. See Henry Charles Lea, *Superstition and Force: Essays on the Wager of Law, the Wager of Battle, the Ordeal, Torture* (New York: Benjamin Bloom, 1971); Maurice Davie, *The Evolution of War* (New Haven, Conn.: Yale University Press, 1929), 123–24. Davie provides a lengthy list of peoples who practiced blood vengeance and what constituted the specific familial practices. See also Erich Fromm, *The Anatomy of Human Destructiveness* (New York: Holt, Rinehart, and Winston, 1973), 272, in which he discusses blood revenge as a sacred duty.

4. In their classic nineteenth-century text, *Ancient Law: Its Connection with the Early History of Society and Its Relation to Modern Ideas* (New York: Scribner, 1864), Sir Henry Maine and Theodore W. Dwight describe early societies as being organized by families rather than individuals. Thus, if "the individual is conspicuously guilty, it is his children, his kinsfolk, his tribesmen, or his fellow-citizens who suffer with him, and sometimes for him" (122).

5. See generally, Harry Elmer Barnes and Negley K. Teeters, *New Horizons in Criminology* (New York: Prentice-Hall, 1943), 391–404; J. E. A. Jolliffe, *The Constitutional History of Medieval England from the English Settlement to 1485* (London: Adam and Charles Black, 1954), 3. Jolliffe indicates that clan blood feuds lasted until the tenth century in England; a man's clan could not disclaim revenge and leave him to bear the feud alone; Davie, 121ff.

6. My analysis of this historical development is based on Western cultures as evidenced largely through some canonical literature. While there is evidence that other cultures have a similar development, this study does not explore them.

7. See, for example, Michael S. Moore, "The Moral Worth of Retribution," in *Responsibility, Character, and the Emotions*, ed. Ferdinand Schoeman (Cambridge: Cambridge University Press, 1987). Moore defines retributivism as "the view that punishment is justified by the moral culpability of those who receive it. A retributivist punishes because, and only because, the offender deserves it" (179).

8. Hubert J. Treston, *Poine: A Study in Ancient Greek Blood Vengeance* (London: Longmans, Green, 1923). Treston avoids the chronology problem by characterizing revenge as falling into four types rather than by attaching a type of revenge to a particular time. The four are (1) barbarous and unrestricted vendetta, an endless series of retaliations that are both collective and hereditary and end only when there is no one left to kill; this type has survived up until recent times, for example, in the Balkan states; (2) personal restricted vendetta in which the right remains with the relatives of the victim, but they do not strike the innocent; this existed among the Achaeans in Homeric Greece and prevailed in Serbia up until recent times; (3) tribal wergeld, which was compensation, fixed by custom or law, paid by the relatives of the slayer to the relatives of the slain; there is ample evidence of its operation in premedieval Germany, Wales, Scotland, Ireland, and among Anglo-Saxons; and (4) homicide as a crime against the body politic; the state enacts the punishment and private vengeance is disallowed (1–4). Theodore Ziolkowski, following A. S. Diamond in *Primitive Law, Past and Present* (London: Methuen, 1971), identifies the stages as Early, Central, and Late Code stages. See Theodore Ziolkowski, *The Mirror of Justice: Literary Reflections of Legal Crisis* (Princeton, N.J.: Princeton University Press, 1997), 11ff.

9. G. R. Driver and John C. Mills, eds. and trans., *The Babylonian Laws* (Oxford: Oxford University Press, 1955), 497.

10. In England, at least, and probably throughout western Europe, attitudes toward private revenge were influenced by the decrees issued by the popes and councils that prohibited private vengeance and trials by combat. Sister Mary Bonaventure Mroz, *Divine Vengeance: A Study in the Philosophical Backgrounds of the Revenge Motif as It Appears in Shakespeare's Chronicle History Plays* (Washington, D.C.: Catholic University Press, 1941), 101, citing Lea, *Superstition and Force*, 206–11 (listing papal decrees).

11. In early English law, a fine, called a *murdrum*, was payable to the king if the murderer was not produced (Treston, 4). In twelfth-century England, an offender could buy back the peace with a *bot* to the offended and a *wite* to the kings. Sir Frederick Pollock and Frederic William Maitland, *The History of English Law Before the Time of Edward I*, vol. 1 (Cambridge: Cambridge University Press, 1923), 48.

12. Although blood feuds had disappeared by the classical period in Greek history, blood feuds were constant in Iceland at least until the twelfth century. See Pollock and Maitland, 47; William Ian Miller, *Bloodtaking and Peacemaking:*

Feud, Law, and Society in Saga Iceland (Chicago: University of Chicago Press, 1990). Blood feud as a system existed among Montenegrin tribes until 1851, when a state was formed. See Christopher Boehm, *Blood Revenge: The Anthropology of Feuding in Montenegro and Other Tribal Societies* (Lawrence: University Press of Kansas, 1984). Boehm cites a 1972 *New York Times* article about blood-feuding among Albanians in Kosovo: "Fears of falling victim to an avenger's bullet are confining about 8,000 Kosovo inhabitants to walled-in, fortresslike households. Fields and vineyards go untended. Workers in new factories dare not go to their jobs and teen-age boys hesitate to go to school" (114). Also, in *Blood Disputes Among Bedouin and Rural Arabs in Israel* (Pittsburgh: University of Pittsburgh Press, 1987), Joseph Ginat discusses the relationship of the power of the state to the practice of blood-feuding in twentieth-century Israel (1973–1983): "Revenge [among the Bedouin tribes] is put off or settlements made because of possible prison terms imposed by the state for acts of blood retribution" (4). In the American South, blood feuds and dueling existed at least until the late nineteenth century. See Edward L. Ayers, *Vengeance and Justice: Crime and Punishment in the 19th Century American South* (New York: Oxford University Press, 1984). As recently as 1999, the *New York Times Magazine* featured an article about a blood feud in northern Albania. Scott Anderson, "The Curse of Blood and Vengeance," *New York Times Magazine*, December 26, 1999, 29.

13. Alasdair MacIntyre, *After Virtue* (Notre Dame, Ind.: University of Notre Dame Press, 1981), 124.

14. MacIntyre, 122.

15. Pollock and Maitland, 31. In addition, the family or clan as the organizing unit of society was gradually replaced, in the western world at least, by the individual. The individual became responsible for his own acts and this responsibility did not automatically extend to his family or clan. See, for example, Maine and Dwight, 180.

16. Judith Mossman, *Wild Justice: A Study of Euripides' Hecuba* (Oxford: Clarendon Press, 1995), 171.

17. Mary Margaret MacKenzie, *Plato on Punishment* (Berkeley: University of California Press, 1981), 106.

18. MacKenzie, 107.

19. Treston, 26.

20. Homer, *Iliad*, book XVI, trans. Stanley Lombardo (Indianapolis: Hackett, 1997), 430.

21. Homer, *Iliad*, book XXI, 32–34.

22. Homer, *Iliad*, book IX, 652–57.

23. The passage depicting the Shield of Achilles depicts two men arguing over blood revenge or blood money and pleading their cases before the elders. Book XVIII, 536–40. Treston, 34, finds this reference to a *wergeld* and arbitration before a council oddly out of place and not typical to the homeric world. A better interpretation, though, is that the greatness and richness of the the *Iliad* lies in the fact that in something like the Shield of Achilles, which depicts routine domestic life as opposed to the scenes of war that dominate the poem, the *Iliad* offers an alternative to itself. See Sheila Murnaghan's introduction in the *Iliad*, xlviii.

24. Homer, *Iliad*, book XXIV, 541–43.

25. James Boyd White calls this an "impossible community" from which Priam and Achilles, products of the heroic society, cannot move: "It is beyond the capacity of the human mind to imagine Achilles and Priam moving out of

this moment as reformers of the world, trying to change their culture or to alter the nature of man. . . . Nor can one imagine Achilles, knowing what he now knows, . . . returning to the battle. . . ." *When Words Lose Their Meaning: Constitutions and Reconstitutions of Language, Character, and Community* (Chicago: University of Chicago Press, 1984), 54. This is one of few depictions of the ending of a cycle of revenge by human rather than divine means.

26. Davie, 210.

27. But see Anne Pippin Burnett, *Revenge in Attic and Later Tragedy* (Berkeley: University of California Press, 1998), 65–98.

28. See, for example, Mossman's discussion of Hecuba's revenge.

29. Homer, *Odyssey*, Albert Cook, trans. and ed. (New York: Norton, 1974), Book IV, lines 38–39.

30. Homer, *Odyssey*, book III, line 306.

31. Treston, 277. Treston posits that two distinct social strata observed different modes of blood-vengeance: the Achaean and the Pelasgian. For the Achaeans, vengeance was a personal duty that required a death. For the Pelasgians, who were more tribal, payment (*wergeld*) was permitted, as was exile; only rarely was the outcome death (26–27ff).

32. MacKenzie notes that the audiences for the Greek tragedians would already have been familiar with the story being dramatized and thus could focus their attention on the characters and the arguments being made by the writer. MacKenzie, 121–22.

33. Euripides, *Orestes*, in *The Complete Greek Tragedies*, vol. 4, ed. David Grene and Richard Lattimore, trans. William Arrowsmith (Chicago: University of Chicago Press,1959), lines 497–507.

34. Aeschylus, *Oresteia, The Libation Bearers*, trans. Richard Lattimore (1953), lines 121, 123.

35. Aeschylus, *The Libation Bearers*, lines 143–44.

36. Aeschylus, *The Libation Bearers*, line 70.

37. Aeschylus, *The Libation Bearers*, line 277.

38. Aeschylus, The Libation Bearers, lines 276–77. That Orestes hesitates to take revenge is somewhat surprising in that he comes from a long line of people who seemingly delighted in it. Orestes' grandfather, Atreus, wreaked grim vengeance on his brother Thyestes after Thyestes seduced Atreus' wife and disputed the throne of Argos. Thyestes was defeated and driven out until he returned as a suppliant with his children. Atreus, in pretended reconciliation, invited Thyestes and his children to a feast. He slaughtered all but one of Thyestes' children and served them in a concealing dish to their father, who ate them. When Thyestes discovered what had happened, he cursed the house of Atreus and fled with his remaining son, Aegisthus. Atreus' sons, Menelaus and Agamemnon, married Helen and Clytemnestra respectively. Clytemnestra bore Orestes, Electra, and Iphigenia. When Paris of Troy seduced Helen and carried her away, Agamemnon and Menelaus organized a great expedition to win her back—the Trojan War. The army, on its way to Troy, gathered at Aulis and was held there by bad weather. A prophet divined that the weather resulted from Artemis' anger and Agamemnon was forced to sacrifice his daughter (and Orestes' and Electra's sister) Iphigenia to appease Artemis. During Agamemnon's absence, Aegisthus (Thyestes' surviving child) returned to Argos, took Clytemnestra as his mistress, and ruled with her. When Agamemnon returned to Argos after the war, bringing with him his mistress Cassandra, Clytemnestra and Aegisthus killed them, in part to avenge Iphigenia's murder.

39. The Furies may have originally been harmless ghosts or even good spirits, who evolved into ghosts of humans who were unjustly killed. The word *Erinyes* (or *Erinnys*) came to mean ghosts who are angry because they have been murdered. In Homer, the Erinyes are no longer human souls, but the avengers of those murdered. See Treston, 109–10; Davie, 121. Davie writes that even in early societies a person who failed in his duty to take blood revenge for a slain relative would be haunted by the slain's enraged ghost.

40. Aeschylus, *The Libation Bearers*, lines 1048–50.

41. Aeschylus, *The Eumenides*, line 46.

42. Aeschylus was the first to bring the Erinyes on stage and to describe them this fully. See Jane Ellen Harrison, *Prolegomena to the Study of Greek Religion* (Cambridge: Cambridge University Press, 1922), 223.

43. Davie, 121.

44. Aeschylus, *The Eumenides*, line 425.

45. Aeschylus, *The Eumenides*, lines 358–68. Since Aeschylus' *Oresteia* was written after the emergence of the pollution doctrine, Orestes' act had to be buttressed by Apollo's intervention or it would have been rejected outright by the audience.

46. Aeschylus, *The Eumenides*, line 470.

47. Aeschylus, *The Eumenides*, lines 471–2.

48. Aeschylus, *The Eumenides*, lines 804–7.

49. Aeschylus, The Eumenides, lines 480–85. This is Aeschylus' version of the establishment of the Areopagus Council at Athens. Aeschylus made a major innovation in that he made the trial of Orestes the first at Areopagus (it was probably the third) and the occasion of the Council's foundation, as well as the first trial for homicide to be held anywhere. See Alan H. Sommerstein's introduction to Aeschylus, *Oresteia* (Cambridge: Cambridge University Press, 1989), 5. Treston reviews various hypotheses about the origin of homicide courts and links the development to the pollution doctrine and the fact that an unrequited murder brought the god's anger on the community or state. Thus a murderer had to appear before a court (92–93).

50. Paul Gewirtz describes the Furies as "emotional forces in life and law" rather than emotion as opposed to reason. He points out that their arguments before Athena's court are reasoned, not emotional. He states: "What the Furies most clearly represent—call it fear, conscience, vengeance—is not a 'threat' to law in the *Oresteia*'s scheme. Rather, Fury is law's partner. It reinforces a respect for legal rights." Paul Gewirtz, "Aeschylus' Law," *Harvard Law Review* 101 (1988): 1043, 1047–48.

51. Athena's vote has given rise to much controversy. Her explanation that she is "always for the male" because no mother gave her birth (lines 735–40) seems unconvincing. A better explanation might be that her vote signals an official approval of Orestes' revenge murder, albeit an approval that is not automatically given as it might have been a century earlier. See, Michael Gagarin, "The Vote of Athena," *American Journal of Philology* 96 (1975): 121 for a bibliography on the topic of Athena's vote.

52. Aeschylus, *The Eumenides*, lines 780–82.

53. Aeschylus, *The Eumenides*, lines 804–7.

54. Aeschylus, *The Eumenides*, lines 824–26.

55. Aeschylus, *The Eumenides*, line 916.

56. Harrison points out that this transformation never explicitly occurs in the play although the title "Eumenides" became attached to the play. Harrison, 252.

57. Harrison, 256.

58. Barnes and Teeters, 399.

59. The Code of Hammurabi (c. 1752 B.C.) provided that "If a man puts out the eye of a free man, they shall put out his eye. If he breaks the bone of a free man they shall break his bone." Diamond, 100.

60. Driver and Mills, 497.

61. Driver and Mills, 409. The authors show a complex chart by which the Babylonian Code regulated composition.

62. Jacoby, 125.

63. Treston, 2.

64. Lea cites an Anglo-Saxon proverb quoted in the laws of Edward the Confessor as collected by William the Conqueror: "Buy off the spear from thy side or endure it" (17).

65. Jolliffe, 3. In some early codes that were the laws of barbarian peoples of western Europe and England from the sixth to the tenth centuries A.D., blood feuds were avoided by payment, for example, of a great number of cattle to a victim's kinship group. Codes set the amount required for adequate compensation for both death and injury. See Diamond, 64–65. The amounts were fixed by social class. Diamond puts the development of composition at the late Early Code stage. Lea, 17, notes that many ancient codes had an appropriate price for every offense against person and property; the Welsh codes rated each eyelash at a penny.

66. Maine and Dwight, 272–73. See also Davie for a discussion of other societies that practiced a version of blood money. Davie also delineates other practices such as rituals, which some societies use to end a blood feud. 211. See also Luke Owen Pike, *A History of Crime in England: Illustrating the Changes of Law in the Progress of Civilization*, vol. 1 (London: Smith, Elder, 1873), 42–43, for a discussion of the development of compensation as an alternative to a blood feud.

67. For example, the Israelites were prohibited by God from accepting payment for a murder. See Numbers 35: 31 (New English Bible translation). Well before the Christian era, both the Jews and the Romans had done away with payment as compensation. See Miller, 144.

68. Diamond, 64.

69. See Jacoby, 67ff. Jacoby dates the change from individual revenge to the pollution doctrine to the seventh century B.C., as does Treston.

70. Diamond, 93.

71. Treston, 174.

72. Recently, a news report appeared about a ten-year-old boy executing the man who had been convicted by an Islamic court of murdering the boy's father. Thousands watched this officially sanctioned act of revenge in a sports stadium in Kandahar, Afghanistan, during the last months of the Taliban's reign there. Under the Taliban's interpretation of Islamic law, relatives of the victim, in this case the eldest male accompanied by his mother, sister, and younger brother, carry out the execution.

73. Treston, 138–41.

74. Numbers 35: 33–34.

75. God, of course, could delegate the taking of revenge as is done in Numbers 31: "The Lord spoke to Moses and said, 'You are to exact vengeance for Israel on the Midianites and then you will be gathered to your father's kin.'" Numbers 31: 1–2.

76. Psalms 103: 8; Joel 2: 13; Jonah 4: 2.

77. Isaiah 34: 6, 8.

78. Isaiah 63:3. See, for example, H. G. L. Peel, *The Vengeance of God: The Meaning of Root NQM and the Function of the NQM-Texts in the Context of Divine Revelation in the Old Testament* (Leiden: E.J. Brill, 1994).

79. Joshua 10: 13. Some scholars suggest that the revenge has a consequentialist function as well as a deontological one in that the revenge purged the wrongdoer and readied him for heaven. See *Encyclopedia Judaica*, vol. 2 (New York: Macmillan, 1972), 1331.

80. Judges 16: 28.

81. Judges 5: 7.

82. Romans 2: 7–9.

83. Often the king incurred not only the right but also the obligation to punish. In some instances, if the king pardoned a wrongdoer, the guilt then fell on the king himself. See Sir Walter Moberly, *The Ethics of Punishment* (New York: Archon Books, 1968), 99.

84. For many, even in contemporary times, this remains a critical distinction between revenge and retribution. See, for example, Robert Nozick, *Philosophical Explanations* (Cambridge, Mass.: Harvard University Press, 1981), 367.

Chapter Two. The Demonizing of Revenge

1. Much has been written about the more subtle differences between revenge and retribution that are not critical to my point. Most agree with my semantic distinction: if the victim or victim's family enacts it, it's called revenge; if the state enacts it, it's called retribution. See, for example, Jeffrie G. Murphy and Jean Hampton, *Forgiveness and Mercy* (Cambridge: Cambridge University Press, 1988); Robert Nozick, *Philosophical Explanations* (Cambridge, Mass.: Harvard University Press, 1981).

2. Cleaver, *A Plaine and Familiar Exposition of the Ten Commandments* (ed. 1618), 267, cited in Fredson Thayer Bowers, *Elizabethan Revenge Tragedy: 1587–1642* (Princeton, N.J.: Princeton University Press, 1940), 13.

3. Daniel Tuvil, *Essayes, Morall and Theologicall* (1609), cited in Bowers, 13.

4. Joseph Butler, "Upon Resentment," in *Butler's Fifteen Sermons* (1726), ed. T. A. Roberts (London: C. Tinling, 1970), 78.

5. Joseph Butler, "Upon Forgiveness of Injuries," in Roberts, 82.

6. Butler, "Upon Forgiveness of Injuries," in Roberts, 83. What is particularly interesting about this remark is the expansion of "family" from a unit related by blood to the entire community, and, along with this expansion, the notion that a wrong is not committed against an individual or kinship unit, but against the community at large.

7. Bowers, 155.

8. Thomas Kyd, *The Spanish Tragedy*, ed. Thomas W. Ross (Berkeley: University of California Press, 1968), 1 (editor's introduction).

9. Kyd, act IV, scene v, lines 1–12, 101.

10. Charles A. Hallett and Elaine S. Hallett, *The Revenger's Madness: A Study of Revenge Tragedy Motifs* (Lincoln: University of Nebraska Press, 1980), 11. Bowers denotes 1587–1607 as the "golden era of the true Kydian revenge tragedy" (109).

11. John Marston, *Antonio's Revenge: The Second Part of Antonio and Mellida*, ed.

G. K. Hunter (Lincoln: University of Nebraska Press, 1965), act I, scene I, lines 17–18.

12. Marston, act III, scene i, line 171.

13. Eleanor Prosser, *Hamlet and Revenge*, 2nd ed. (Stanford, Calif.: Stanford University Press, 1971), 63. Other scholars of the revenge plays, however, claim that the suppression of the urge for revenge had a class bias and that "an Elizabethan gentlemen disregarded without a qualm the ethical and religious opinion of his day which condemned private revenge, and felt obliged by the more powerful code of honor to revenge personally any injury offered him." Bowers, 37.

14. Prosser, 5.

15. In 1610, James I issued a proclamation against dueling, and the drama from 1620–1630 is described as "propaganda plays." See, generally Bowers, 186 ff.

16. Immanuel Kant, "On the Right to Punish and Grant Clemency," in *The Metaphysical Elements of Justice*, Part 1 of *The Metaphysics of Morals*, trans. John Ladd, 2nd ed. (Indianapolis: Hackett, 1999), sec. 49 [6:331]. I do not mean to oversimplify Kant's writing on punishment, which continues to be widely (and hotly) debated. See, for example, Tom Sorrell, "Punishment in a Kantian Framework," in *Punishment and Political Theory*, Matt Matravers, (Portland, Ore.: Hart, 1999), 20–23.

17. Immanuel Kant, "The Doctrine of Virtue," in *The Metaphysics of Morals* (1785), trans. and ed. Mary Gregor (Cambridge: Cambridge University Press, 1996), sec. 36 [6: 461], 208. Despite Kant's overt eschewing of emotions, some commentators have remarked that his choice of language when discussing punishment reveals someone greatly influenced by them: "Indeed, the zeal with which Kant advocated retribution may excuse a doubt whether he was not himself much influenced on this matter by rather primitive emotion." James Heath, *Elizabethan-Century Penal Theory* (London: Oxford University Press, 1963), 10. Nietzsche noted parenthetically that "the categorical imperative smells of cruelty." Friedrich Nietzsche, "Second Treatise: Guilt, Bad Conscience, and Related Matters," in *On the Genealogy of Morality: A Polemic* (1887), trans. Maudemarie Clark and Alan J. Swenson (Indianapolis: Hackett, 1980), sec. 6: 23, 41.

18. G. W. F. Hegel, *Elements of the Philosophy of Right* (1821), ed. Allen W. Wood, trans. H. B. Nisbet (Cambridge: Cambridge University Press, 1991), sec. 101, 129.

19. Hegel, *Elements*, sec. 101, 129.

20. Hegel, *Elements*, sec. 100, 126.

21. Hegel, *Elements*, sec. 100, 126.

22. Hegel, *Elements*, sec. 101, 129.

23. Michael S. Moore, "The Moral Worth of Retribution," in *Responsibility, Character, and the Emotions*, ed. Ferdinand Schoeman (Cambridge: Cambridge University Press, 1987) 82; see also Herbert Morris, "Persons and Punishment," in *On Guilt and Innocence: Essays in Legal Philosophy and Moral Psychology* (Berkeley: University of California Press, 1976), 46; and for an interesting critique of Moore and Morris, see David Dolinko, "Three Mistakes of Retributivism," *UCLA Law Review* 39 (1992): 1623.

24. Moore. This insightful piece first alerted me to the connection between the demonizing of revenge and retribution and Nietzsche's *ressentiment*.

25. Nietzsche, II, 11, 49.

26. Nietzsche, II, 11, 49.

27. Nietzsche, II, 11, 48.

28. John R. Reed, *Dickens and Thackeray: Punishment and Forgiveness* (Athens: Ohio University Press, 1995), 132.

29. F. H. Bradley in a 1894 essay, cited in H. B. Acton in *The Philosophy of Punishment: A Collection of Papers* (London: Macmillan,1969), 10.

30. Herbert L. Packer, *The Limits of the Criminal Sanction* (Stanford, Calif.: Stanford University Press, 1968), 9.

31. A. C. Ewing, *The Morality of Punishment* (London: Kegan Paul, 1929), 32.

32. 32. K. G. Armstrong, "The Retributivist Hits Back," in Acton, 139.

33. Acton, 71.

34. See, generally, H. B. Acton's Introduction to *The Philosophy of Punishment* (1969), 9–38. Also see Dolinko, 1634–42, for a recent discussion of the problem of making penalties proportional to crimes under a retributivist theory.

35. John David Mabbott, "Punishment," *MIND* 48 (1939): 152.

36. *Williams v. New York*, 337 U.S. 241, 248 (1949) (Justice Black).

37. Wayne R. LaFave and Austin W. Scott, Jr., *Handbook on Criminal Law* (St. Paul, Minn.: West, 1972), 24. The latest edition of LaFave and Scott deletes those words.

38. Murphy and Hampton, 2–3. Other scholars, however, argue that retributivism is enjoying a comeback. See, for example, Dolinko, who sees the resurgence of retributivism as being responsible for inflexible sentencing and lack of compassion for the social conditions that can produce criminals, as well as for the increased support of the death penalty; and Michael S. Moore, who attempts to rehabilitate retributivism in part by distinguishing between retributive urges that are legitimate moral outrage at criminals and those that are pathological cases of emotion run amok. Moore, "The Moral Worth of Retributivism," 191. While this debate is important and worthwhile, my interest is in the link between retributivism and the need to respect genuine feelings of anger and resentment that victims have toward their wrongdoers. The recent restorative justice movement can be seen as moving toward this end. Restorative justice "is based on the assumption that the response to crime cannot be effective without the joint involvement of victims, offenders, and the community . . . [and] on the principle that justice is best served when each of these parties receive fair and balanced attention, are actively involved in the justice process and gain tangible benefits from their interactions." Gordon Bazemore, "Three Paradigms for Juvenile Justice," in *Restorative Justice: International Perspectives*, ed. Burt Galaway and Joe Hudson (Monsey, N.Y.: Criminal Justice Press, 1996), 37, 46.

39. See, for example, Russell L. Christopher, "Deterring Retributivism: The Injustice of 'Just' Punishment," *Northwestern Law Review* 96 (2002): 843.

40. Niccolo Machiavelli, *The Discourses of Niccolo Machiavelli*, I, 7, trans. Leslie J. Walker, S.J. (London: Routledge and Kegan Paul, 1975), 228.

41. Francis Bacon, "Of Revenge," in *Essays and Apothegms of Francis Lord Bacon* (1624), ed. John Buchan (London: Walter Scott,1922), 11.

42. Bacon, 11.

43. *The Whole Treatise of the Cases of Conscience . . . by M. W. Perkins*, cited in Bowers, 36.

44. Adam Smith, *The Theory of Moral Sentiment* (1759), reprint (Oxford: Clarendon Press, 1976), 320.

45. Smith, 38.

46. Smith, 86.

47. Smith, 71.

48. An interesting literary example of the urge toward revenge residing in the gentlest of hearts, which was brought to my attention by Jean Hampton, can be found in Dostoyevsky's *The Brothers Karamazov*. The cynical brother, Ivan, tells the gentle Christian brother, Alyosha, a gruesome story of cruelty and injustice. When Ivan asks him what should be done to the wrongdoer, Alyosha instinctively responds, "Shoot him!" Fyodor Dostoyevsky, *The Brothers Karamazov*, trans. David Magarshack (New York: Penguin, 1982), 284, cited in Jean Hampton, "Correcting Harms Versus Righting Wrongs: The Goal of Retribution," *UCLA Law Review* 39 (1992).

49. Thomas Carlyle, "Latter-Day Pamphlet on Model Prisons" (No. 2, March 1850), in *Carlyle's Latter-Day Pamphlets*, ed. M. K. Goldberg and J. P. Seigel (Port Credit, Ont.: Canadian Federation for the Humanities, 1983), 99.

50. James Fitzjames Stephen, *Liberty, Equality, Fraternity* (London: Smith, Elder, 1874), 162. Moreover, this sense that the desire for revenge lies in the nature of humankind has maintained its hold. The United States Supreme Court has more than once acknowledged the likelihood that state failure can result in the taking back of the "right" to take revenge: "The instinct for retribution is part of the nature of man, and channeling that instinct in the administration of criminal justice serves an important purpose in promoting the stability of a society governed by law. When people begin to believe that organized society is unwilling or unable to impose upon criminal offenders the punishment they 'deserve,' then there are sown the seeds of anarchy—of self-help, vigilante justice, and lynch law." *Furman v. Georgia*, 408 U.S. 238, 308 (1972) (Stewart, J., concurring).

51. Stephen, 162.

52. Hallett and Hallett, 8; Bowers, 104.

53. Harold Bloom observes that "Shakespeare created him [Hamlet] to be as ambivalent and divided a consciousness as a coherent drama could sustain." Harold Bloom, *Shakespeare: The Invention of the Human* (New York: Riverhead Books, 1998), 387.

54. William Shakespeare, *The Tragedy of Hamlet: Prince of Denmark*, ed. Sylvan Barnet (New York: Signet, 1998), I, v, lines 23–25.

55. *Hamlet*, I, v, line 81.

56. *Hamlet*, I, ii, line 188. Hamlet compares his father to Hyperion, Jove, Mars and Mercury in III, iv, lines 57–59. Maynard Mack writes in *Killing the King* (New Haven, Conn.: Yale University Press, 1973), 79: the "conjunction of Hyperion with Jove, Mars with Mercury, makes old Hamlet a true Renaissance ideal, displaying the perfect balance of virtues—and indeed the seal of every god."

57. *Hamlet*, I, v, line 85.

58. *Hamlet*, I, v, line 86.

59. Hallett and Hallett describe Senecan ghosts as "intermediaries between supernatural forces and mankind. They stress with an urgency that arises from man's most primitive instincts the need to right an imbalance resulting from some unnatural violation of human life" (21).

60. Hallett and Hallett, 38.

61. *Hamlet*, IV, vii, lines 107–9.

62. *Hamlet*, IV, vi, line 126.

63. See, for example, Lily B. Campbell, "Theories of Revenge in Renaissance England," in *Collected Papers of Lily B. Campbell* (New York: Russell and Russell, 1968), 155.

64. Some argue for a clear contrast between the two Hamlets, father and son,

in that the ghost is a warrior fit for Icelandic saga and the prince is a university intellectual, representative of a new age. See, Peter Alexander, *Hamlet, Father and Son* (Oxford: Clarendon Press, 1955).

65. *Hamlet*, I, v, lines 29–31.
66. *Hamlet*, II, ii, lines 593–597.
67. *Hamlet*, I, v, line 187.
68. *Hamlet*, II, ii, line 247.
69. Erich Fromm, *The Anatomy of Human Destructiveness* (New York: Holt, Rinehart, and Winston, 1973), 273.
70. *Hamlet*, I, v, line 91.
71. *Hamlet*, I, v. lines 95–112.
72. *Hamlet*, V, ii, lines 345–49.
73. *Hamlet*, I, v, line 172.
74. *Hamlet*, V, ii, line 357.
75. *Hamlet*, V, ii, lines 380–81.

Chapter Three. Language, Violence, and Oppression

1. Pietro Marongiu and Graeme Newman, *Vengeance: The Fight Against Injustice* (Totowa, N.J.: Rowman and Littlefield, 1987), 164. One has only to look at contemporary movies to see how widespread the urge for revenge and the approval of it are, especially when the state fails to act. Since 2000, widely seen (and award-winning) movies that celebrate revenge include *Collateral Damage, The Patriot, Gladiator,* and *In the Bedroom.* In a *New York Times* article entitled "Vigilante Vengeance: Hollywood's Response to Primal Fantasies," David Edelstein writes of the acclaimed *In the Bedroom* in which a mild-mannered small-town doctor played by actor Tom Wilkinson coldbloodedly kills his son's killer. Edelstein notes that "Many people, this writer included . . . felt a surge of satisfaction when Mr. Wilkinson pulled the trigger." *New York Times,* Arts and Leisure Section, February 10, 2002, 15.

2. This is not to say that forgiveness, should an individual decide to follow this course, is not a good thing, only that forgiveness is personal and not something a state can or should demand of its citizens. See Jeffrie G. Murphy and Jean Hampton, *Forgiveness and Mercy* (Cambridge: Cambridge University Press, 1988).

3. Richard Goldstone, Foreword to Martha Minow, *Between Vengeance and Forgiveness: Facing History After Genocide and Mass Violence* (Boston: Beacon Press, 1998), x.

4. The Bible contains a story in which a parade is held for the victim as a means of balancing the harm done to her. Jean Hampton relates it thus (footnotes omitted): "the Persian King Ahasuerus marries the Hebrew woman Esther, whose uncle Mordecai had helped the King in the past to defeat two would-be usurpers of his throne. Mordecai offended one of the King's highest counsellors, named Haman, by refusing to show obeisance to him. Haman then decided to destroy not only Mordecai, but also all the Jewish people, and was permitted by the King to construct a plan to do so after Haman convinced him that these people were dangerous and disrespectful of his rule. However, the King began to feel guilty about the treatment Mordecai had received, given Mordecai's previous help to him. So the King decided to honor Mordecai in some way, and asked Haman, 'What shall be done to the man whom the king delights to honor?' Assuming he would be the honoree, Haman said, 'For the man whom

the king delights to honor, let royal robes be brought, which the king has worn, and the horse on which the king has ridden, and on whose head a royal crown is set; and . . . [find a servant to] conduct the man on horseback through the open square of the city, proclaiming before him; "Thus shall it be done to the man whom the king delights to honor." The King agreed to Haman's plan, only the man he honored was Mordecai, and the servant he chose to escort him through the city was Haman. Haman's reaction? Following the parade he 'hurried to his house, mourning' and was told by his wife and friends that he had begun to 'fall' before Mordecai." Hampton argues that this is a "successful retributive response" because the parade conveyed the message of Mordecai's value and supplanted Haman's message of superiority over him. Jean Hampton, "Correcting Harms Versus Righting Wrongs: The Goal of Retribution," *UCLA Law Review* 39 (1992): 1695–96. Hampton argues elsewhere that even forgiveness can be a kind of getting back.

5. Elaine Scarry, *The Body in Pain: The Making and Unmaking of the World* (New York: Oxford University Press, 1985), 4.

6. Scarry, 19.

7. Terence Coonan (quoting Lawrence Weschler) calls this the "ultimate message of the torturer"—that any utterance the victim makes is not heard. Terence S. Coonan, "Rescuing History: Legal and Theological Reflections on the Task of Making Former Torturers Accountable," *Fordham International Law Journal* 20 (1996): 512.

8. Jacobo Timerman, *Prisoner Without a Name, Cell Without a Number* (New York: Knopf, 1981), 32–3.

9. *Nunca Más: The Report of the Argentine National Commission on the Disappeared* (1984), English trans. (New York: Farrar Straus Giroux, 1986), 30.

10. *Nunca Más*, 36.

11. In *Unspeakable Acts, Ordinary People: The Dynamics of Torture* (New York: Knopf, 2000), 255, John Conroy calls torture "infectious"—that one country learns to torture from another and the incidence of torture increases.

12. Scarry, 27.

13. *Nunca Más*, 20.

14. Scarry, 20. In *Torture and Eucharist: Theology, Politics, and the Body of Christ* (Malden, Mass.: Blackwell, 1998), 28, William Cavanaugh makes the same point about the situation in Chile under Pinochet: "in most cases the [torture] victim cannot tell the agents anything they do not already know, and certainly nothing that could be of even minimal importance to the regime." Lawrence Weschler, in *A Miracle, a Universe: Settling Accounts with Torturers* (New York: Pantheon, 1990), 125, quotes a Uruguyan torture victim: "They weren't really after any information—they knew everything already, and had everybody's name. It was all just part of the process." A torture victim in Ireland reported: "I felt so helpless and isolated that I would have told anybody anything. The interrogations were nothing for me because I wasn't in the position to tell them what they wanted to know. I admitted to being in everything but the crib [with the baby Jesus in Bethlehem], and if they had asked me I would have said, 'Yes, the crib as well." Conroy, 7. In *Nunca Más*, victims reveal that they did not even understand the questions they were asked because the questions were phrased in the jargon of the torturers. One torture victim testified that "If they wanted you to reply that you had seen San Martin on horseback the previous day they succeeded" (29, 43). George Orwell, of course, knew that torture could destroy the personality and force the victim to confess to anything. In *1984*, Winston Smith,

the would-be rebel against the new order is tortured and the book concludes with Winston "in the public dock, confessing everything, implicating everybody." George Orwell, *1984* (New York: New American Library, 1981), 245.

15. *Truth and Reconciliation Report of South Africa* (1998), extract 4, sec. 13.

16. Scarry, 35.

17. Cavanaugh, 31.

18. Cavanaugh, 30.

19. Scarry, 57.

20. *Nunca Más,* 22–25.

21. Scarry, 40–41. In Argentina, torture victims were taken to the "kitchen" and to the "operating theatre." One torture device was called a "telephone." A metal bed frame, called a *parilla* (grill), was often used. *Nunca Más,* 23, 29. Police in Chicago allegedly used a radiator to burn a suspect. Conroy, 69–70.

22. Amos Funkenstein has suggested that "the systematic destruction of self-identity of inmates in concentration camps was also the attempt to destroy their narrative of themselves." Cited in Saul Friedlander, ed., *Probing the Limits of Representation: Nazism and the "Final Solution",* (Cambridge, Mass.: Harvard University Press, 1992), 77.

23. *Nunca Más,* 52.

24. According to Scarry, medicine is typically present by inversion in torture. She cites instances from Russia, Greece, the Philippines, Chile, Portugal, Brazil, Israel, and Uruguay in which doctors and medical procedures were used as part of the technology of torture. Scarry, 42. A interesting variation on this is revealed in *Nunca Más,* 38, where a prisoner says he was taken to a " 'Priest', who would be in charge of 'taking my confession'."

25. Paulina's psychological state is illustrated by testimony from real torture victims. See Anibal Quijada, "Barbed Wire Fence," trans. Jo Carrillo, in *Chilean Writers in Exile: Eight Short Novels,* ed. Fernando Alegria (Trumansburg, N.Y.: Crossing Press, 1982), 45; Conroy, 169–83.

26. Murphy and Hampton, 25.

27. Jean Hampton, "An Expressive Theory of Retribution," in *Retributivism and Its Critics,* ed. Wesley Cragg (Stuttgart: Steiner, 1992), 9.

28. Hampton, "An Expressive Theory," 12.

29. Jean Hampton, "Correcting Harms," 1672.

30. *Nunca Más,* 25.

31. Hampton uses as an example a story told by Bill T. Jones of a heinous act committed by a white farmer on his four black farmhands. The story, while grippingly unforgettable and an excellent example for Hampton's purposes, is easily rivaled by stories of torture that come out of the oppressive regimes considered here. See Hampton, "Correcting Harms," 1675ff.

32. Hampton, "Correcting Harms," 1677.

33. *Death and the Maiden,* Act One, scene three.

34. Hampton, "Correcting Harms," 1678.

35. Arthur Ripstein, "Responses to Humiliation," *Social Research* 64, 1 (Spring 1997). Ripstein writes that a state's "failure to punish means that the criminal's assessment of the appropriate way to treat the victim stands uncontested" (102).

36. See also, Robert E. Rodes, Jr., *The Legal Enterprise* (Port Washington, N.Y.: Kennikat Press, 1976), in which Rodes justifies retribution by an analysis of the disbalance of power that occurs in a harm: "I find an answer [as to whether punishment is justified] in looking at crime and punishment in light of what they have in common, the exercise of power. The criminal has exercised an

unjust power, a power to which he is not entitled, over a specific victim, over the community in general. . . . In punishing him, the government, on behalf of the community . . . exercises a just power over him. What the punishment restores is not the abstract metaphysical balance between what is and what is not subject to the will of the criminal, but a highly concrete superiority of just over unjust power" (85–86).

37. Murphy and Hampton, *Forgiveness and Mercy*, 12.

38. Scarry, 172–73.

39. *Death and the Maiden*, Act Two, scene one.

40. James Boyd White, *When Words Lose Their Meaning: Constitutions and Reconstitutions of Language, Character, and Community* (Chicago: University of Chicago Press, 1984), 5.

41. *Death and the Maiden*, Act Two, scene one.

42. *Death and the Maiden*, Act Two, scene one.

43. White, 284.

44. Ana Julia Cienfuegos and Cristina Monelli, "The Testimony of Political Repression As a Therapeutic Instrument," *American Journal of Orthopsychiatry* 53, no. 1 (January 1983): 43, 49.

45. Cienfuegos and Monelli, 46.

46. *Truth and Reconciliation Report of South Africa* (1998), extract 4, sec. 54.

47. Susan Bandes makes the crucial distinction between what victims desire and what the legal system ought to provide in "When Victims Seek Closure," *Fordham Urban Law Journal* 27 (2000): 1605.

48. In describing the situation under Pinochet in Chile, Cavanaugh writes that the regime's activity "atomizes the citizenry through fear, thereby dismantling other *social* bodies which would rival the state's authority over *individual* bodies" (2).

49. In South Africa, it was the Special Branch, in Nazi Germany the Gestapo (using a project tellingly called "Nacht und Nebel"—night and fog), in East Germany the Stasi.

50. Bruce B. Campbell, "Death Squads: Definitions, Problems, and Historical Context," in *Death Squads in Global Perspective: Murder with Deniability*, ed. Bruce B. Campbell and Arthur D. Brenner (New York: St. Martin's Press, 2000), 4.

51. Veena Das, "Sufferings, Theodicies, Disciplinary Practices, Appropriations," *International Science Journal* 154 (1997): 563, 567.

52. *Report of the Chilean National Commission on Truth and Reconciliation*, trans. Philip E. Berryman (Notre Dame, Ind.: Center for Civil and Human Rights, 1993), vol. 2, 795. See generally 133, 143.

53. In *Torture and Eucharist*, Cavanaugh cites the reply given by Chilean officials when the Interamerican Commission on Human Rights inquired on a mother's behalf about the whereabouts of Manuel Edgardo Cortez Joo: "Presumably this person has gone into hiding with the purpose of joining the clandestine extremist movement" (52). Manuel Edgardo was never seen again.

54. Belisario Betancur, Reinaldo Figueredo Planchart, and Thomas Buergenthal, *From Madness to Hope: The 12-Year War in El Salvador: Report of the Commission on the Truth for El Salvador* (New York: United Nations, 1993), 110.

55. *Nunca Más*, 131.

56. *Getting Away with Murder: Political Killings and "Disappearances" in the 1990s* (New York: Amnesty International, 1993), 8.

57. *Getting Away with Murder*, 51.

58. Timerman, 51.

59. *From Madness to Hope*, 110. This woman never saw her daughter again and the daughter is presumed to have been killed while in the custody of the air force (113).

60. Cavanaugh, 54.

61. Timerman, 43.

62. *Report of the Chilean National Commission on Truth and Reconciliation*, vol. 2, 778.

63. Cavanaugh, 53.

64. Glenn R. Randall and Ellen L. Lutz, *Serving Survivors of Torture: A Practical Manual for Health Professionals and Other Service Providers* (Waldorf, Md.: American Association for the Advancement of Science, 1991), 40.

65. Randall and Lutz, 69.

66. Interview with the mothers of Stompie Seipei and Koekie Zwane. July 2000, Johannesburg, South Africa, Notes on file with the author.

67. *Nunca Más*, 233.

68. Aeschylus, *Oresteia, The Libation Bearers*, trans. Richmond Lattimore (Chicago: University of Chicago Press, 1953), ll. 143–44.

69. Cavanaugh, 31. Cavanaugh uses the language of pollution: "the system of torture . . . seep[s] like poison into the groundwater of the subject classes" (46).

70. *Truth and Reconciliation Report of South Africa* (1998), extract 4, paragraph 124.

71. *Truth and Reconciliation Report of South Africa* (1998), extract 4, paragraph 22.

72. Carina Perelli, "Memoria de Sangre: Fear, Hope, and Disenchantment in Argentina," in *Remapping Memory: The Politics of TimeSpace*," ed. Jonathan Boyarin (Minneapolis: University of Minnesota Press, 1994), 43–44. See also Jaime Malamud-Goti, *Game Without End: State Terror and the Politics of Justice* (Norman: University of Oklahoma Press, 1996), 122–45.

73. Perelli, 45. Perelli notes that some groups such as the Madres of the Plaza de Mayo and some human rights organizations did manage to band together, but their action was very limited and "had no noticeable impact on the population" (46).

74. *Guatemala, Never Again*, REMHI, Recovery of Historical Memory Project: The Official Report of the Human Rights Office, Archdiocese of Guatemala (Maryknoll, N.Y.: Orbis Books, 1999), 45. Translation of *Guatemala, Nunca Más*.

75. Primo Levi writes that circumstances in Auschwitz were designed to make the prisoners isolated and alienated: "One entered hoping at least for the solidarity of one's companions in misfortune, but the hoped for allies, except in special cases, were not there; there were instead a thousand sealed off monads." Primo Levi, *The Drowned and the Saved*, trans. Raymond Rosenthal (New York: Simon and Schuster, 1988), 38.

76. Timerman, 51.

77. *Truth and Reconciliation Report of South Africa* (1998), extract 4, sec. 138.

78. Cavanaugh, 72–73. The word "martyr" derives from the word for "witness," and martyrs characteristically are able to voice opposition. (This, in fact, is usually why they are killed.) The oppressive regimes I write about here silenced any potential martyrs so that no one could bear witness. Robert Cover makes a similar point about violence, silence, and martyrdom in "Violence and the Word," in *Narrative, Violence, and the Law: The Essays of Robert Cover* (Ann Arbor, Mich.: University of Michigan Press, 1992), 207.

79. "La tortura: practica estatal mas fuerte que el amor," *Colleccion Reflexion y Debate*, Series Derechos Humanos, no. 5 (Nov. 1987), cited in Cavanaugh, 72.

Chapter Four. What Can Stories Do?

1. For an excellent survey and discussion of truth commissions and reports, see Priscilla B. Hayner, *Unspeakable Truths: Confronting State Terror and Atrocity* (New York: Routledge, 2001).

2. José Zalaquett, "Balancing Ethical Imperatives and Political Constraints: The Dilemma of New Democracies Confronting Past Human Rights Violations," *Hastings Law Journal* 43 (1992): 1425, 1430, citing Max Weber, "Politics as Vocation," *Essays in Sociology*, trans. H. H. Gerth and C. Wright Mills (New York: Oxford University Press, 1946). Weber elaborates the distinction: "This is not to say that an ethic of ultimate ends is identical with irresponsibility, or that an ethic of responsibility is identical with unprincipled opportunism. . . . However there is an abysmal contrast between conduct that follows the maxim of an ethic of ultimate ends—that is, in religious terms, 'The Christian does rightly and leaves the results with the Lord'—and conduct that follows the maxim of an ethic of responsibility, in which case one has to give an account of the foreseeable results of one's actions" (120–22). Ruti Teitel also makes this point in *Transitional Justice* (Oxford: Oxford University Press, 2000) writing: "What emerges is a pragmatic balancing of ideal justice with political realism" (213).

3. Zalaquett, 1433.

4. Jeanne M. Woods, "Reconciling Reconciliation," *UCLA Journal of International Law & Foreign Affairs* 3 (1998): 81, 89.

5. A major South African case, *Azanian Peoples Organization (AZAPO) and Others v. President of the Republic of South Africa and Others*, 1996, SALR 671 (CC), had, arguably and cynically, this result. AZAPO and the relatives of some of the best-known victims of the apartheid regime—Steven Biko, Griffith and Victoria Mxenge, and Dr. and Mrs. Fabian Ribeiro—challenged the portion (Sec. 20[7]) of the Promotion of National Unity and Reconciliation Act (which established the Truth and Reconciliation Commission) that allowed for amnesty in exchange for the truth from a perpetrator on the ground that their constitutional right to have a dispute settled by a court of law was violated. The Constitutional Court found that the provision was constitutional because the amnesty provision was critical to the political settlement and because it provided an incentive for truth-telling. These values trumped the plaintiffs' rights.

6. Richard Goldstone, "Justice as a Tool for Peace-Making: Truth Commissions and International Criminal Tribunals," *NYU Journal of International Law and Policy* 28 (1996): 485, 486.

7. Goldstone, 491.

8. Peter Goodrich, "Justice and the Trauma of Law: A Response to George Pavlich," *Studies in Law, Politics, and Society* 18 (1998): 271, 274. Others also take a more expansive view of justice. See, for example, Paul van Zyl, "Dilemmas of Transitional Justice: The Case of South Africa's Truth and Reconciliation Commission," *Journal of International Affairs* 52 (1999): 648, 659, who writes that "prosecutions and punishment are important components of justice, but they are only post hoc interventions. Justice encompasses the truth."

9. Goodrich, 274.

10. Goodrich, 275. Others also take the "justice as process" position. Bernard P. Dauenhauer writes that "for Ricoeur, the justice that ought to be the aim of responsible politics is one that is always in the making. It calls for an ongoing conversation about justice itself, a conversation that always calls upon and contests both convictions and criticisms of them." Bernard P. Dauenhauer, *Paul*

Ricoeur: The Promise and Risk of Politics (Lanham, Md.: Rowman and Littlefield, 1998), 319.

11. These seven are not meant to be exhaustive; there may well be other benefits. Additionally, they are *potential* benefits and are not necessarily realized in every or even any truth reports.

12. The line between victim and perpetrator, victim and nonvictim is not always clear. In Chile, for example, many of those who testified before the Commission, giving valuable details about those who disappeared, came out of guilt at having given over names under torture. They were indeed victims but came seeing themselves as guilty perpetrators.

13. See generally, Judith Lewis Herman, *Trauma and Recovery* (New York: Basic Books, 1992), 173–95; Frank M. Ochberg, ed., *Post-Traumatic Therapy and Victims of Violence* (New York: Bruner/Mazel, 1988).

14. Glenn R. Randall and Ellen L. Lutz, *Serving Survivors of Torture: A Practical Manual for Health Professionals and Other Service Providers* (Waldorf, Md.: American Association for the Advancement of Science, 1991), 117.

15. Ana Julia Cienfuegos and Cristina Monelli, "The Testimony of Political Repression as a Therapeutic Instrument, *American Journal of Orthopsychiatry* 53 (January 1983): 43, 50.

16. Richard Mollica, "The Trauma Story: The Psychiatric Care of Refugee Survivors of Violence and Torture," in Ochberg, ed., 304.

17. Susan J. Brison, "The Uses of Narrative in the Aftermath of Violence," in *On Feminist Ethics and Politics*, ed. Claudia Card (Lawrence: University of Kansas Press, 1999), 214.

18. Brison cites J. L. Austin's definition of "speech acts" as performative utterances: "the uttering of the sentence is . . . the doing of an action." Brison, 215, citing J. L. Austin, *How To Do Things with Words* (Cambridge, Mass.: Harvard University Press, 1962), 5.

19. Randall and Lutz, 101.

20. David Carr, *Time, Narrative, and History* (Bloomington: Indiana University Press, 1986), 91.

21. Paul Ricoeur, *Time and Narrative*, vol. 1, trans. Kathleen McLaughlin and David Pellauer (Chicago: University of Chicago Press, 1984), 31.

22. Walter R. Fisher, *Human Communication as Narration: Toward a Philosophy of Reason, Value, and Action* (Columbia: University of South Carolina Press, 1987), 62.

23. Carr, 65.

24. Hayden White, *The Content of the Form: Narrative Discourse and Historical Representation* (Baltimore: Johns Hopkins University Press, 1987). 1.

25. Roland Barthes, "Introduction to the Structural Analysis of Narratives," in *Image, Music, Text*, trans. Stephen Heath (London: Fontana, 1987), 79.

26. Alasdair MacIntyre, "How to Be a North American," lecture to the National Conference of State Humanities Councils, Chicago, Nov. 14, 1987.

27. Carr, 97.

28. Carr, 93–94.

29. That all victims feel healed is, of course, an overly simplistic conclusion, as Priscilla Hayner wisely points out. Some of those who testify feel retraumatized, rather than experiencing their testifying as cathartic. Post-traumatic stress syndrome symptoms can result from testifying, and some people worry that their testimony can result in acts of revenge from the people they name as perpetrators. Hayner recommends that support networks, some of which already exist, be expanded to help victims after they testify. Hayner, 53.

30. Marth Minow, *Between Vengeance and Forgiveness: Facing History After Genocide and Mass Violence* (Boston: Beacon Press, 1998), 66.

31. Minow, *Between Vengeance and Forgiveness*, 67. Those who treat survivors of human rights abuses note that some survivors can become trapped in the trauma story and need help in integrating the personal story into a larger picture. See, for example, Randall and Lutz, 101.

32. See, Desmond Tutu, *No Future Without Forgiveness* (London: Rider, 1999), chapter 6.

33. Minow, *Between Vengeance and Forgiveness*, 4.

34. Jean Hampton, "Correcting Harms Versus Righting Wrongs: The Goal of Retribution," *UCLA Law Review* 39 (1992): 1677.

35. Jacques Derrida defines justice as a relation or debt from one person to another and an "incalculable demand to treat the other on the other's terms." Derrida convincingly maintains that "To address oneself in the language of the other is, it seems, the condition of all possible justice."Jacques Derrida, "Force of Law: The 'Mystical Foundation of Authority,'" in *Deconstruction and the Possibility of Justice*, ed. Drucilla Cornell, Michael Rosenfeld, David Gray Carlson (New York: Routledge, 1992), 17. Thus even a trial, in which traditional notions of justice are enacted and perpetrators are punished, falls short of full and adequate justice if victims have not been able to tell their stories, if their ability to relate events in their own words has not been allowed (as it usually has not).

36. Hampton, "Correcting Harms," 1686.

37. See note 5 for a discussion of the AZAPO suit.

38. Interview with George Bizos, Johannesburg, South Africa, July 10, 2000 (notes on file with the author). Asmal, Asmal, and Roberts, in their observations of the postapartheid situation in South Africa agree, seeing the trials that had occurred in South Africa as expensive and largely ineffective in discovering the truth or adequately punishing the perpetrators. Kader Asmal, Louise Asmal, and Ronald Suresh Roberts, *Reconciliation Through Truth: A Reckoning of Apartheid's Criminal Governance*, 2nd ed. (New York: St. Martin's Press, 1997), 19–24.

39. Justice Albie Sachs, in *Dealing with the Past: Truth and Reconciliation in South Africa*, ed. Alex Boraine, Janet Levy, and Ronel Scheffer (Capetown: Institute for Democracy in South Africa,1995) (cited on TRC Homepage—www.truth.org.za/reading/beyond.htm). Sachs elaborates on these kinds of truth and two others in "The South African Truth Commission," *Montana Law Review* 63 (2002): 25.

40. Sachs, 25.

41. Telford Taylor writes that the legacy of Nuremberg differs from the actual trials: "Today, 'Nuremberg' is both what actually happened there and what people think happened, and the second is more important than the first. . . . It is not the bare record but the ethos of Nuremberg that we must reckon today." Telford Taylor, *Nuremberg and Vietnam: An American Tragedy* (Chicago: Quadrangle Books, 1970), 13–14.

42. See (for criticism of Nuremberg proceedings), William J. Bosch, *Judgment on Nuremberg: American Attitudes Toward the Major German War-Crime Trials* (Chapel Hill, N.C.: University of North Carolina Press, 1970). Additionally, the charter for the Tokyo trials, Japan's counterpart to Nuremberg, provided that "The Tribunal shall not be bound by technical rules of evidence . . . and shall admit any evidence that it deems to have probative value." Charter of the International Military Tribunal for the Far East, January 19, 1946, art. 13, T.I.A.S. No. 1589, 4 Bevans 20, 25 (as amended April 26, 1946, 4 Bevans 27, 30).

43. Graciela Fernandez Meijide et al., "The Role of Historical Inquiry in Cre-

ating Accountability for Human Rights Abuses," *Boston College Third World Law Journal* 12 (1992): 269. On the other hand, Tina Rosenberg, in *The Haunted Land: Facing Europe's Ghosts After Communism* (New York: Random House, 1995), 403, maintains that trials are crucial in Latin America: "while trials may endanger democracy's short term prospects in Latin America, they are crucial to its long-term health. The cycle of repression and impunity has continued for centuries because a class of powerful people holds itself above the law. Taking the military to account for its abuses in a court of law, thus establishing civilian control of the military and the primacy of law over force, is the only way to break that cycle."

44. Carina Perelli, "Memoria de Sangre: Fear, Hope, and Disenchantment in Argentina," in *Remapping Memory: The Politics of TimeSpace,* ed. Jonathan Boyarin (Minneapolis: University of Minnesota Press, 1994), 47.

45. See, Carlos Santiago Nino, *Radical Evil on Trial* (New Haven, Conn.: Yale University Press, 1996), 60–104.

46. Perelli, 49. In addition, a group of English-speaking moral and legal philosophers, in a "rather Athenian climate," discussed the legal and philosophical issues raised by the trial in public lectures. Nino, 84.

47. Nino, 90.

48. Perelli, 50. See also, Nino, 82–84, for some specific details of who testified and what they said.

49. Perelli, 50.

50. Terence S. Coonan, "Rescuing History: Legal and Theological Reflections on the Task of Making Former Torturers Accountable," *Fordham International Law Journal* 20 (1996): 522–53. The Punto Final Law established a sixty-day period beyond which no new charges could be brought; the Due Obedience Law established an irrebuttable presumption of innocence for soldiers and officers up to the rank of lieutenant colonel who had acted in due obedience to orders from superiors. See also Nino, 101.

51. Jaime Malamud-Goti, *Game Without End: State Terror and the Politics of Justice* (Norman: University of Oklahoma Press, 1996), 7.

52. Mark Osiel, *Mass Atrocity, Collective Memory, and the Law* (New Brunswick, NJ: Transaction, 1997), 3. Carlos Nino also lists as a critical benefit of trials the opportunity for public deliberation that they accord. Nino, 147.

53. Osiel, 3.

54. Osiel, 3.

55. Erna Paris, *Long Shadows: Truth, Lies, and History* (New York: Bloomsbury, 2001), 411.

56. In March of 2000, I attended a few days of the beginning of the trial of General Radislav Krstic at the International Criminal Tribunal for the Former Yugoslavia at The Hague. On the opening day, the general public and members of the press lined up for seats and the limited seating area was full. By the third day, there were only two or three observers. Krstic was being tried for masterminding and supervising the massacre of nearly 8,000 Muslims at the UN safe haven of Srebrenica and was at that time the highest ranking military person to have been tried at The Hague. A reporter who was the Paris bureau chief for the *Los Angeles Times* explained to me the fall-off in press attendance. He said that on the first day the story would be on the front page. The second day he could do a follow-up that would appear on page five. But by the third day, unless something unusual happened, there would be nothing new to say. The Hague is hard to get to. He just couldn't give it time. In *Long Shadows,* her recent book about

the shaping of historical memory, Erna Paris relates a similar experience when she observed the trial of Kupreskic and others at the ICTY: "A fair trial in the British Continental tradition is a tedious process that bogs down in the detail of evidence, and barring news of a sensation in the offing, the press will show up only at the beginning and the end" (399).

57. Eugene de Kock Amnesty Hearing, Pretoria, South Africa, July 10, 2000.

58. Jerry Richardson Amnesty Hearing, Johannesburg, South Africa, July 11–13, 2000.

59. Michael Ignatieff, "Articles of Faith," *Index on Censorship* 5, (1996): 113.

60. Zalaquett, "Balancing," 1437.

61. In a recent book, Adam Nossiter tells the story of the trial of Maurice Papon in Bordeaux in 1997. The use of a trial as a means of establishing the truth about the collaboration of some French bureaucrats and providing an official memory for France was undercut by legalistic maneuverings and grandstanding by lawyers. Not until the testimony of the descendants of the victims was truth articulated and recognized. Adam Nossiter, *Algeria Hotel: France, Memory and the Second World War* (Boston: Houghton Mifflin, 2001). France, of course, has resources beyond that of most, if not all, transitional democracies.

62. Mikhail M. Bakhtin, *Rabelais and His World*, trans. Helene Iswolsky (Cambridge, Mass.: MIT Press, 1965), 10.

63. Bakhtin, *Rabelais*, 8.

64. Bakhtin, *Rabelais*, 10.

65. Bakhtin, *Rabelais*, 10.

66. Bakhtin, *Rabelais*, 9.

67. Bakhtin, *Rabelais*, 10.

68. Bakhtin, *Rabelais*, 10.

69. Mikhail Bakhtin, *Problems of Dostoevsky's Poetics*, ed. And trans. Caryl Emerson (Minneapolis: University of Minnesota Press, 1984), 123.

70. Gillian Slovo, *Red Dust* (New York: Norton, 2002), 84.

71. Bakhtin, *Problems*, 124.

72. Bakhtin, *Problems*, 6.

73. Bakhtin, *Problems*, 110.

74. Hayden White, 1.

75. Hayden White, 1.

76. Martha Nussbaum, "Rational Emotion," in *Literature and Legal Problem Solving*, ed. Paul J. Heald (Durham, N.C.: Carolina Academic Press, 1998), 99.

77. Jean-François Lyotard, *The Différend: Phrases in Dispute*, trans. Georges Van Den Abbeele (Minneapolis: University of Minnesota Press, 1988), 9.

78. The idea that narratives provide a means by which an oppressed class can speak to the powerful has taken hold in the American legal community in the discussion of "outsider" narratives in the work of such legal scholars as Patricia Williams, Richard Delgado, Mari Matsuda, Derrick Bell, and many others.

79. Terence Coonan, 544. Coonan cites a definition provided by theologian Richard McBrien: "No theological principle or focus is more characteristic of Catholicism or more central to its identity than the principle of sacramentality. The Catholic vision sees God in and through all things: other people, communities, movements, events, places, objects, the world at large, the whole cosmos. The visible, the tangible, the finite, the historical—all these are actual or potential carriers of the divine presence." Richard P. McBrien, *Catholicism*, Study Edition (Minneapolis, Minn.: Winston Press, 1981), 1180.

80. Coonan, 544.

81. Coonan, 544.

82. Robert Jay Lifton, *The Broken Connection: On Death and the Continuity of Life* (New York: Simon and Schuster, 1979), 179. Susan Brison's description of the trauma of rape discussed earlier in this chapter also uses metaphors of dismemberment and fragmentation.

83. *Bullfinch's Mythology* (New York: Thomas Y. Crowell, 1970), 294.

84. McBrien, 758.

85. McBrien, 759, citing 1 Corinthians 11: 24–25.

86. McBrien, 762.

87. By sacrament, I mean a formal religious act that is sacred as a sign or symbol of a spiritual reality and by sacramental having the character of a sacrament.

88. In the play, Miranda maintains to Gerardo that he is not Paulina's torturer and thus cannot "confess." To placate Paulina and end the night of terror, Gerardo asks Paulina for the story and passes it on to Miranda, who then delivers the "confession" she requires. Paulina, however, plants small errors in her story (names of people, etc.) that Miranda inadvertently corrects in his rendering, making it quite likely that Paulina has correctly identified him.

89. Osiris, Bacchus, etc. The sacramental sense of storytelling is also related to the use of ritual for healing in some societies. In Zimbabwe, for example, the ritualistic telling of stories of harm rests "upon the assumption that what is known, consciously articulated, and confessed before a legitimate public authority . . . has been defused of its . . . power to harm." Pamela Reynolds, *Traditional Healers and Childhood in Zimbabwe* (Athens: Ohio University Press, 1996), xxxi.

Chapter Five. Telling Stories in a Search for Justice: The Argentinian, Chilean, and Salvadoran Truth Commissions

1. See, for example, Kathryn Abrams, "Hearing the Call of Stories," *California Law Review* 79 (1991): 971; Richard Delgado, "Storytelling for Oppositionists and Others: A Plea for Narrative," *Michigan Law Review* 87 (1989): 2411.

2. Hayden White, *The Content of the Form: Narrative Discourse and Historical Representation* (Baltimore: Johns Hopkins University Press, 1987), x–xi.

3. See, for example, Eric Alfred Havelock, *Preface to Plato* (Cambridge, Mass.: Harvard University Press, 1963).

4. Martha Nussbaum, *Love's Knowledge: Essays on Philosophy and Literature* (New York: Oxford University Press, 1990), 10–23.

5. Nussbaum, *Love's Knowledge*, 15.

6. Nussbaum, *Love's Knowledge*, 17.

7. Hayden White, ix.

8. Nussbaum, *Love's Knowledge*, 7.

9. See generally, Elaine Scarry, *The Body in Pain: The Making and Unmaking of the World* (New York: Oxford University Press, 1985), 60ff.

10. See generally, Mikhail M. Bakhtin, *The Problems of Dostoevsky's Poetics*, ed. and trans. Caryl Emerson (Minneapolis: University of Minnesota Press, 1984).

11. Bakhtin, *Problems*, 24.

12. Carlos Santiago Nino, *Radical Evil on Trial* (New Haven, Conn.: Yale University Press, 1996), 3.

13. The interethnic wars that broke out in the former Yugoslavia in 1991 are

a recent example of an unresolved past in which hatred and resentment festered and finally erupted.

14. Some, including Churchill, favored summary execution of the major Nazi figures. Many felt that the enormity of the atrocities exceeded the ken of any civilized judicial process. Nino, 5–6. See also Telford Taylor, *The Anatomy of the Nuremberg Trials: A Personal Memoir* (New York: Knopf, 1992); Drexel A. Sprecher, *Inside the Nuremberg Trial: A Prosecutor's Comprehensive Account* (Lanham, Md.: University Press of America, 1999).

15. "The new paradigm [begun at Nuremberg] empowers the individual, endowing her with legal personality and human rights enforceable against the state." Jeanne M. Woods, "Reconciling Reconciliation," *UCLA Journal of International Law & Foreign Affairs* 3 (1998): 81, 85.

16. Although prosecutions may be the traditional and perhaps expected response, "Many fledgling democracies have simply not had the power, popular support, legal tools, or conditions necessary to prosecute effectively." Stephen Landsman, "Alternative Responses to Serious Human Rights Abuses: Of Prosecutions and Truth Commissions," *Law & Contemporary Problems* 59 (1996): 84.

17. A number of recent books deal with the considerations involved in a country's deciding what measures to take; see, for example, Neil J. Kritz, ed., *Transitional Justice: How Emerging Democracies Reckon with Former Regimes*, 2 vols. (Washington, D.C.: United States Institute of Peace Press, 1995); A. James McAdams, ed., *Transitional Justice and the Rule of Law in New Democracies* (Notre Dame, Ind.: University of Notre Dame Press, 1997). In an article in the latter book, Juan Méndez writes: "The hardest question of all is how to pursue the objectives of justice and of reconciliation without falling into tokenism and a false morality that only thinly disguises the perpetuation of impunity." "In Defense of Transitional Justice," McAdams, 1.

18. Truth commission reports should not be seen as an exclusive remedy. They may and do certainly coexist with trials, reparations, and other responses. There is also a growing consensus that international law requires an investigation of human rights abuses, but little consensus exists about what precise form this investigation should take. See, Jo M. Pasqualucci, "The Whole Truth and Nothing But the Truth: Truth Commissions, Impunity and the Inter-American Human Rights System," *Boston University International Law Journal* 12 (1994): 321, 323; Priscilla Hayner, *Unspeakable Truths: Confronting State Terror and Atrocity* (New York: Routledge, 2001), 30–31.

19. Priscilla B. Hayner, "Fifteen Truth Commissions—1974 to 1994: A Comparative Study," *Human Rights Quarterly* 16 (1994): 607.

20. Some commissions turn over their findings (including names that may not have been published in the report) to the judiciary for possible prosecution.

21. Hayner, "Fifteen Truth Commissions," 637.

22. The notion of plot comes from Aristotle's *Poetics*. Plot is a combination of temporal succession and causality. E. M. Forster explained it this way: "'The king died and then the queen died' is a story. 'The king died, and then the queen died of grief' is a plot." E. M. Forster, *Aspects of the Novel* (New York: Harcourt, Brace, 1927).

23. Emplotment is what is employed when one writes a "full-fledged historical narrative, a coherent emplotment linking beginning, middle, and end within a specific *framework of interpretation*" (italics original). Saul Friedlander, ed., *Probing the Limits of Representation: Nazism and the "Final Solution"* (Cambridge, Mass.: Harvard University Press, 1992), 6.

24. Hayden White, 5. White differentiates between narratives and annals and chronicles, two other possibilities for the representation of historical reality. Annals consist of a list of events in chronological sequence. The chronicle, while it may wish to tell a story, usually fails to do so because it lacks narrative closure. "It does not so much conclude as simply terminate. It starts out to tell a story but breaks off *in medias res* . . . it leaves things unresolved" (5).

25. Graciela Fernandez Meijide et al, "The Role of Historical Inquiry in Creating Accountability for Human Rights Abuses," *Boston College Third World Law Journal* 12 (1992): 277; see also Charles S. Maier, "Doing History, Doing Justice: The Narrative of the Historian and of the Truth Commission," in *Truth v. Justice: The Morality of Truth Commissions*, ed. Robert I. Rotberg and Dennis Thompson (Princeton, N.J.: Princeton University Press, 2000), 261.

26. Meijede et al., 278.

27. G. W. F. Hegel, *Introduction to the Philosophy of History: With Selections from a Philosophy of Rights*, trans. Leo Rauch (Indianapolis, Ind.: Hackett, 1988), 64. A country that "is in the process of shaping itself . . . produces an intelligent and definite record of (and interest in) actions and events whose results are lasting" (65).

28. Paul Ricoeur, "Reflections on a New Ethos for Europe," *Philosophy and Social Criticism* 21 (1995): 516.

29. Cited in Brandon Hamber, "Will Reconciliation Follow Disclosure?"; http://www.csvr.org.za/articles/artrcbr.htm.

30. Perelli, 39.

31. Detailed discussions of the events leading up to the Argentinian commission may be found in Nino and in Wolfgang S. Heinz and Hugo Fruhling, *Determinants of Gross Human Rights Violations by State and State-Sponsored Actors in Brazil, Uruguay, Chile, and Argentina* (The Hague: Nijhoff , 1999).

32. Hayner, "Fifteen Truth Commissions," 597. Richard Goldstone, "Exposing Human Rights Abuses—A Help or Hindrance to Reconciliation?" *Hastings Constitutional Law Quarterly* 22 (1995): 607, 610, gives a slightly different history of truth commissions, seeing versions of them shortly after World War II in Denmark and Australia.

33. Nino, 60.

34. *Nunca Más: The Report of the Argentine National Commission on the Disappeared*, intro. Ronald Dworkin (New York: Farrar Straus Giroux, 1986), 428.

35. *Nunca Más*, 429.

36. *Nunca Más*, 431. After a while, the Depositions Department had to leave Fridays open to process the material collected during the week.

37. *Nunca Más*, 432.

38. *Nunca Más*, 435.

39. Congress successfully nullified the self-amnesty law, and several trials, including the "big trial" against the commanders, began in 1985. The Argentinian trials are discussed briefly in Chapter 4, 21–23. Also see, Nino, 81 ff.

40. Nino, 81.

41. Hayden White, 201.

42. *Nunca Más*, 1.

43. *Nunca Más*, 1.

44. *Nunca Más*, 1.

45. *Nunca Más*, 1.

46. *Nunca Más*, 5.

47. *Nunca Más*, 5–6.

48. *Nunca Más*, 2.

49. *Nunca Más*, 2.

50. Jaime Malamud-Goti, who as secretary of state was one of the architects of the trials, makes a similar point about the trials in Argentina. Jaime Malamud-Goti, *Game Without End: State Terror and the Politics of Justice* (Norman: University of Oklahoma Press, 1996).

51. *Nunca Más*, 9–10.

52. Frank Kermode, *The Sense of an Ending: Studies in the Theory of Fiction* (New York: Oxford University Press, 1966). Kermode defines "plot" as "an organization that humanizes time by giving it form" (45).

53. *Nunca Más*, 11.

54. *Nunca Más*, 9.

55. Kermode is helpful again: plot provides us a way "of bundling together perception of the present, memory of the past, and expectation of the future . . . that which was conceived of as merely successive becomes charged with past and future: what was *chronos* [passing time] becomes *kairos* [significant, teleological time]" (46).

56. *Nunca Más*, 9.

57. *Nunca Más*, 9.

58. *Nunca Más*, 7.

59. *Nunca Más*, 229.

60. *Nunca Más*, 53 (statement of Jorge Rafael Videla, December 22, 1977, *Gente* magazine).

61. *Nunca Más*, 53 (statement of Roberto Viola, September 7, 1978).

62. *Nunca Más*, 53 (statement of Luciano Benjamin Menendez, March 15, 1984, *Gente* magazine).

63. *Nunca Más*, 148.

64. *Nunca Más*, 15.

65. *Nunca Más*, 23.

66. Full discussions of the events that led to the Chilean Commission may be found in Heinz and Fruhling, eds.; Jorge Correa Sutil, "'No Victorious Army Has Ever Been Prosecuted . . .': The Unsettled Story of Transitional Justice in Chile," in McAdams, ed.; José Zalaquett's introduction to the English translation of the Chilean report; and Alexandra Barahona de Brito, "Passion, Constraint, Law, and *Fortuna*: The Human Rights Challenge to Chilean Democracy," in *Burying the Past: Making Peace and Doing Justice After Civil Conflict*, ed. Nigel Biggar (Washington, D.C.: Georgetown University Press, 2001).

67. Sutil, in McAdams, ed., 132.

68. Many other alternatives were considered and discarded, and the decision to go with a truth commission was not easily made. See "Gross Human Rights Violations in Chile, 1960–1990," in Heinz and Fruhling, eds., 566.

69. Heinz and Fruhling, eds., 566.

70. Jorge Correa, "Dealing With Past Human Rights Violations: The Chilean Case After Dictatorship," *Notre Dame Law Review* 67 (1992): 1455, notes 38–40. He lists Patricia Verdugo's *Los Zarpazos del puma* and Eugenio Ahumada's *Chile la memoria prohibida* as the most prominent examples of popular books detailing human rights violations during this period.

71. The Commission was given six months to deliver its report, with a possible three month extension, which it used.

72. José Zalaquett, "Balancing Ethical Imperatives and Political Constraints: The Dilemma of New Democracies Confronting Past Human Rights Violations," *Hastings Law Journal* 43 (1992): 1425, 1434.

73. *Report of the Chilean National Commission on Truth and Reconciliation*, vol. 1, 16–17. (Hereafter *Chilean Report*).

74. Zalaquett, 1437.

75. Correa, 1471. Correa writes: "The same flag that was used so many times by the propaganda of the military was being recovered."

76. *Chilean Report*, 17.

77. Correa, 1472.

78. Three political assassinations occurred within three weeks of the report's release, diverting the public's attention and curtailing public discussion of the report. See Cynthia Brown, *Human Rights and the "Politics of Agreement": Chile During President Aylwin's First Year* (New York: Americas Watch, 1991), 29–30.

79. Barahona de Brito, 151.

80. *Chilean Report*, 1.

81. *Chilean Report*, 430.

82. *Chilean Report*, 4.

83. *Chilean Report*, 101.

84. *Chilean Report*, 126.

85. *Chilean Report*, 153.

86. *Chilean Report*, 469.

87. *Chilean Report*, 469.

88. *Chilean Report*, 505.

89. *Chilean Report*, 777.

90. *Chilean Report*, 777.

91. *Chilean Report*, 780.

92. *Chilean Report*, 779.

93. *Chilean Report*, 800.

94. A typical example: "On *October 12, 1973*, **Pedro Pascual CEA CABEZAS**, 49, a farmer, was arrested at the El Pedregal estate. Police arrested him and another person. They were taken to the El Alamo checkpoint and then transferred to the First police station in Los Angeles. The other person was taken to the regiment and at that point lost contact with Pedro Cea, who remains disappeared to this day. Since it is established that he was arrested, this Commission holds the conviction that Pedro Pascual Cea, underwent forced disappearance at the hands of government agents who violated his human rights." *Chilean Report*, 373.

95. For a fuller discussion of the events leading up to the Salvadoran truth commission, see Hayner, *Unspeakable Truths*, 38–40; Margaret Popkin, *Peace Without Justice: Obstacles to Building the Rule of Law in El Salvador* (University Park: Pennsylvania State University Press, 2000); Cynthia Arnson, *El Salvador: Accountability and Human Rights: The Report of the United Nations Commission on the Truth for El Salvador, News from Americas Watch* 5, no. 7 (New York: Human Rights Watch Americas, 1993).

96. The FMLN believed that any Salvadoran daring to investigate the government abuses would be in danger; the UN probably favored foreigners for reasons of security, impartiality, and the prestige of the commission. The government agreed as long as another panel—the Ad Hoc Commission to review the records of military officers—was comprised of Salvadorans. See *El Salvador: Accountability and Human Rights*, 6–7.

97. The final peace accord was signed eight months later.

98. Belisario Betancura, Reinaldo Figueredo, and Thomas Buergenthal, *From Madness to Hope: The 12-Year War in El Salvador: Report of the Commission on the Truth for El Salvador* (New York: United Nations, 1993), 14.

99. *From Madness to Hope*, 14.

100. Article 5, Chapultepec Peace Agreement, quoted in *From Madness to Hope*, 11.

101. The testimony was kept confidential, although transcripts of it are archived at the International Rule of Law Center at George Washington University in Washington, D.C., under the control of a special international foundation. See *From Madness to Hope*, 16.

102. *From Madness to Hope*, 23.

103. Thomas Buergenthal, "The United Nation Truth Commission for El Salvador," *Vanderbilt Journal of Transnational Law* 27 (1994): 497, 506.

104. Buergenthal, 506.

105. Buergenthal, 517.

106. *From Madness to Hope*, 10.

107. *From Madness to Hope*, 10.

108. *From Madness to Hope*, 10.

109. *From Madness to Hope*, 10.

110. *From Madness to Hope*, 10.

111. *From Madness to Hope*, 10.

112. *From Madness to Hope*, 14.

113. *From Madness to Hope*, 17.

114. *From Madness to Hope*, 26.

115. *From Madness to Hope*, 29.

116. *From Madness to Hope*, 43.

117. The focus on cases perpetrated by state agents resulted in criticism of the report by the Lawyers Committee for Human Rights. See *Improvising History: A Critical Examination of the United Nations Observer Mission in El Salvador*, Report by the Lawyers Committee for Human Rights (New York: Lawyers Committee for Human Rights, 1995), 129.

118. The Commission explains in the Mandate section that it selected two kinds of cases on which to focus: "Individual cases or acts which, by their nature, outraged Salvadoran society and/or international opinion" and "individual cases with similar characteristics revealing a systematic pattern of violence or ill-treatment which, if taken together, equally outraged Salvadoran society, especially since their aim was to intimidate certain sectors of society." *From Madness to Hope*, 19.

119. *From Madness to Hope*, 47.

120. *From Madness to Hope*, 46–47.

121. *El Salvador: Accountability and Human Rights*, 20.

122. Buergenthal, 535–36.

123. For a more detailed criticism of the choice to use outsiders to investigate and write the report, see Popkin, 122.

124. Andre du Toit, "Perpetrator Findings as Artificial Even-Handedness? The TRC's Contested Judgements of Moral and Political Accountability for Gross Human Rights Violations," paper presented at conference "The TRC: Commissioning the Past," cited in Charles Villa-Vicencio, "On the Limitations of Academic History: The Quest for Truth Demands Both More and Less," in *After the TRC: Reflections on Truth and Reconciliation in South Africa*, ed. Wilmot James and Linda van de Vijver (Athens: Ohio University Press, 2001), 29.

Chapter Six. Telling Stories in a Search for More Than Justice: The South African Truth and Reconciliation Commission

Epigraph: Excerpt from Seamus Heaney, *The Cure at Troy: A Version of Sophocles' Philoctetes*, copyright © 1990 Seamus Heaney, reprinted by permission of Farrar, Straus and Giroux, LLC.

1. Constitution of the Republic of South Africa Act, 1993, sec. 232(4).

2. Excerpts were published in special newspaper editions by the Independent Newspapers and the Institute for Democracy in South Africa. The full report was put on line. Nonetheless, when I visited in South Africa in 2002, and I asked nearly everyone I encountered if he or she had read the report, none of those not officially associated with the Commission had done so.

3. Many books provide a fuller background of the events leading up to the South African Truth and Reconciliation Commission. A few are Sanford J. Ungar, *Africa: The People and Politics of an Emerging Continent* (New York: Simon and Schuster, 1986); Steven Mufson, *Fighting Years: Black Resistance and the Struggle for a New South Africa* (Boston: Beacon Press, 1990); Nelson Mandela, *Long Walk to Freedom* (London: Little, Brown, 1994), Desmond Tutu, *No Future Without Forgiveness* (London: Random House, 1999). Institutionalized racism preexisted 1948, as early as the founding of the Union of South Africa in 1910 and the Land Act of 1913. See, for example, Kader Asmal, Louise Asmal, and Ronald Suresh Roberts, *Reconciliation Through Truth: A Reckoning of Apartheid's Criminal Governance*, 2nd ed. (New York: St. Martin's Press, 1997), 7ff.

4. These experiences and the conferences are chronicled in eds., Alex Borain, Janet Levy, and Ronel Scheffer *Dealing with the Past: Truth and Reconciliation in South Africa*, (Capetown: Institute for Democracy in South Africa, 1994) and Alex Borain and Janet Levy, eds., *The Healing of a Nation?* (Capetown: Justice in Transition, 1995).

5. Truth and Reconciliation Commission, Interim Report, June 1996, Section 2: Origins and Objectives (http://www.truth.org.za/reports/repl-all.htm). The amnesty requirement was a "twelfth hour" compromise that came at the very end of the negotiations. See Emily H. McCarthy, "South Africa's Amnesty Process: A Viable Route Toward Truth and Reconciliation?" *Michigan Journal of Race and Law* 3 (1997): 183. McCarthy attributes this information to George Bizos. The decision to attach the amnesty requirement to the truth commission process came later. Antjie Krog reports that Tutu explained to reporters in "all the languages he could muster": "*We* [the commissioners] did not decide on amnesty. The political parties decided on amnesty. Amnesty made our election possible. The amnesty clause was inserted in the early hours of the morning after an exhausted night of negotiating. The last thing, the last sentence was added: amnesty shall be granted through a process of reconciliation. And it was only when *that* was put in, that the *boere* signed the negotiations, opening the door to our election (italics added)." Antjie Krog, *Country of My Skull: Guilt, Sorrow, and the Limits of Forgiveness in the New South Africa* (Johannesburg: Random House, 1998), 23.

6. Chapter 4 in Volume 1 of the report itself offers a detailed description of the Commission's mandate and the decisions it made about that mandate. *Truth and Reconciliation Commission of South Africa Report*, vol. 1, 48–93 (hereafter *S.A. Report*).

7. See, generally, Krog, 22–23.

8. The HRV hearings lasted until June 1997; the Amnesty Committee hearings continued after that date.

9. The audience for the TRC's hearings was not limited to South Africa; the international community listened in as well, although sometimes years later. For example, in March 1999, PBS telecast *Facing the Truth: With Bill Moyers* (produced and directed by Gail Pellett, Films for the Humanities and Sciences, 1999).

10. See, for example, Sarah Nuttall and Carli Coetzee, eds., *Negotiating the Past: The Making of Memory in South Africa* (Capetown: Oxford University Press, 1998); Charles Villa-Vicencio and Wilhelm Verwoerd, eds., *Looking Back, Reach-*

ing Forward: Reflections on the Truth and Reconciliation Commissions of South Africa (Capetown: University of Capetown Press, 2000); Tutu. There are also documentaries about the hearings: Bill Moyers' *Facing the Truth* and the award-winning *Long Night's Journey into Day* (produced and directed by Frances Reid and Deborah Hoffman, Iris Films, 2000).

11. Krog, 26. The religious overtones of the hearings became a matter of contention. Before the Johannesburg hearings opened, some TRC officials voiced concerns: "The previous hearing, in East London, as well as numerous TRC ceremonies of the previous weeks . . . were far too 'religious' for their taste. The many prayers, the hymn-singing before and during the hearings and the religious wrappings of the process were out of place. The TRC process was a legal process and should be conducted in a juridical style." Tutu accepted the suggestion that the next hearing begin with a moment of silence instead of a prayer. But when the hearing occurred, Tutu was unable to begin without praying. Piet Meiring, "The *Baruti* Versus the Lawyers: The Role of Religion in the TRC Process," in Villa-Vicencio and Verwoerd, 123.

12. *S.A. Report*, vol. 5, 2–3.

13. Susan VanZanten Gallagher, "Cry with a Beloved Country: Restoring Dignity to the Victims of Apartheid," *Christianity Today*, February 9, 1998, 1 (http://www.christianitytoday.com/ct/8t2/8t218a.html).

14. As a result, the Commission was criticized for elevating its role as a "sympathetic listening post" over its role as an investigatory body. See, for example, "Closing the Door on SA's Dark Past," *Reports from SAPA*, May 11, 1996 (http://www.doj.gov.za/trc/media/1996/9605/s960511b.htm).

15. James Solheim, "South African Truth Commission Staggers Under Horrifying Testimony," Episcopal News Service, June 6, 1996 (http://www.umr.org/HTsoutha.htm).

16. For example, Mary Burton in response to the testimony of Sandra Adonis, May 22, 1997. "Truth and Reconciliation Commission: Youth Hearings: Submissions—Questions and Answers." (http://www.doj.gov.za/trc/special/children/adonis.htm).

17. Reports from SAPA, April 9, 1996 (http://www.truth.org.za/sapa/9604/s960409b.htm)

18. *S.A. Report*, vol. 5, 3.

19. The requests were surprisingly modest: a plaque where someone died, money for college, or just knowing who had committed the act. Gallagher, 2.

20. Krog, 42–43.

21. William Kentridge, Director's Note to Jane Taylor, *Ubu and the Truth Commission* (Capetown: University of Capetown Press, 1998), ix. This is not to say that the hearings were received uncritically. Some Afrikaners, skeptical from the beginning, dubbed the commission the "Crying and Lying" Commission ("Lieg en Bieg Kommissie"). Krog, 214–15. Others have criticized the hearings for the ways victims were selected to testify, for the TRC's "top-down" approach that favored national action over local dynamics, and for other reasons. Indeed the TRC has been among the most-commented-on events of the late twentieth century. See, Hugo van der Merwe, "National and Community Reconciliation: Competing Agendas in the South African Truth and Reconciliation Commission," in *Burying the Past: Making Peace and Doing Justice After Civil Conflict*, ed. Nigel Biggar (Washington, D.C.: Georgetown University Press, 2001), 85.

22. Ebrahim Moosa, "Truth and Reconciliation as Performance: Spectres of Eucharistic Redemption," in Villa-Vicencio and Verwoerd, 117–18.

23. Krog, 259.

24. See Paul Lansing and Julie C. King, "South Africa's Truth and Reconciliation Commission: The Conflict Between Individual Justice and National Healing in the Post-Apartheid Age," *Arizona Journal of International and Comparative Law* 15 (1998): 753 for a complete discussion of the perceived failures of the hearings.

25. *Hamlet*, act 5, scene ii, lines 380–81.

26. Timothy Garton Ash, "True Confessions," *New York Review of Books*, July 17, 1997, 36–37.

27. Fiona Ross, "From a 'Culture of Shame' to a 'Circle of Guilt'" (http://www.uni-ulm.de/~rturrell/sarobnewhtml/ross.html).

28. Krog, 43.

29. The Commission's governing act limited its investigations to gross violations of human rights defined as the "killing, abduction, torture or severe ill-treatment" and the "attempt, conspiracy, incitement, instigation, command or procurement to commit" such acts.

30. *S.A. Report*, vol. 1, 24.

31. *S.A. Report*, vol. 1, 1.

32. *S.A. Report*, vol. 1, 2.

33. *S.A. Report*, vol. 1, 22.

34. *S.A. Report*, vol. 1, 22.

35. *S.A. Report*, vol. 1, 23.

36. *S.A. Report*, vol. 1, 29.

37. Volume 2 is organized largely around geography: outside South Africa, inside, and the homelands; and around certain special topics (liberation movements) and special investigations. Volume 3, which focuses on victims, is also organized by geography, gathering the victim stories into five regions: the Eastern Cape, Natal and KwaZulu, the Orange Free State, the Western Cape, and the Transvaal.

38. *S.A. Report*, vol. 4, 58.

39. *S.A. Report*, vol. 4, 91.

40. *S.A. Report*, vol. 4, 101.

41. *S.A. Report*, vol. 5, 129.

42. *S.A. Report*, vol. 5, 131.

43. *S.A. Report*, vol. 5, 291.

44. This is the case except for a brief minority position report written by Commissioner Wynand Malan, which is an attack on the "moral-ethical approach" of this new master narrative that names apartheid itself as a human rights abuse. He proposed delaying the report because its "sheer volume . . . much of which I haven't read" made it difficult to endorse. More specifically, he defended the system of apartheid, although not the abuses it engendered, as a logical framework for midcentury South Africa.

45. See, for example, Wilmot James and Linda van de Vijver, eds., *After the TRC: Reflections on Truth and Reconciliation in South Africa* (Athens: Ohio University Press, 2001); Biggar, ed.; Robert I. Rotberg and Dennis Thompson, eds., *Truth v. Justice: The Morality of Truth Commissions* (Princeton, N.J.: Princeton University Press, 2000).

Chapter Seven. The Truth Must Dazzle Gradually

The title phrase comes from Emily Dickinson's poem No. 427 (1129), "Tell all the Truth but tell it slant—." The final two lines are "the Truth must dazzle gradually / Or every man be blind—." *Final Harvest: Emily Dickinson's Poems,* selection and introduction by Thomas H. Johnson (Boston: Little, Brown, 1961), 248.

1. T. S. Eliot, *Murder in the Cathedral* (New York: Harcourt, Brace and Co., 1935), 44.

2. Reed Brody, "Justice: The First Casualty of Truth?" *Nation* 272, no. 17, April 30, 2001, 28.

3. See, for example, Michael Scharf, "The Case for a Permanent International Truth Commission," *Duke Journal of Comparative & International Law* 7 (1997): 375.

4. Jonathan D. Tepperman, "Truth and Consequences," *Foreign Affairs* 81 (March/April 2002): 128.

5. Brody, 29.

6. Sebastien Brett, *Argentina: Reluctant Partner: The Argentine Government's Failure to Back Trial of Human Rights* Violators, Human Rights Watch Report 13, 5 (New York: Human Rights Watch, December 2001).

7. Carolyn J. Mooney, "Studying the Struggle for Memory in Latin America," *Chronicle of Higher Education,* December 8, 2000, A56.

8. *Argentina: Reluctant Partner.*

9. *New York Times,* June 22, 2003, Editorials, section 4, page 10.

10. Noted author and niece of Pinochet's most prominent victim, former President Allende, Isabel Allende reflected on Garzon's action: "By pursuing the general, assembling a strong legal case and issuing the extradition request, Garzon has already achieved the salutary result of Pinochet's moral ruin. Henceforth, the man who had the gall to pose as his nation's savior will take his place alongside Caligula and Idi Amin. Even if Pinochet never faces a tribunal, justice has been done." Isabel Allende, "Pinochet Without Hatred," *New York Times Magazine,* January 17, 1999, 24.

11. *Chile: Human Rights Developments,* Human Rights Watch Report (New York: Human Rights Watch, 2001) (http://www.hrw.org/wr2k1/americas/chile-.html).

12. Clifford Krauss, "Shadows of Torment / A Special Report: Pinochet Case Reviving Voices of the Tortured," *New York Times,* January 3, 2000, A10.

13. Brody, 25.

14. *Chicago Tribune,* July 4, 2003, 10.

15. *Amnesty International On-Line, El Salvador* (http://www.web.amnesty.org/ai.nsf/index/amr290012001).

16. *Chicago Tribune,* July 25, 2002, 3.

17. This occurs despite attempts by the government to shut down popular protests. In a discouraging incident that occurred not too long after the truth report became widely known, President Alfonsín threatened a protesting crowd with government response.

18. An excellent example of the mixed responses may be found in Martin Meredith, *Coming to Terms: South Africa's Search for Truth* (New York: Public Affairs, 1999). In her foreword, Tina Rosenberg discusses the different opinions that she and Meredith have about the success of the TRC. Meredith believes that the TRC "left South Africa ultimately unsatisfied." Rosenberg sees the TRC as a "huge achievement, and its impact may seem even greater as time goes on" (xi).

19. Nigel Biggar, ed., *Burying the Past: Making Peace and Doing Justice After Civil Conflict* (Washington, D.C.: Georgetown University Press, 2001), 8.

20. Portrayed in *Facing the Truth: With Bill Moyers* (produced and directed by Gail Pellett, Films for the Humanities and Sciences, 1999).

21. Charles Villa-Vicencio, "Restorative Justice in Social Context: The South African Truth and Reconciliation Commission," in Biggar, ed., 207.

22. Brody, 31. Also see Tepperman.

23. Robert Jay Lifton, *Death in Life: Survivors of Hiroshima* (New York: Random House, 1967), 500.

24. Robert J. Lifton and Greg Mitchell, "The Age of Numbing," *Technology Review* 98 (1997): 58.

25. Frank Kermode, *The Sense of an Ending: Studies in the Theory of Fiction* (New York: Oxford University Press, 1966), 17.

26. Antjie Krog, *Country of My Skull: Guilt, Sorrow, and the Limits of Forgiveness in the New South Africa* (Johannesburg: Random House, 1998), 237.

27. Veena Das, "Sufferings, Theodicies, Disciplinary Practices, Appropriations," *International Social Science Journal* 154 (1997): 563, 570.

28. Arthur Kleinman and Joan Kleinman, "The Appeal of Experience; The Dismay of Images: Cultural Appropriations of Suffering in Our Times," *Daedalus* 125, no. 1 (Winter 1996): 1.

29. Kleinman and Kleinman, 18.

30. Das, 570.

31. Colin Bundy, "The Beast of the Past: History and the TRC," in *After the TRC: Reflections on Truth and Reconciliation in South Africa,* ed. Wilmot James and Linda van de Vijver (Athens: Ohio University Press, 2001), 14.

32. Herman Melville, *Billy Budd, Sailor: An Inside Narrative* (Chicago: University of Chicago Press, 1962), 128.

33. Krog, 38.

Bibliography

Abrams, Kathryn. "Hearing the Call of Stories." *California Law Review* 79 (1991): 971.

Acton, H. B. *The Philosophy of Punishment: A Collection of Papers.* London: Macmillan, 1969.

Aeschylus. *Oresteia.* Trans. Richmond Lattimore. Chicago: University of Chicago Press, 1953.

———. *Eumenides. Oresteia.* Intro. Alan H. Sommerstein. Cambridge: Cambridge University Press, 1989.

Alexander, Peter. *Hamlet, Father and Son.* Oxford: Clarendon Press, 1955.

Allende, Isabel. "Pinochet Without Hatred." *New York Times Magazine,* January 17, 1999, 24.

Anderson, Scott. "The Curse of Blood and Vengeance." *New York Times Magazine,* December 26, 1999, 29.

Arnson, Cynthia. *El Salvador: Accountability and Human Rights.* The Report of the United Nations Commission on the Truth for El Salvador. *News from Americas Watch* 5, no. 7. New York: Americas Watch, August 10, 1993.

Ash, Timothy Garton. "True Confessions." *New York Review of Books,* July 17, 1997, 33.

Askin, Kelly Dawn. *War Crimes Against Women: Prosecution in International War Crimes Tribunals.* The Hague: Nijhoff, 1997.

Asmal, Kader, Louise Asmal, and Ronald Suresh Roberts. *Reconciliation Through Truth: A Reckoning of Apartheid's Criminal Governance.* 2nd ed., New York: St. Martin's Press, 1997.

Ayers, Edward L. *Vengeance and Justice: Crime and Punishment in the 19th Century American South.* New York: Oxford University Press, 1984.

Azanian Peoples Organization (AZAPO) and Others v. President of the Republic of South Africa and Others, 1996 (8). Butterworths Constitutional Law Reports 1015 (CC).

Bacon, Lord Francis. "Of Revenge." 1624. In *Essays and Apothegms of Francis Lord Bacon,* ed. John Buchan. London: Walter Scott, 1922.

Bakhtin, Mikhail M. *Problems of Dostoevsky's Poetics.* Ed. and trans. Caryl Emerson. Minneapolis: University of Minnesota Press, 1984.

———. *Rabelais and His World.* Trans. Helene Iswolsky. Cambridge, Mass.: MIT Press, 1965.

Bandes, Susan. "When Victims Seek Closure." *Fordham Urban Law Journal* 27 (2000): 1599.

Barnes, Harry Elmer, and Negley K. Teeters. *New Horizons in Criminology.* New York: Prentice-Hall, 1943.

Barthes, Roland. "Introduction to the Structural Analysis of Narratives." In *Image, Music, Text.* Trans. Stephen Heath. London: Fontana Press, 1987.

Bass, Gary Jonathan. "War Crimes and the Limits of Legalism." *Michigan Law Review* 97 (1999): 2103.

Bazemore, Gordon. "Three Paradigms for Juvenile Justice." In *Restorative Justice: International Perspectives,* ed. Burt Galaway and Joe Hudson. Monsey, N.Y.: Criminal Justice Press, 1996.

Betancur, Belisario, Reinaldo Figueredo, and Thomas Buergenthal. *From Madness to Hope: The 12-Year War in El Salvador.* Report of the Commission on the Truth for El Salvador. New York: United Nations, 1993.

Biggar, Nigel, ed. *Burying the Past: Making Peace and Doing Justice After Civil Conflict.* Washington, D.C.: Georgetown University Press, 2001.

Bloom, Harold. *Shakespeare: The Invention of the Human.* New York: Riverhead Books: 1998.

Boehm, Christopher. *Blood Revenge: The Anthropology of Feuding in Montenegro and Other Tribal Societies.* Lawrence: University Press of Kansas, 1984. Reprint Philadelphia: University of Pennsylvania Press, 1987.

Borain, Alex, and Janet Levy, eds. *The Healing of a Nation?* Capetown: Justice in Transition, 1995.

Borain, Alex, Janet Levy, and Ronel Scheffer, eds. *Dealing with the Past: Truth and Reconciliation in South Africa.* Capetown: Institute for Democracy in South Africa, 1994.

Bosch, William J. *Judgment on Nuremberg: American Attitudes Toward the Major German War-Crime Trials.* Chapel Hill: University of North Carolina Press, 1970.

Bowers, Fredson Thayer. *Elizabethan Revenge Tragedy: 1587–1642.* Princeton, N.J.: Princeton University Press, 1940.

Boyarin, Jonathan, ed. *Remapping Memory: The Politics of TimeSpace.* Minneapolis: University of Minnesota Press, 1994.

Brett, Sebastien. *Argentina: Reluctant Partner: The Argentine Government's Failure to Back Trials of Human Rights Violators.* Human Rights Watch Report 13, no. 5 (B). New York: Human Rights Watch, December 2001. http://www.hrw.org/reports/2001/argentina/index.html

Brison, Susan J. "The Uses of Narrative in the Aftermath of Violence." In *On Feminist Ethics and Politics,* ed. Claudia Card. Lawrence: University Press of Kansas, 1999.

Brody, Reed. "Justice: The First Casualty of Truth?" *Nation,* 272, no. 17, April 4, 2001.

Brown, Cynthia. *Human Rights and the Politics of Agreement: Chile During President Aylwin's First Year.* New York: Americas Watch, 1991.

Buergenthal, Thomas. "The United Nations Truth Commission for El Salvador." *Vanderbilt Journal of Transnational Law* 27 (1994): 497.

Bullfinch's Mythology. New York: Thomas Y. Crowell, 1970.

Burnett, Anne Pippin. *Revenge in Attic and Later Tragedy.* Berkeley: University of California Press, 1998.

Butler, Joseph. *Butler's Fifteen Sermons.* Ed. T. A. Roberts. London: C. Tinling, 1970.

Campbell, Bruce B., and Arthur D. Brenner, eds. *Death Squads in Global Perspective: Murder with Deniability.* New York: St. Martin's Press, 2000.

Campbell, Lily B. "Theories of Revenge in Renaissance England." In *Collected Papers of Lily B. Campbell.* New York: Russell and Russell, 1968.

Carlyle, Thomas. "Latter-Day Pamphlet on Moral Prisons" (No. 2, Mar. 1850).

In *Carlyle's Latter-Day Pamphlets*, ed. M. K. Goldberg and J. P. Seigel. Port Credit, Ont.: Canadian Federation for the Humanities, 1983.

Carr, David. *Time, Narrative, and History*. Bloomington: Indiana University Press, 1986.

Cavanaugh, William. *Torture and Eucharist: Theology, Politics, and the Body of Christ*. Malden, Mass: Blackwell, 1998.

Chile: Human Rights Developments. Human Rights Watch World Report. New York: Human Rights Watch, 2001. http://www.hrw.org/wr2k1/americas/chile .html.

Christopher, Russell L. "Deterring Retributivism: The Injustice of 'Just' Punishment." *Northwestern University Law Review* 96 (2002): 843.

Cienfuegos, Ana Julia, and Cristina Monelli. "The Testimony of Political Repression as a Therapeutic Instrument." *American Journal of Orthopsychiatry* 53, no. 1 (January 1983): 43.

"Closing the Door on SA's Dark Past," *Reports from SAPA*, May 11, 1996. http:// www.doj.gov.za/trc/media/1996/9605/s960511b.htm.

Conroy, John. *Unspeakable Acts, Ordinary People: The Dynamics of Torture*. New York: Knopf, 2000.

Coonan, Terence S. "Rescuing History: Legal and Theological Reflections on the Task of Making Former Torturers Accountable." *Fordham International Law Journal* 20 (1996): 512.

Correa, Jorge. "Dealing with Past Human Rights Violations: The Chilean Case After Dictatorship." *Notre Dame Law Review* 67 (1992): 1455.

Cover, Robert. "Violence and the World." In *Narrative, Violence, and the Law: The Essays of Robert Cover*. Ann Arbor: University of Michigan Press, 1992.

Currie, Mark. *Postmodern Narrative Theory*. New York: St. Martin's, 1998.

Das, Veena. "Sufferings, Theodicies, Disciplinary Practices, Appropriations." *International Social Science Journal* 154 (1997): 563.

Dauenhauer, Bernard P. *Paul Ricoeur: The Promise and Risk of Politics*. Lanham, Md.: Rowman and Littlefield, 1998.

Davie, Maurice H. *The Evolution of War*. New Haven, Conn: Yale University Press, 1929.

Delgado, Richard. "Storytelling for Oppositionists and Others: A Plea for Narrative." *Michigan Law Review* 87 (1989): 2411.

Derrida, Jacques. "Force of Law: The 'Mystical Foundation of Authority'." In *Deconstruction and the Possibility of Justice*, ed. Drucilla Cornell, Michael Rosenfeld, and David Gray Carlson. New York: Routledge, 1992.

Diamond, A. S. *Primitive Law, Past and Present*. London: Methuen, 1971.

Dolinko, David. "Three Mistakes of Retributivism." *UCLA Law Review* 39 (1992): 1623.

Dorfman, Ariel. *Death and the Maiden*. London: Duke of York Theatre, 1992.

Driver, G. R., and John C. Mills, eds. and trans. *The Babylonian Laws*. Oxford: Oxford University Press, 1955.

Edelstein, David. "Vigilante Vengeance: Hollywood's Response to Primal Fantasies." *New York Times*, February 10, 2002, Arts and Leisure section, 15.

"El Salvador: Peace Can Only Be Achieved with Justice," *Amnesty International Online*, April 5, 2001. http://www.web.amnesty.org/ai.nsf/index/amr 290012001.

Euripides. *Orestes*. In *The Complete Greek Tragedies*, vol. 4, ed. David Grene and Richard Lattimore. Trans. William Arrowsmith. Chicago: University of Chicago Press, 1959.

Ewing, A. C. *The Morality of Punishment.* London: Kegan Paul, 1929.

Facing the Truth: With Bill Moyers. Prod. and dir. Gail Pellett. Princeton, N.J.: Films for the Humanities & Sciences, 1999. Videocassette.

Fisher, Walter R. *Human Communication As Narration: Toward a Philosophy of Reason, Value, and Action.* Columbia: University of South Carolina Press, 1987.

Forster, E. M. *Aspects of the Novel.* New York: Harcourt, Brace, 1927.

Friedlander, Saul, ed. *Probing the Limits of Representation: Nazism and the "Final Solution".* Cambridge, Mass.: Harvard University Press, 1992.

Fromm, Erich. *The Anatomy of Human Destructiveness.* New York: Holt, Rinehart, and Winston, 1973.

Gagarin, Michael. "The Vote of Athena." *American Journal of Philology* 96 (1975): 121.

Galaway, Burt, and Joe Hudson, eds. *Restorative Justice: International Perspectives.* Monsey, N.Y.: Criminal Justice Press, 1996.

Gallagher, Susan VanZanten. "Cry with a Beloved Country: Restoring Dignity to the Victims of Apartheid." *Christianity Today,* February 9, 1998, 1. http://www.christianitytoday.com/ct/8t2/8t218a.html.

Getting Away with Murder: Political Killings and "Disappearances" in the 1990s. New York: Amnesty International, 1993.

Gewirtz, Paul. "Aeschylus' Law." *Harvard Law Review* 101 (1988): 1043.

Ginat, Joseph. *Blood Disputes Among Bedouin and Rural Arabs in Israel.* Pittsburgh: University of Pittsburgh Press, 1987.

Goldstone, Richard. "Exposing Human Rights Abuses—A Help or Hindrance to Reconciliation?" *Hastings Constitutional Law Quarterly* 22 (1995): 607.

———. "Justice as a Tool for Peacemaking: Truth Commissions and International Criminal Tribunals." *New York University Journal of International Law and Politics* 28 (1996):485.

Goodrich, Peter. "Justice and the Trauma of Law: A Response to George Pavlich." *Studies in Law, Politics, and Society* 18 (1998): 271.

Guatemala, Never Again! REMHI, Recovery of Historical Memory Project : The Official Report of the Human Rights Office, Archdiocese of Guatemala. Maryknoll, N.Y.: Orbis Books, 1999. Translation of Nunca Más.

Hallett, Charles A., and Elaine S. Hallett. *The Revenger's Madness: A Study of Revenge Tragedy Motifs.* Lincoln: University of Nebraska Press, 1980.

Hamber, Brandon. "Will Reconciliation Follow Disclosure?" http://www.csvr.org.za/articles/artrcbr.htm.

Hampton, Jean. "Correcting Harms Versus Righting Wrongs: The Goal of Retribution." *UCLA Law Review* 39 (1992): 1659.

———. "An Expressive Theory of Retribution" In *Retributivism and Its Critics. Canadian Section of the International Society for Philosophy of Law and Social Philosophy (CS, IVR): Papers of the Special Nordic Conference Held at the University of Toronto, June 25–27, 1990,* ed. Wesley Cragg. Stuttgart: Steiner, 1992.

Harrison, Jane Ellen. *Prolegomena to the Study of Greek Religion.* Cambridge: Cambridge University Press, 1922.

Havelock, Eric Alfred. *Preface to Plato.* Cambridge, Mass.: Harvard University Press,1963.

Hayner, Priscilla B. "Fifteen Truth Commissions–1974 to 1994: A Comparative Study." *Human Rights Quarterly* 16 (1994): 597.

———. *Unspeakable Truths: Confronting State Terror and Atrocity.* New York: Routledge, 2001.

Heald, Paul J., ed. *Literature and Legal Problem Solving: Law and Literature as Ethical Discourse,* Durham, N.C.: Carolina Academic Press, 1998.

Heath, James. *Eighteenth Century Penal Theory.* London: Oxford University Press, 1963.

Hegel, G. W. F. *Introduction to the Philosophy of History: With Selections from a Philosophy of Right.* Trans. Leo Rauch. Indianapolis: Hackett, 1988.

Heinz, Wolfgang S., and Hugo Fruhling. *Determinants of Gross Human Rights Violations by State and State-Sponsored Actors in Brazil, Uruguay, Chile, and Argentina.* The Hague: Nijhoff, 1999.

Herman, Judith Lewis. *Trauma and Recovery.* New York: Basic Books, 1992.

Homer. *The Iliad.* Trans. Stanley Lombardo. Indianapolis: Hackett, 1997.

———. *The Odyssey.* Trans. and ed. Albert Cook. New York: Norton, 1974.

Horney, Karen. "The Value of Vindictiveness." In *The Unknown Karen Horney: Essays on Gender, Culture, and Psychoanalysis,* ed. Bernard J. Paris. New Haven, Conn.: Yale University Press, 2000.

Ignatieff, Michael. "Articles of Faith." *Index on Censorship* 5 (September 1996): 113.

Improvising History: A Critical Examination of the United Nations Observer Mission in El Salvador. A Report by the Lawyers Committee for Human Rights. New York: Lawyers Committee for Human Rights, 1995.

Jacoby, Susan. *Wild Justice: The Evolution of Revenge.* New York: Harper and Row, 1983.

James, Wilmot, and Linda van de Vijver, eds. *After the TRC: Reflections on Truth and Reconciliation in South Africa.* Athens: Ohio University Press, 2001.

Jolliffe, J. E. A. *The Constitutional Law of Medieval England from the English Settlement to 1485.* London: Adam and Charles Black, 1954.

Kant, Immanuel. *The Metaphysics of Morals.* Trans. and ed. Mary Gregor. Cambridge: Cambridge University Press, 1996.

———. On the Right to Punish and Grand Clemency. In *The Metaphysical Elements of Justice,* part 1 of *The Metaphysics of Morals.* Trans. John Ladd. 2nd ed. Indianapolis: Hackett, 1999, sec. 49 [6: 331].

Kermode, Frank. *The Sense of an Ending: Studies in the Theory of Fiction.* New York: Oxford University Press, 1966.

Keyishian, Harry. *The Shapes of Revenge: Victimization, Vengeance, and Vindictiveness in Shakespeare.* Atlantic Highlands, N.J.: Humanities Press, 1995.

Kleinman, Arthur, and Joan Kleinman. "The Appeal of Experience: The Dismay of Images: Cultural Appropriations of Suffering in Our Times." *Daedalus* 125 (Winter 1996): 1.

Krauss, Clifford. "Shadows of Torment: A Special Report: Pinochet Case Reviving Voices of the Tortured." *New York Times,* January 3, 2000, A1.

Kritz, Neil J. ed. *Transitional Justice: How Emerging Democracies Reckon with Former Regimes.* 2 vols. Washington, D.C.: United States Institute of Peace Press, 1995.

Krog, Antjie. *Country of My Skull: Guilt, Sorrow, and the Limits of Forgiveness in the New South Africa.* Johannesburg: Random House, 1998.

Kyd, Thomas. *The Spanish Tragedy.* Ed. Thomas W. Ross. Berkeley: University of California Press, 1968.

LaFave, Wayne R., and Austin W. Scott, Jr. *Handbook on Criminal Law.* St. Paul, Minn: West Publishing, 1972.

Landsman, Stephen. "Alternative Responses to Serious Human Rights Abuses: Of Prosecutions and Truth Commissions." *Law & Contemporary Problems* 59 (1996): 81.

Lansing, Paul, and Julie C. King. "South Africa's Truth and Reconciliation Commission: The Conflict Between Individual Justice and National Healing in the

Post-Apartheid Age." *Arizona Journal of International and Comparative Law* 15 (1998): 752.

Lea, Henry Charles. *Superstition and Force: Essays on the Wager of Law, the Wager of Battle, the Ordeal, Torture.* 1866. Reprint, New York: Benjamin Bloom, 1971.

Levi, Primo. *The Drowned and the Saved.* Trans. Raymond Rosenthal. New York: Simon and Schuster, 1988.

Lifton, Robert Jay. *The Broken Connection: On Death and the Continuity of Life.* New York: Simon and Schuster, 1979.

———. *Death in Life: Survivors of Hiroshima.* New York: Random House, 1967.

Lifton, Robert Jay, and Greg Mitchell. "The Age of Numbing." *Technology Review* 98 (1997): 58.

Luban, David. "On Dorfman's *Death and the Maiden.*" *Yale Journal of Law and the Humanities* 10 (1998): 115.

Lyons, William. *Emotion.* Cambridge: Cambridge University Press, 1980.

Lyotard, Jean-François. *The Differend: Phrases in Dispute.* Trans. Georges Van Den Abbeele. Minneapolis: University of Minnesota Press, 1988. Translation of *Le différend.*

Mabbott, John David. "Punishment." *MIND* 48 (1939): 152.

Machiavelli, Niccolo. *The Discourses of Niccolo Machiavelli.* Trans. Leslie J. Walker, S.J. London: Routledge and Kegan Paul, 1975.

MacIntyre, Alasdair. *After Virtue.* Notre Dame, Ind.: University of Notre Dame Press, 1981.

———. "How to Be a North American." lecture to the National Conference of State Humanities Councils, Chicago November 14, 1987. Published as a booklet by the Federation of State Humanities Councils, 1012 14th St. N.W., #1207, Washington, D.C.: 2005. Pub. no. 2-88, Humanities Series (1988).

Mack, Maynard, Jr. *Killing the King.* New Haven, Conn.: Yale University Press, 1973.

MacKenzie, Mary Margaret. *Plato on Punishment.* Berkeley: University of California Press, 1981.

Maier, Charles S. *"Doing History, Doing Justice: The Narrative of the Historian and of the Truth Commission."* In *Truth v. Justice: The Morality of Truth Commissions,* ed. Robert I. Rotberg and Dennis Thompson. Princeton, N.J.: Princeton University Press, 2000.

Maine, Sir Henry, and Theodore W. Dwight. *Ancient Law: Its Connection with the Early History of Society, and Its Relation to Modern Ideas.* New York: Scribner, 1864.

Malamud-Goti, Jaime. *Game Without End: State Terror and the Politics of Justice.* Norman: University of Oklahoma Press, 1996.

Mandela, Nelson. *Long Walk to Freedom.* London: Little, Brown, 1994.

Marongiu, Pietro, and Graeme Newman. *Vengeance: The Fight Against Injustice.* Totowa, N.J.: Rowman and Littlefield, 1987.

Marston, John. *Antonio's Revenge: The Second Part of Antonio and Mellida.* Ed. G. K. Hunter. Lincoln: University of Nebraska Press, 1965.

McAdams, A. James, ed. *Transitional Justice and the Rule of Law in New Democracies.* Notre Dame, Ind.: University of Notre Dame Press, 1997.

McBrien, Richard P. *Catholicism.* Study Edition, Minneapolis: Winston Press, 1981.

McCarthy, Emily H. "South Africa's Amnesty Process: A Viable Route Toward Truth and Reconciliation?" *Michigan Journal of Race and Law* 3 (1997): 183.

Meijide, Graciela Fernandez et al. "The Role of Historical Inquiry in Creating Accountability for Human Rights Abuses." *Boston College Third World Law Journal* 12 (1992): 269.

Melville, Herman. *Billy Budd, Sailor: An Inside Narrative.* Chicago: University of Chicago Press, 1962.

Meredith, Martin. *Coming to Terms: South Africa's Search for Truth.* New York: Public Affairs, 1999.

Miller, William Ian. *Bloodtaking and Peacemaking: Feud, Law, and Society in Saga Iceland.* Chicago: University of Chicago Press, 1990.

Minow, Martha. *Between Vengeance and Forgiveness: Facing History After Genocide and Mass Violence.* Boston: Beacon Press, 1998.

———. "Institutions and Emotions: Redressing Mass Violence." In *The Passions of Law*, ed. Susan Bandes. New York: New York University Press, 1999.

Moberly, Sir Walter. *The Ethics of Punishment.* New York: Archon Books, 1968.

Mollica, Richard. "The Trauma Story: The Psychiatric Care of Refuge Survivors of Violence and Torture." In *Post-Traumatic Therapy and Victims of Violence*, ed. Frank M. Ochberg. New York: Bruner/Mazel, 1988.

Mooney, Carolyn J. "Studying the Struggle for Memory in Latin America." *Chronicle of Higher Education*, December 8, 2000, A56.

Moore, Michael S. "Moral Death: A Kantian Essay on Psychopathy." In *Retribution, Justice, and Therapy: Essays in the Philosophy of Law*, ed. Jeffrie G. Murphy. Boston: D. Reidel, 1979.

———. "The Moral Worth of Retribution." In *Responsibility, Character, and the Emotions*, ed. Ferdinand Schoeman. Cambridge: Cambridge University Press, 1987.

Moosa, Ebrahim. "Truth and Reconciliation as Performance: Spectres of Eucharistic Redemption." In *Looking Backward, Reaching Forward Reflections on the Truth and Reconciliation Commission of South Africa*, ed. Charles Villa-Vicencio and Wilhelm Verwoerd. Capetown: University of Capetown Press, 2000.

Morris, Herbert. "Persons and Punishment." *The Monist* 52 (Oct. 1968): 475.

Mossman, Judith. *Wild Justice: A Study of Euripides' Hecuba.* Oxford: Clarendon Press, 1995.

Mroz, Sister Mary Bonaventure. *Divine Vengeance: A Study in the Philosophical Backgrounds of the Revenge Motif as It Appears in Shakespeare's Chronicle History Plays.* Washington, D.C.: Catholic University of America Press, 1941.

Mufson, Steven. *Fighting Years: Black Resistance and the Struggle for a New South Africa.* Boston: Beacon Press, 1990.

Murphy, Jeffrie G. and Jean Hampton. *Forgiveness and Mercy.* Cambridge: Cambridge University Press, 1988.

Nietzsche, Friedrich. *On the Genealogy of Morality: A Polemic.* Trans. Maudemarie Clark and Alan J. Swenson. Indianapolis, Ind.: Hackett, 1998.

Nino, Carlos Santiago. *Radical Evil on Trial.* New Haven, Conn.: Yale University Press, 1996.

Nossiter, Adam. *Algeria Hotel: France, Memory, and the Second World War.* Boston: Houghton Mifflin, 2001.

Nozick, Robert. *Philosophical Explanations.* Cambridge, Mass.: Harvard University Press, 1981.

Nunca Más: The Report of the Argentine National Commission on the Disappeared: Intro. Ronald Dworkin. New York: Farrar Straus Giroux, 1986.

Nussbaum, Martha. *Love's Knowledge: Essays on Philosophy and Literature.* New York: Oxford University Press, 1990.

———. "Rational Emotions." In *Literature and Legal Problem Solving: Law and Literature as Ethical Discourse*, ed. Paul J. Heald. Durham, N.C.: Carolina Academic Press, 1998.

Nuttall, Sarah and Carli Coetzee, eds. *Negotiating the Past: The Making of Memory in South Africa.* Capetown: Oxford University Press, 1998.

Ochberg, Frank M., ed. *Post-Traumatic Therapy and Victims of Violence.* New York: Bruner/Mazel, 1988.

Orentlicher, Diane F. "Settling Accounts: The Duty to Prosecute Human Rights Violations of a Prior Regime" *Yale Law Journal* 100 (1991): 2537.

Orwell, George. *1984.* New York: New American Library, 1981.

Osiel, Mark. *Mass Atrocity, Collective Memory, and the Law,* New Brunswick, N.J.: Transaction Publishers, 1997.

Packer, Herbert L. *The Limits of the Criminal Sanction.* Stanford, Calif: Stanford University Press, 1968.

Paris, Erna. *Long Shadows: Truth, Lies, and History.* New York: Bloomsbury, 2001.

Pasqualucci, Jo M. "The Whole Truth and Nothing but the Truth: Truth Commissions, Impunity, and the Inter-American Human Rights System." *Boston University International Law Journal* 12 (1994): 321.

Peel, H. G. L. *The Vengeance of God: The Meaning of the Root NQM and the Function of NQM-Texts in the Context of Divine Revelation in the Old Testament.* Leiden: E.J. Brill, 1994.

Perelli, Carina. "Memorial de Sangre: Fear, Hope, and Disenchantment in Argentina." In *Remapping Memory: The Politics of TimeSpace,* ed. Jonathan Boyarin. Minneapolis: University of Minnesota Press, 1994.

Pike, Luke Owen. *A History of Crime in England: Illustrating the Changes of Law in the Progress of Civilization.* Vol. 1. London: Smith, Elder, 1873.

Pollock, Sir Frederick, and Frederic William Maitland. *The History of English Law Before the Time of Edward I.* Vol. 1. Cambridge: Cambridge University Press, 1923.

Popkin, Margaret. *Peace Without Justice: Obstacles to Building the Rule of Law in El Salvador.* University Park: Pennsylvania State University Press, 2000.

Prosser, Eleanor. *Hamlet and Revenge.* 2nd ed. Stanford, Calif.: Stanford University Press, 1971.

Quijada, Anibal. "Barbed Wire Fence." Trans. Jo Carrillo. In *Chilean Writers in Exile: Eight Short Novels,* ed. Fernando Alegria. Trumansburg, N.Y.: Crossing Press, 1982.

Randall, Glenn R., and Ellen L. Lutz. *Serving Survivors of Torture: A Practical Manual for Health Professionals and Other Service Providers.* Waldorf, Md.: American Association for the Advancement of Science, 1991.

Reed, John R. *Dickens and Thackeray: Punishment and Forgiveness.* Athens: Ohio University Press, 1995.

Report of the Chilean National Commission on Truth and Reconciliation. Trans. Phillip E. Berryman. Notre Dame, Ind.: Center for Civil and Human Rights, 1993.

Reynolds, Pamela. *Traditional Healers and Childhood in Zimbabwe.* Athens: Ohio University Press, 1996.

Ricoeur, Paul. "Reflections on a New Ethos for Europe." *Philosophy and Social Criticism* 21 (1995): 516.

———. *Time and Narrative.* Vol. 1. Trans. Kathleen McLaughlin and David Pellauer. Chicago: University of Chicago Press, 1984.

Ripstein, Arthur. "Responses to Humiliation." *Social Research* 64, no. 1 (Spring 1997).

Rodes, Robert E., Jr. *The Legal Enterprise.* Port Washington, N.Y.: Kennikat Press, 1976.

Roht-Arriaza, Naomi, ed. *Impunity and Human Rights in International Law and Practice.* New York: Oxford University Press, 1995.

Rosenberg, Tina. *The Haunted Land: Facing Europe's Ghosts After Communism*, New York: Random House, 1995.

Ross, Fiona. "From a 'Culture of Shame' to a 'Circle of Guilt'." Review of *Country of My Skull*, by Antjie Krog. *South African Review of Books*, June 1998. http://www.uni-ulm.de/~rturrell/sarobnewhtml/ross.html.

Rotberg, Robert I., and Dennis Thompson, eds. *Truth v. Justice: The Morality of Truth Commissions*. Princeton, N.J.: Princeton University Press, 2000.

Sachs, Albie. "The South African Truth Commission." *Montana Law Review* 63 (2002): 25,

Scarry, Elaine. *The Body in Pain: The Making and Unmaking of the World*. New York: Oxford University Press, 1985.

Scharf, Michael. "The Case for a Permanent International Truth Commission." *Duke Journal of Comparative & International Law* 7 (1997): 375.

Shakespeare, William. *The Tragedy of Hamlet: Prince of Denmark*, ed. Sylvan Barnet. New York: Signet, 1998.

Shklar, Judith N. *Legalism: Law, Morals, and Political Trials*. Cambridge, Mass.: Harvard University Press, 1986.

Sieff, Michelle, and Leslie Vinjamuri. "Reconciling Order and Justice: New Institutional Solutions in Post-Conflict States." *Journal of International Affairs* 52 (1999): 758.

Slovo, Gillian. *Red Dust*. New York: W.W. Norton, 2002.

Smith, Adam. *The Theory of Moral Sentiments*, Oxford: Clarendon Press, 1976.

Solheim, James. "South African Truth Commission Staggers Under Horrifying Testimony." *Episcopal News Service*, June 6, 1996. http://www.umr.org/HTsoutha.htm.

Sorrell, Tom. "Punishment in a Kantian Framework." In *Punishment and Political Theory*, ed. Matt Matravers. Portland, Ore.: Hart Publishing, 1999.

Sprecher, Drexel A. *Inside the Nuremberg Trial: A Prosecutor's Comprehensive Account*. Lanham, Md.: University Press of America, 1999.

Stephen, James Fitzjames. *Liberty, Equality, Fraternity*. London: Smith, Elder, 1874.

Taylor, Jane. *Ubu and the Truth Commission*. Director's note by William Kentridge. Capetown: University of Capetown Press, 1998.

Taylor, Telford. *The Anatomy of the Nuremberg Trials: A Personal Memoir*. New York: Knopf, 1992.

———. *Nuremberg and Vietnam: An American Tragedy*. Chicago: Quadrangle Books, 1970.

Teitel, Ruti. *Transitional Justice*. Oxford: Oxford University Press, 2000.

Tepperman, Jonathan D. "Truth and Consequences." *Foreign Affairs* 81 (March/April 2002): 128.

Timerman, Jacobo. *Prisoner Without a Name, Cell Without a Number*. New York: Knopf, 1981.

Treston, Hubert J. *Poine: A Study in Ancient Greek Blood Vengeance*. London: Longmans, Green, 1923.

Troeltsch, Ernst. *The Social Teaching of Christian Churches*. Vol. 2. Trans. Olive Wyon. New York: Harper Torchbooks, 1960.

Truth and Reconciliation Commission: Youth Hearings: Submissions—Questions and Answers, May 22, 1997. http://www.doj.gov.za/trc/special/children/adonis.htm.

Truth and Reconciliation Commission, Interim Report, June 1996. Section 2: Origins and Objectives. http://www.doj.za/the/indes.html/repl-all.htm.

Tutu, Desmond. *No Future Without Forgiveness.* London: Random House, 1999.
————. *Truth and Reconciliation Commission of South Africa Report.* 5 vols. New York: Truth and Reconciliation Commission, 1998.
"Tutu Hears the Story of Son's Shooting in Gugulethu." *Reports from SAPA*, April 9, 1996. http://www.doj.gov.za/trc/media/1996/9604/s960409b.htm.
Ungar, Sanford J. *Africa: The People and Politics of an Emerging Continent.* New York: Simon and Schuster, 1986.
Van der Merwe, Hugo. "National and Community Reconciliation: Competing Agendas in the South African Truth and Reconciliation Commission." In *Burying the Past: Making Peace and Doing Justice After Civil Conflict,* ed. Nigel Biggar. Washington, D.C.: Georgetown University Press, 2001.
van Zyl, Paul. "Dilemmas of Transitional Justice: The Case of South Africa's Truth and Reconciliation Commission." *Journal of International Affairs* 52 (1999): 648.
Villa-Vicencio, Charles and Wilhelm Verwoerd, eds. *Looking Back, Reaching Forward: Reflections on the Truth and Reconciliation Commission of South Africa.* Capetown: University of Capetown Press, 2000.
Weber, Max. "Politics as Vocation." In *From Max Weber: Essays in Sociology,* ed. and trans. H. H. Gerth and C. Wright Mills. New York: Oxford University Press, 1946.
Weschler, Lawrence. *A Miracle, a Universe: Settling Accounts with Torturers.* New York: Pantheon Books, 1990.
White, Hayden. *The Content of the Form: Narrative Discourse and Historical Representation.* Baltimore: Johns Hopkins University Press, 1987.
White, James Boyd. *When Words Lose Their Meaning: Constitutions and Reconstitutions of Language, Character, and Community.* Chicago: University of Chicago Press, 1984.
Woods, Jeanne M. "Reconciling Reconciliation. *UCLA Journal of International Law & Foreign Affairs* 3 (1998): 81.
Zalaquett, José. "Balancing Ethical Imperatives and Political Constraints: The Dilemma of New Democracies Confronting Past Human Rights Violations." *Hastings Law Journal* 43 (1992): 1425.
Ziolkowski, Theodore. *The Mirror of Justice: Literary Reflections of Legal Crisis.* Princeton, N.J.: Princeton University Press, 1997.

Index

Acknowledgments

My first debt of gratitude is owed to two people I have never met: Ariel Dorfman and Juliet Stevenson. Dorfman's words and Stevenson's performance combined to create a Paulina Salas who haunted me until I listened to her questions. Like the ghost in *Hamlet*, she insisted, "Remember me." *Death and the Maiden* is a perfect example of the power of art to move people, and of the role that artists can play in the aftermath of violence.

As I worked through the ideas in this book, I was assisted and challenged by other academics to whom I spoke. Thank you to Alice Perlin for inviting me to present an annual Law and Literature lecture at the Loyola University, Chicago, School of Law; to Janis Johnston for inviting me to give a faculty colloquium at the University of Illinois Law School; to Margaret Doody for asking me to join in her chair inaugural conference on narrative at Notre Dame; to Rachel May for inviting me to deliver lectures at the University of Washington; to the Notre Dame Center for Civil and Human Rights for inviting me to be part of their transitional justice series; and to the Von Hugel Institute at St. Edmund's College, Cambridge, for allowing me to present my ideas to an international audience. Each time I was asked provocative and insightful questions that compelled me to clarify and refine the material that ended up as *Shattered Voices*.

In addition, the participants at the 2000 Legal Discourse Colloquium heard some of *Shattered Voices* as a work-in-progress and offered helpful suggestions as well as needed encouragement to see the project through.

Through all this engagement with my fellow academics, I came to see both the promise and the limitations of my project. The promise was evidently opening new ways of thinking and talking about the work of truth commissions; the discussions were lively and sometimes helpfully contentious. As to the limitations, there is much that *Shattered Voices* does *not* do: it does not take on the many-headed hydra question of what "truth" is in truth reports. I leave that in the capable hands of other scholars working on the issue. Nor does it investigate actual victim responses to truth reports. Although I know and have talked to some victims, I purposely left this book theoretical. Empirical work is a welcome next step, as is an investigation of other ways in which countries continue to advance the discussion of the past—through websites and art, for example.

To Notre Dame Law School for giving me a sabbatical year so that I could fully devote my attention to reading truth reports, I am deeply grateful; and to my colleagues at the Law School, for their interest in my work and their inspiring dedication to justice, as well as for their suggestions and gentle critiques, I am most thankful. I have been fortunate to have been part of a community of scholars at Notre Dame who believe that achieving justice, however we may variously define it, is the work of everyone. My colleague, Garth Meintjes, graciously guided me through a visit to South Africa and has endlessly discussed the South African hearings with me. His longtime dedication to combating apartheid and to insisting that his native South Africa become a just society have spurred me on. My long-time colleague Bob Rodes painstakingly read the final manuscript and pushed me toward perfection. And I particularly appreciate the contributions of two friends: Stuart Greene for reminding me about *carnival* and aiding me in seeing the connection to truth commission hearings; and Jill Godmilow, the talented film maker, for frequently challenging me and constantly reminding me that we must be wary of stories.

A number of research assistants worked with me at various stages: thanks to Michael Harte, who took up the challenge of reading philosophy; Lisa-Jo Baker, whose insights into life in post-apartheid South Africa were immensely helpful; Quinn Vandenberg, who cheerfully chased down elusive footnotes; and the incomparable Daniel Pratt, who never met a page number he couldn't find, and who told me that it was "interesting" that I noted a "well known article" from a book called *The Unknown Karen Horney*" (I deleted "well known").

To Bill Krier—advisor and confidante, best friend and finest editor—my profound gratitude for having challenged me intellectually for as long as I can remember and for giving me the courage (and support) to write the book I wanted to write. It's a cliché (and you would be quick to point it out) to say that I could not have done it without you, but I could and would not have written the same book without your patiently serving as a sounding board and reader. Thank you for your unceasing attention to detail and your unflagging encouragement.